# REBUILDING FAMILIES
# ONE DOLLAR AT A TIME

*Achieving Financial Stability
In Spite of an Uncertain Economy*

---

**Maxine Marsolini
with Charlie Marsolini, CPA**

Rebuilding Families®
Portland, Oregon

Copyright © 2011 Maxine Marsolini
All rights reserved. Except for brief quotations in printed reviews, no part of this publication may be reproduced, stored in a retrieval system, or transmitted in any form or by any means without prior permission. For information about permission to quote larger sections of this book, go to www.rebuildingfamilies.net to submit your request.

ISBN: 0615476740
ISBN-13: 9780615476742

Published by Rebuilding Families®
Portland, Oregon

Rebuilding Families® is a registered United States trademark # 3,267,110

Back cover photo by Yuen Lui Studio, Inc.

This book is put together as a resource providing high quality, thought-provoking money talk. Its purpose is to impart useful financial information to the reader. The helps given are not intended to replace or prevent anyone from seeking other forms of professional advice. The author assumes no liability for how this material is put into practice. At times names and places have been changed to protect the privacy of individuals.

*There is no practice more dangerous than that of borrowing money; for when money can be had in this way, repayment is seldom thought of in time, the interest becomes a loss, exertions to raise it by dent of industry cease, it comes easy and is spent freely, and many things {are} indulged in that would never be thought of if {they were} to be purchased by the sweat of the brow.*

—George Washington

# Foreword

Money problems are meant to be worked through. *Rebuilding Families One Dollar at a Time* presents an encouraging message full of the hope families are looking for today. Financial stress is a problem for far too many people today. Money remains the number one cause of marital and family conflict. In this outstanding book, Charlie and Maxine Marsolini share simple, practical ways to understand the broader economic picture and become successful money managers at home.

I first met Charlie and Maxine in 1989 when Crown Ministries was in its formative years, and I was looking for a Pacific Northwest director. Fortunately, they were looking for a place to serve that was helping people overcome money problems. Since 1990, Charlie and Maxine have been part of the Crown Financial Ministries leadership team. I can truthfully say not many people know how to handle money as well as Charlie. His story intrigued me from the day we met. Growing up in the rough and tumble North End of Boston, he often saw the destructive use of money. Later, as a Certified Public Accountant, he served his clients brilliantly as he motivated many to create true financial success.

Charlie and Maxine Marsolini have written a gem. I heartily recommend this book because you have an opportunity to learn from an expert and a bottom line kind of couple. The truths you'll find in these pages will bless you and your family's finances for generations to come. But start reading right now! The sooner you put this into practice the sooner your financial story will improve!

—Howard Dayton
Compass—finances God's way Founder
Crown Financial Ministries Cofounder

# What the People are Saying

## About Charlie
*Charlie Marsolini is an excellent and highly motivating speaker. So glad to have been here. It was a completely valuable experience.*

*I really appreciated you talking about saving before being out of debt. I have been disciplined to pay off debt and not splurge but got better insight on the principles of saving.*

*After hearing Charlie talk, I feel like I have hope and I can start a budget. Charlie really broke things down so I could understand.*

*Charlie made excellent points through his life stories. He was transparent about himself and money and showed himself a good steward of his God-given abilities.*

*I expected to gain information and understanding on how to stay out of debt, as well as to get out. Not only did that happen, but I was challenged to know God better in the areas of finances, giving and debt.*

*I came to the seminar on scholarship from my church and in need of wise counsel. As a result of poor planning and unique circumstances, my husband and I are prepared to go bankrupt. I now have a move forward plan that will allow us to not make the same mistake twice. Thank you.*

*I learned from Charlie that we are not as bad off as I thought. There is hope for us. We will apply the financial principles. Then we will be okay.*

## About Maxine
*Maxine's presentation was more than I expected. She brought light and perspective about family to me. I will make a conscious effort to use what I have learned today.*

*Useful information in all aspects of life, relationships, and work. It just seems to work for all situations.*

*One of the crucial principles I learned from this seminar is the importance of sharing and maintaining the history of the children in a blended family.*

*I am thankful for your transparency! Very good! We need more seminars like this.*

*Very personal. Shows she cares to be here. My wife and I feel like we learned a lot.*

*Kept me interested. I appreciate that what you and Charlie went through brought you to work at spreading the information to help others. Thank you.*

# Meet the Authors: The Perfect Team

Maxine Marsolini writes this book with the help of her favorite financial expert and husband of thirty-six years, Charlie Marsolini. Charlie's lifelong career in the financial arena substantiates the content.

From the narrow cobblestone streets of Boston's North End, to apprenticeship with a Jewish accounting firm, to the ownership of his own successful accounting practice in southern Oregon, Charlie reveals how the poor get poorer and the rich get richer. Instructing others in the fine art of money management is second nature to him. From his youth, Charlie's been deeply involved in the business world and keenly aware of what's happening in the streets. Groomed as the only child of a shrewd Mafia loan shark and bookie, he saw the power of money wielded in terrifying ways. And yet Charlie's career path followed the money as a Certified Public Accountant, Series Seven (Securities) Broker, Registered Investment Advisor, Financial Planner, Pastor, Seminar Instructor and Area Director with Crown Financial Ministries. His extensive insight into the world of money from both sides of the coin continues to garner the respect of businessmen, pastors, and individuals alike.

Maxine's experience as an author of family books, a life coach, and a web broadcaster, attests to her ability to address family issues. And money is one subject all families must face.

Together, this perfect team has witnessed many financial success stories. With a little coaching help, they've seen precious couples, who fought over money, pick up, clean up, or correct, earlier financial mistakes and become confident money managers.

For more information, or to contact the Marsolini's, visit www.rebuildingfamilies.net.

# Acknowledgements

*"With God all things are possible."* Matthew 19:26

We express gratitude to those who have unselfishly allowed their stories to be told. You are the heroes within these pages. Some of the accounts are upbeat. Others tell of serious financial struggles. Your openness, without a doubt, substantiates the need for such a book and communicates hope to many people.

Our deepest thanks go to Sue Miholer, freelance editor and owner of Picky, Picky, Ink, for her expert eyes and picky edits, and to Pamala J. Vincent, Lindy Batdorf, and Tom Fuller, whose candid critiques provided just the right tweaks to move this book to completion. Your careful scrutiny, enthusiasm, and contributions to the printed matter strengthened the content and delivered encouragement to us in ways we cannot adequately express. Without a reading audience, a book has no future. We are grateful for those of you who will buy this book. We firmly believe you will profit from what is written in these pages.

A word to our readers: Whatever the financial concern, we've got something for anyone and everyone who wants to know more about taking charge of their money. If your goal is to dig out from under financial chaos, or to improve upon what is already a good plan, or to direct plenty of dollars to their highest good, or to be informed about the larger global economy, this book is for you. Money is universal. Managing money well is personal.

—Charlie and Maxine Marsolini

# Table of Contents

| | |
|---|---|
| Foreword by Howard Dayton | v |
| What the People are Saying | vii |
| Meet the Authors: The Perfect Team | ix |
| Acknowledgements | xi |
| **One: On the Brink of Financial Collapse** *A pivotal moment in history* | 3 |
| In the News . . . Timeline | 10 |
| **Two: After the Bubble Burst—Now What?** *Waking up in a contracting economy* | 17 |
| **Three: Four Words Show Up Big in the New Economy** *Recession, Depression, Deflation, and Contraction* | 25 |
| **Four: From the Streets to Streetwise** *How a Mafia son come out a winner in the money game* | 39 |
| **Five: Marketing Slick Talk Sets the Trap** *Are you tired of scams, tricks, and lies?* | 47 |
| **Six: What Creates a Bubble in the First Place?** *Caught up in the Wealth Effect* | 55 |
| **Seven: Know the Score** *What is a credit score—why is it important?* | 69 |
| **Eight: Cover Your Backside** *The super amazing benefits of savings* | 81 |
| **Nine: Count the Costs** *What is the true cost of spending?* | 97 |
| **Ten: Why Games of Chance Are a Poor Bet** *Do you want the real truth about the gaming industry?* | 109 |

Eleven: Families that Blend—Should the Money Merge?
*Stepfamilies and their unique money issues*     123

Twelve: Sharks in the Shadows
*Wising up to hidden fees, scams, and malicious fraud*     141

Thirteen: All Eyes on a World Economy
*What does it mean to live in a global marketplace?*     165

Fourteen: Invest Beyond the Local Bank
*The basics of stocks, bonds, 401(k)s and swindlers like Ponzi*     179

Fifteen: Pass Along Smart Money Habits
*Groom children to be streetwise with money*     199

Sixteen: Spread Some Green Around
*Sharing with others produces a harvest of joy*     213

Seventeen: There's No U-haul Behind the Hearse
*Living today with tomorrow's legacy in mind*     221

Eighteen: Feel the Urgency
*Act streetwise—know the Players—know the language*     233

Notes     243

# Pivotal: Piv· ot· al \ˈpi-və-tᵊl\

Vitally important, critical

Merriam-Webster's Online Dictionary, 2007-2008, Merriam-Webster Incorporated

# One

## On the Brink of Financial Collapse

## A pivotal moment in history

*The best protection you can have against the misuse of credit is to determine that you will control the use of credit and refuse to allow it to control you ... there is no substitute for personal discipline and self-control in the area of credit.* [1]
—Larry Burkett

Money is so necessary to daily life that a lack of money can weigh heavily on emotional and physical health. Pam's story is a striking example.

"When did the chest pains begin?" the ER doctor asked me.

"Just a couple of hours ago. I feel like I can't breathe. I'm sweating and I haven't done anything and I'm really light-headed. I was just sitting in the car," I said as medical equipment began to record information from all the wires now attached to me. There was a flurry of activity and then as quickly as it had begun, it all stopped. With a wave of the ER doctor's hand, everyone left the room. Now alone with me, he handed me a cup with a straw and said, "Drink this and try to hit the back of your throat." Within moments all the pain stopped, my breathing calmed down, and I asked, "What happened to me?"

Sitting on a stool next to me, the doctor said, "You did the right thing. If you ever have these kinds of symptoms again, you should not hesitate to come to the emergency room. But today is your lucky day; this was not a heart attack. This was an anxiety attack mixed with acid reflux. It feels just like a heart attack. Have you had some stress in your life lately?"

"Anxiety attack . . . could worrying about our bills have made me sick?" I said, feeling stupid for causing everyone so much alarm.

"Anxiety attacks are typically physical reactions to emotional or mental stress," the doctor explained. "They tend to start small and build up to what you just had—a full-blown episode. But I have bad news and good news."

"What's the bad news?" I asked, waiting for the bomb to drop.

"This is self-inflicted," he said, writing on my chart.

"And the good news," I asked, hoping for some magical fix.

He winked, handed me notes for my personal physician, "This is self-inflicted," and left the exam room.

That was the day I learned being in debt is *more* than a financial problem.

Maybe you can identify with Pam's story; or perhaps know someone who could. She's not unusual. Lots of us delay correcting a problem until after a serious wakeup call grabs our attention and gives us a hunger for change. The only way to keep health and finances in proper balance is to have a game plan that limits negative stressors and cultivates positive solutions.

Financial mistakes are costly. So why don't more people do what it takes to avoid obvious blunders? The *Red Tape Chronicles*, December 2009, provides a simple answer: Millions of Americans are severely lacking in financial basics, and this shortcoming played a major role in the housing bubble and the resulting economic collapse. There is no way to function in our society without understanding money, percentages, interest calculation.[2]

The *Red Tape Chronicles* place blame squarely on our shoulders and make no bones about the need to fix this pressing problem or suffer the consequences. In this book, Charlie and Maxine Marsolini bring forth current financial conditions, historical data, step-by-step concepts, future trends, and a unique learning opportunity for you to make use of. With or without a college education, just about anyone who wants to be a smart money manager can accomplish that objective. Paying no attention to what's being spent becomes the pastime of fools.

The authors firmly believe this generation is tired of the status quo and ready to possess financial integrity. Inquiring minds will have their hearts set on finishing well with debt under control, money in the bank, and an enduring layer of financial stability and peace in place.

## This Particular Financial Crisis

The nature of this particular financial crisis ranks among the most pivotal moments in the history of the world. *Never* before has so much debt been owed by individuals, business entities, governments, and sovereign nations. The result is an economy that has been rudely shoved to the brink of financial disaster—and, in some cases, total collapse.

For the first time in decades, we are living in a period of economic contraction rather than expansion—a contraction possessing the ability to deliver an even greater sting than did the Great Depression.

There's an urgent need to grab onto the basics of good money management and to seize a working familiarity with the larger complex 24/7 world of finance that affects how we live every single day. The purpose of is to get people ready for what lies ahead.

How money is spent should not be left to chance. All dollars need a boss. That's you. That's me. Shame, or failed past experiences, don't have to get in the way. Today is a new day complete with a brand-new opportunity to succeed. Believe it or not, most people don't know what they don't know until there is a desperate need to look for better answers. Dire circumstances drive fresh thinking into place. The same is true of money troubles. The road to financial stability begins to map a course in the right direction when its owners begin to manage money wisely.

## Living Beyond Sustainable Means

Beginning in 2008, living beyond sustainable means came home to roost as the housing market collapsed, causing a foreclosure pandemic to spread across the land, and it continues to bear down on property owners. Prestigious banks collapsed beneath the economic strain as did iconic brokerage firms on Wall Street.

Trouble for banks persists. The *Washington Post* reported: More banks failed in the United States this year [2010] than in any year since 1992, during the savings-and-loan crisis, according to the Federal Deposit Insurance Corporation.[3]

Second to be hard-hit were the auto manufacturers. Many were forced to shut their doors and pass out pink slips to faithful employees. From there, the dominoes began to topple in many other directions. To date 14,800,000 Americans have been added to the nation's unemployed. And no real jobs are on the horizon to replace those that were lost.

In 2009, California issued IOUs for state tax refunds. Pennsylvania came close to insolvency; stimulus money saved them for now. New Jersey's governor affirmed a spending freeze. March 13, 2010's edition of *USA Today* gave us more reason for concern: The recession has tied up cash and caused officials in half a dozen states to consider freezing refunds, in one case for as long as five months. "It's an indicator of how bad it is," says Scott Pattison, executive director of the National Association of State Budget Officers.[4]

States in trouble see their bond ratings drop and the cost of borrowing rise. When more and more interest is paid to bondholders, there are less budgeted monies available to provide for public services. Servicing debt feels a whole lot like throwing money to the wind. There's no way to utilize a dollar's fullest potential when so much of its worth is pledged elsewhere. There is no escaping a lower standard of living for the future. That means our kids and grandkids will struggle beneath the weight of a prior generation's poor money management and overindulgent lifestyle.

The same holds true for the federal government. The thought of a sovereign nation like the United States of America going into default is no longer unthinkable. It's possible. Our beloved country, founded on the strong principles of freedom, has forfeited its financial independence beneath a staggering, growing, multi-trillion dollar debt. By 2020, the United States is predicted to spend more than one trillion dollars annually just to service the national debt! This is a saturation point we do not want to come to. In case anyone is curious, a trillion dollars is a one followed by *twelve* zeros ($1,000,000,000,000). Numbers this big are unsustainable and hard to wrap the average mind around, but we must. Otherwise, money paid on interest will squeeze out other budget items that run our society—things like Medicaid, defense, government and so much more.

## Limit Stress—Cultivate Solutions

Money management and the impact of consumer debt on Main Street is where the rubber meets the road for you and me. When it's our bills that have to be paid, it's only natural for uncertain economic times to birth anxiety about what will happen tomorrow. The sad news is that people who are not prepared to endure a downturn in the economy sometimes choose irrational behaviors. Some act out in desperate ways because they feel trapped and vulnerable. As a rule, financial problems multiply stresses at home and result in added bouts of depression, domestic violence, neighborhood crime, and suicides.

## What the Experts Predict

A large group of leading economists see a time when the stimulus stops, quantitative easing has run its course, governments can no longer borrow, and the picture is one of depression, *not* inflation. Depression is far more dangerous than inflation because debt balloons while assets continue to lose value.

Many experts say our problems will not go away any time soon.
1. Additional banks will close—and always on a Friday afternoon so panic doesn't erupt and bank regulators have the weekend to close things down and offload the failing bank to a viable one. On Monday morning the doors open under a new name (Washington Mutual became Chase).
2. Unemployment will remain a problem for the indefinite future. 150,000 new jobs are needed every month *just* to keep up with population growth. We're nowhere near that quota and there's a dire need to get over 14,800,000 people who've already lost jobs back to work!
3. Millions of manufacturing jobs will never return.
4. Rules to the money game are being manipulated as the power of influence or the influence of power (and there is a big difference between the two) being wielded from the White House decides which businesses are too big to fail and which ones are allowed to go under—at the taxpayers' expense.

## Hold Capitol Hill Accountable

Don't be fooled. A stimulus package is *not* free money. Government coffers are filled from the fount of taxpayer dollars, investors monies, and government shenanigans. Doling out dollars to keep up public morale isn't smart. There is no surplus to spend! Giving out borrowed money only leads to a larger national debt that gets passed along to our children.

The private sector already funds lots of charitable programs and research. Neighbors still help neighbors. The USA is the most charitable nation in the world. Our people have a heart to help and will deliver compassion to others without government involvement. We are generous givers.

The average person would be busted for the same shoddy business practices taking place behind closed doors on Capitol Hill. Politicians have swept aside prudent accounting rules meant to govern free market enterprise to gain a win in the political arena. That's troubling.

The constructs of the Constitution of the United States are being disregarded. For instance, there is no constitutional provision empowering elected representatives to arrogantly sign their will into law without a discussion before the people. But this abuse of power has taken place within the Obama administration. The voice of the people has fallen on deaf ears while the option to exercise "Executive Privilege" was held up as the President's power card. Chicago-style politics is allowed to shamelessly drive the United States ever deeper into a black hole of unsustainable debt.

For that reason, the Tea Party movement showed up. People want to preserve the freedoms America's founding fathers fought so hard to create. For them, it makes no sense to accept the government's example of financial mismanagement. Legislation that places people at risk for economic implosion deserves to be protested by citizens who believe the job of elected representatives is to create financial stability, surplus budgets, and opportunities for growth.

Good money management is always a matter of putting basic financial principles into practice day-after-day, month-after-month, year-after-year. God's best for His children is to not be careless with money, end up bankrupt, become homeless, live hand-to-mouth, become dependent on charity, or wind up in jail. His wisdom will lead His kids to become wise stewards (administrators) over money and possessions. In doing so, financial success in spite of an uncertain economy is well within reach.

## The Bottom Line

- This financial crisis is unlike any other, at any time, in history.
- Stimulus money will not solve our problems.
- Debt is no friend; it has an unsustainable saturation point.
- Money problems contribute to family stress and compromise health.
- Paying no attention to what's being spent is the pastime of fools.
- 150,000 *new* jobs are needed every month to keep up with population growth.
- Learning to manage money well is a gift you give yourself.

## Increase the Wealth Challenge

What troubles you the most after reading this chapter? What facts surprised you? Take an honest look at how this pivotal financial crisis has affected your emotional and physical health. If money troubles have led you to thoughts of desperation, or to act out in aggressive unacceptable behaviors, admit it. Don't lose hope. Get help now.

## Common "Cents" Sense

*Let us be self controlled, putting on faith and love as a breastplate.*[5]

## In the News ... Timeline

April 25, 2011 MarketWatch columnist Brett Arends posted this story: For the first time, the international organization (International Monetary Fund) has set a date for the moment when the "Age of America" will end and the U.S. economy will be overtaken by that of China. According to the latest IMF official forecasts, China's economy will surpass that of America in real terms in 2016—just five years from now. Most people aren't prepared for this. What we have done is traded jobs for profit. The jobs have moved to China. The capability erodes in the U.S. and grows in China. That's very destructive.

April 4, 2011 *USA Today* (Christine Dugas) reported: The economy may be on firmer footing, but many American families are still in financial distress and lack the financial skills they need to climb out of debt, according to the fifth annual Financial Literacy Survey released Tuesday by the National Foundation for Credit Counseling. When parents were asked how they would grade themselves as financial role models for their children, 34% gave themselves a C or lower, according to a survey of 1,008 parents, called Parents, Kids & Money, by T. Rowe Price.

April 4, 2011 Smartmoney.com informs us as of January [2011], the average interest rate paid on relatively safe vehicles such as short-term savings accounts, time deposits and money-market funds stood at only 0.24%. That's one-tenth the level of late 2007 and the lowest on records dating back to 1959. "Americans who have done everything right, have worked hard, saved their money and stayed out of debt are the ones being punished by low interest rates," says Richard Fisher, president of the Federal Reserve Bank of Dallas and a voting member of the Fed's policy-making open market committee. "That state of affairs is not sustainable for a long period of time."

March 29, 2011 Jonathan M. Seidl of www.theblaze.com reported on China's "ghost cities." "It's estimated that 10 new cities are being built every year," Australian news program *SBS Dateline* says. That may sound impressive, until you realize that many of the cities remain vacant long after they're built. See, even though China has become the leader in development, it's adopted the idea that "If you build it they will come." There's just one problem: they're not coming. And so China has a problem—ghost cities: According to Business Insider, some estimates say that nearly 64 million properties are vacant in China. The country is plagued with empty homes, malls, and businesses.

March 9, 2011 Joel Rosenberg tells why The Joshua Fund is ready to open its 8$^{\text{th}}$ Food Distribution Center: Israel's economy is growing faster than any other country in the industrialized world, but not everyone is benefiting. Poverty in Israel is rising, yet with so much of the government's budget going towards national security, social welfare budgets are shrinking and many families are really struggling. Fully 25% of Israelis live under the poverty level (which is less than $900 for a family of four per month), up from 23.7% in 2008. www.joshuafund.net

December 28, 2010 David S. Hilzenrath, Washington Post Staff Writer, informed readers: More banks failed in the United States this year than in any year since 1992, during the savings-and-loan crisis, according to the Federal Deposit Insurance Corp. Amid high unemployment, a struggling economy and a still-devastated real estate market, the nation is closing out the year with 157 bank failures, up from 140 in 2009. As recently as 2006, before the bubble burst, there were none.

November 23, 2010 Fitch Ratings said: Bank-owned homes that are in limbo are called "Shadow Inventory" in the real estate industry. It's unclear how many bank-owned homes are sitting empty, but not yet for sale, around the country, because banks don't necessarily have to report them on their balance sheets. But attempts to quantify this Shadow Inventory have led to alarming conclusions. Earlier this month, Fitch Ratings said there are an estimated 7 million homes in this shadow inventory pipeline—and that it would take more than three years to sell all those bank-owned homes.

May 21, 2010 EconomicPolicyJournal.com has learned that 32 states have run out funds to make unemployment benefit payments and that the federal government has been supplying these states with funds so that they can make their payments to the unemployed. In some cases, states have borrowed billions. As of May 20, the total balance outstanding by 32 states (and the Virgin Islands) is $37.8 billion.

April 23, 2010 Christine Dugas, *USA Today*, reports: "Generation Y"—teens and twentysomethings known stereotypically for their coddled upbringing, confidence, opinionated dialogue, free-spending habits and openness to change. Now, stagnant wages, job insecurity, the decline in employer-sponsored health insurance and retirement benefits, the rapid increase in basic expenses, soaring debt and minimal savings have jeopardized the economic security of the entire generation, according to a recent report by Demos, a public policy research and advocacy think tank. Their generation is the first in a century that is unlikely to end up better off financially than their parents.

April 15, 2010 Associated Press reporter Alex Veiga wrote: More homes were taken over by banks and scheduled for a foreclosure sale than in any quarter going back to at least January 2005, when RealtyTrac began reporting the data, the firm said. "We're right now on pace to see more than 1 million bank repossessions this year," said Rick Sharga, a RealtyTrac senior vice president.

March. 12, 2010, Remae Merle, as told in the *Washington Post*: Borrowers in trouble now are, for the most part, people who have better credit and safer loans and have become delinquent because they've lost their jobs or are dealing with other economic setbacks, economists said. More than 75 percent of the borrowers who are now seriously delinquent—they have missed at least three monthly payments—have traditional prime loans, according to First American CoreLogic. Most have not made a mortgage payment in six months.

January 1, 2010 Neil Irwin, *Washington Post* Staff Writer reports: There has been zero net job creation since December 1999. No previous decade going back to the 1940s had job growth of less than 20 percent. Economic output rose at its slowest rate of any decade since the 1930s as well.

December 18, 2009 financial expert John Mauldin reports: This recession was caused not by too much inventory but by too much credit and leverage in the system. And now we are in the process of deleveraging. It is a process that is nowhere near complete. Total consumer debt is shrinking for the first time in 60 years. And the decline shows no sign of abating.

December 7, 2009 *Bloomberg News* reports: Federal Reserve Chairman Ben S. Bernanke said, "The U.S. economy confronts some formidable headwinds that seem likely to keep the pace of expansion moderate."

November 24, 2009 CNNMoney.com reports: Almost 10.7 million U.S. mortgages were "underwater" as of September...another 2.3 million homeowners are within 5% of negative territory.

November 23, 2009 CNNMoney.com reports Americans have conducted more transactions and spent more money using debit cards than credit cards this year (reluctant to take on more debt) —the first time that's ever happened.

November 19, 2009 *USA Today* reports: There will be about 2.4 million homes lost next year through foreclosure, short sales and deeds in lieu of foreclosure. That compares with 2 million homes lost in 2009.

October 29, 2009 Laura Rowley, *Money and Happiness* reports: Moody's says that 2010 loan charge-offs by banks, on an annualized rate, are exceeding the levels of the Great Depression, and will increase in the coming year.

October 26, 2009 Bloomberg reports: The U.S. Standard & Poor's 500 Index is about 40 percent overvalued and headed for a drop as central banks pull back on securities purchases that pushed up asset prices.

October 7, 2009 Reuters reports: "The private sector needs to start growing on its own for a sustainable recovery to take place." Timothy Geithner (current Secretary of the Treasury)

# Economy: \i-kä-nə-mē

The management of household or private affairs and especially expenses; the structure or conditions of economic life in a country, area, or period

Merriam-Webster's Online Dictionary, 2007-2008, Merriam-Webster Incorporated

# Two

## After the Bubble Burst—Now What?

## Waking up in a contracting economy

*Consumers are beginning to regard payments on home equity, credit card, auto and other loans as discretionary outlays. When the choice is between making the credit card payment and putting bread on the table, financial integrity loses out.* [6]
—A. Gary Shilling

Ever wonder how some of the brightest financial minds in America were able to shepherd such a large population into a dreadful housing crisis and debt-driven contracting economy? If you answered "Yes" and you're losing sleep over money, this book is for you. There's a lot to be said about knowing how to play the money game and being empowered to launch a winning offense.

A long chain of irresponsible events was set in motion right under our noses, using the availability of easy money as the bait. Lenders, eager to line their pockets with the profit from a new generation of creative loans, lured borrowers into a seductive web of subprime, adjustable-rate, interest-only kinds of mortgages. Marketers were at the top of their game by playing a tune that spoke more to human emotions than to common sense. The message was that dreams could come true for anyone wanting to own a home or to live the good life—all you needed was a home equity line of credit. Income level became a moot point. Paperwork could be surreptitiously prepared to sufficiently reflect positive numbers to qualify. And the down payment? Not to worry. No longer necessary. It was even acceptable to borrow more than the house was worth. The message was heard. Millions of consumers poured into mortgage companies and banking institutions to grab their chunk of easy cash.

Because money proved simple to get, the demand for things (cars, vacations, homes and second homes, designer clothing, dining in the finest restaurants) increased dramatically. People spent and spent using any kind of credit available: home equity payouts, credit cards attached to home equities, and consumer credit. The demand for more stuff drove the ever-increasing use of credit, which in turn drove developers to build more commercial projects—also on credit. Credit had become *the drug of choice* and debt piled on. Soon Starbucks, Macaroni Grill, Cinema Complex, REI and Coldwater Creek were given the go-ahead to build in multiple locations. In the suburbs of Portland, Oregon alone, four destination shopping villages emerged within the past six years. The names are fittingly sophisticated: Bridgeport Village to the south, West Village at Clackamas Towne Center to the east, Streets of Tanasbourne to the west and Cascade Station to the north, near the airport, and just before you cross over the Columbia River into Vancouver, Washington. Shoppers no longer needed to drive into the city center of Portland or Vancouver. The developers brought the shopping centers to them.

By 2008 people were spending a $1.40 for every dollar earned. Debt wasn't taken seriously because homes were expected to keep rising in value with no ceiling in sight. The widespread result of the Wealth Effect was to cause people to feel rich and plant the belief they'd continue to grow richer by the day.

But home equity was only a gain on paper, not real money in our wallets.

**Part two of the story:** Once written up, these same high-risk mortgages, commercial real estate lending, and car loans were bundled and sold into investment pools. More bright minds, this time on Wall Street, sliced them up into smaller portions and spread the toxic pieces into mortgage-backed securities sold 24/7 around the world. The homeowner didn't know his mortgage was no longer in one piece. And, unknown to investors, these financial instruments were not the healthy assets their issuers touted them to be. Portfolios grew fat with a product rated to succeed but destined to fail.

Mortgage bankers, stockbrokers, investment bankers, CEOs, COOs—men and women full of financial expertise—must have closed their eyes to the dangerous economic climate being set into motion. Financially street-wise individuals would not have purposefully planned a tsunami! But when greed runs the ship, look out. Treacherous icebergs lie just below the surface. The moral compass can be thrown overboard with Titanic proportion repercussions.

**Part three of the story:** Little was known in the public sector about the true content of these investment bundles. Buyers, hungry to accumulate wealth, trusted the ratings and their broker's advice. These instruments were purchased in good faith. For a while, the market rode the bubble. No one imagined what could happen if the bubble burst—if borrowers should reach a day when they found themselves unable to repay those ill-considered loans.

**Part four of the story** takes us to that pivotal day in the fall of 2008 when an avalanche of default mortgages roared across the nation. Millions of borrowers who purchased homes during the housing bubble or refinanced, thinking mortgage values would never come down, recklessly brushed aside caution and signed contracts only to discover mortgage payments were on the rise and income was not. This perfect storm turned into a knockout punch to many a family and lender alike. Mortgages will continue to reset through 2015 along with a large inventory of commercial property loans. Communities will feel the impact of lost revenue for years to come.

## Our Future

The wiggling tentacles of this financial drama have spread far and wide, beyond America and into the global economy. Shock and disbelief are all around. Wall Street's tumbling giant Bear Stearns came first, followed by many top banks and auto manufacturers who begged to be rescued. Only quick government intervention—the injecting of hundreds of billions of TARP (Toxic Asset Relief Program) dollars at taxpayers' expense—kept the monetary system from total collapse.

When debt is rampant, the future standard of living is destined to be much lower. All the excess demand for goods and services created by living on borrowed money has backpedaling effects. If the contractor has no house to build or remodel, the plumber has no need to install a kitchen sink, and the sink manufacturer is forced to cut back production. That's how jobs are lost—like dominoes, they topple.

There's only one real way to come to grips with an economy in decline. **Rein in spending**. Learn how to make do with the dollars you have. If you can't pay for it, you don't buy it.

Sounds easy, but too many people are still desperate for another dollar fix when the real solution is rehab. The quicker you accept that this financial crisis is a serious one and begin to change your ways, the quicker the pressure will be released and a more stable future can be secured. Reining in will require commitment, training, and sacrifice. But without radical change, personal finances, community services, and national security are at stake.

Over time, servicing debt grows big enough to squeeze out necessary budgeted items like food, clothing, shelter, fire departments, and funding for military strength. Paying interest on borrowed money is a *really* big deal.

When the money supply runs short, and payments cannot be made, embarrassment and default come next. Legal proceedings move into place. And, worst case scenario, it's possible for a lender to ask the court's permission to garnish your wages—if you've still got a job.

Although we all want to take the high road, not understanding the true value of debt and defaulting on loans have more far-reaching effects than we might first understand. Part of money rehab is to begin to understand those things "they" don't want you to know, and being proactive will avoid the sinking of the Titanic.

## A Sad but Stark Reality

Closer to home is news of evictions, foreclosures, shrunken equities, retirement funds hard hit, store closures, millions of jobs lost, and suicide that saturate media broadcasts and publications. These terrible truths represent another stark reality. Financial hardship for a family can't help but put our children at greater risk.

> *...Children will be directly impacted by the mortgage crisis as their families lose their homes due to foreclosures. These children are not just losing their homes, but they also risk losing their friends, schools, and in many ways, their childhood.*[7]

The average person living today does not understand a contracting economy. For the past sixty years, the euphoria of growth and expansion has driven the economy forward. Today the opposite is true as we circumvent downsizing, bank failures, foreclosures—all because the appetite to borrow money was not controlled.

We've never lived like this before today. Let's borrow from the pages of history. Post-World War II, the lion's share of the economy was driven with real dollars. Most families were not in financial trouble and did not live lavishly. Credit was limited, was not easily accessible, and certainly not a popular choice. If money was borrowed, there was great respect for paying it back and a real fear of consequences if one could not. Years passed and hand-shake integrity faded. Thinking changed and borrowing money became a more and more acceptable practice.

Today, sixty plus years after World War II, two-thirds of Americans are strapped with massive debt. Financial freedom appears elusive—not because the goal is unattainable, but because most people aren't sure how to start or what to do. This book is ready to help resolve that dilemma.

## Opportunity Awaits

In adversity opportunity awaits. Yes, the economy has made a major shift and will continue to evolve into a new paradigm. This generation is the one poised to start a new thing. It's up to you to usher in a more frugal and stable set of economic principles. You are being challenged to set an economic climate capable of sustaining generations to come. It will not be an easy task. It will take courageous people who are determined to lead the family and the nation into solid, sustainable, streetwise money management.

Have no doubt. Strong leaders, even statesmen, will emerge from this crisis as families lessen stress and increase peace because financial integrity has been brought onboard.

Charlie often says, "A dollar can only be spent once." It is the author's deepest desire that this book will equip you with the tools you'll need to take back the financial power many of us have unknowingly given away. Uniting stewardship tools with a learners heart allows us to look forward with great anticipation to building financial integrity, personal peace and family stability. Shall we?

### The Bottom Line
- Lenders cultivate a consumer's desire to borrow.
- Bubbles are artificially created; don't follow the herd—lambs get slaughtered.
- Interest on debt grows—daily!
- Finances in trouble put children at greater risk.
- There is no substitute for possessing a good amount of financial knowledge.
- Don't spend more than you make.
- Prepare for this financial crisis to continue.

## Increase the Wealth Challenge

Take an honest look at how the current financial crisis has affected your family's life. What has changed? With hindsight, what could you have done differently? Don't get stuck on any of yesterday's shame or regret. Release the past. Learn from what's happened. Determine to walk into the future armed with a teachable spirit and a new attitude—one that's ready to cultivate smart sustainable habits with your dollars.

## Common "Cents" Sense

*May he give you the desire of your heart and make all your plans succeed.*[8]

# Contraction: \kən-ˈtrak-shən\

A reduction in business activity or growth

Merriam-Webster's Online Dictionary, 2007-2008, Merriam-Webster Incorporated

# **Three**

## Four Words Show up Big in the New Economy

## Recession, Depression, Deflation, and Contraction

*We have put holes in the bucket of our economy, and the "water" or GDP(Gross Domestic Product) is leaking out. We are going to settle at some new lower level of GDP and consumer spending.* [9]

—John Mauldin

Recession. Depression. Deflation. Contraction. All four words are being tossed about to describe the state of today's economy. What do they mean? What are their differences? What role do they play in our day-to-day lives?

None of these four words conjure up a happy picture of upward motion. Instead, they bring uneasiness and thoughts of a wild ride down a steep hill into the depths of uncertainty. That's where these words are similar—after that, boy, do they differ in meaning.

In the larger economic picture, a series of benchmarks defines the onset of a recession, a depression, a deflation, or an economic contraction. Economists, who work on behalf of the government, extract pertinent information from multiple economic sectors including unemployment numbers, gross domestic product (GDP), international trade, housing starts, as well as the fluctuations of Wall Street.

The average person will never know everything there is to know about the inner workings of the national economy, but regular people can come to understand the basics of economic volatility in the broader financial system in order to adequately protect finances on the home front.

Where do we start? Let's get real about the economy. The government has misled people when declaring an official end to the recession in June 2009. Federal Reserve maneuvers have long been at work painting a more positive picture than truly exists by pouring large sums of money into the economy in an attempt to keep businesses afloat. As a result, the trusting people of America have been given a false sense of hope.

The United States is truthfully still in a recession and also experiencing deflationary times while simultaneously contraction is more descriptive of the economy going forward.

*We are permanently destroying jobs in this recession, all up and down the food chain and in numerous industries. There will be fewer cars made, for a long time. Less demand for financial service jobs. Housing construction will be a long time recovering.*[10]

When the national economy takes a hit, society shoulders the impact. Taxpayers are left with the burden of big deficits to pay. In a tough economy things get personal really fast. The loss of businesses and jobs that provided paychecks are happening not just on the news; they are happening to people we know. Foreclosure and nasty calls from creditors demanding payment create insecurity for families. Future dreams of being financially stable in our golden years have collapsed for too many seniors. Nest eggs have shrunk dramatically or vanished altogether. Seniors fortunate to have something left are finding interest rates so low that income earned from investments is no longer enough to provide for their needs. Savings have eroded.

Times are tough, but don't lose heart—things can improve.

A *cash flow snag* is an opportunity to restructure the way money is managed. Personal finances must learn how to dance to the beat of a different drum. The end results depend on how well the composer learns to write the score and expertly play the music. With a little practice all of us can learn to play the notes.

Start by accepting the fact that living in a contracting economy is a new paradigm. For decades, expansion has been the norm. Not so now. To continue to do business as usual and ignore the new shape of the economy will prove foolish. To come out a winner some things must change.

A good place to start this change is to understand four words that influence the new economy: Recession, Depression, Deflation, and Contraction.

## Recession

Recession, simply defined, is a significant decrease in economic activity due to overleveraging dollars. In technical terms, recession occurs after three consecutive quarters of negative employment growth (job losses).

Overleveraging dollars is the key cause—the tipping point, the perfect storm—that collapses a financial system and creates a recession.

What is overleveraging? In a nutshell, it's like stretching dollars too thin. Lenders—like banks, mortgage companies, and investment corporations—who loaned out capital monies at thirty, forty, or sixty times its true value, took on extreme risk with every dollar deposited into their care. Consider a $100,000 of banked dollars being loaned out sixty times over, or to the equivalent of $6,000,000. Sixty borrowers were given a full portion of each dollar held in reserve. That's crazy! That's overleveraging. Remember, only $100,000 truly sits in reserve to back the $6,000,000 worth of loans. The lender placed the institution in a perilous position.

Two things happen next. A large number of loans go into default at the very same time people, who fear going broke or need money to live on, withdraw large chunks of cash from banks and stock market portfolios.

The house of cards topples. Suddenly the economy, as we know it, implodes.

This is a short explanation of how our financial security rug got yanked out from under us in the fall of 2008. Banking institutions and large brokerage houses did not have enough cash held in reserve to cover both the risk and the demand for cash. Red flags flew high and the stock market looked a lot like a bloodbath.

Our government came riding in like a knight on a shiny white horse to manipulate the economy in desperate ways. All in hopes of bringing life support to a gasping economy.

Questions abound. Where were the overseers? Why were regulations meant to prevent such a large tsunami ignored? What was the reasoning behind such a risky shift in financial policy? To answer these questions correctly, we'll need to step into history for a moment. There are three stepping stones to this whodunit.

## The First Stone

Once upon a time, in 1933, regulations were in place to keep the public safe from banking practices thought to be too speculative in nature.

After the 1929 stock market crash and commercial bank failures, the Glass-Steagall Act (GSA) was endorsed. Senator Glass was a former Treasury Secretary and the founder of the U.S. Federal Reserve System. Congressman Steagall once served as chairman of the House Banking and

Currency Committee. The goal of GSA was to regulate the banking industry in such a way as to protect the economy from a future collapse.

GSA set up a regulatory firewall between commercial and investment bank activities. A commercial bank could not also sell investments. An investment bank would not manage checking accounts. A savings and loan bank was limited to savings and loans. These businesses were to be kept independent of one another—no one-stop shopping as we have today.

## The Second Stone

In 1956, Congress made another wise decision to add more regulations to the banking sector. This time the effort was to prevent financial conglomerates from amassing too much power. Some banks were involved in selling and underwriting insurance to customers. Selling insurance was okay—underwriting insurance was not. Congress believed underwriting insurance was not a good banking practice. In the government's opinion, there were too many risks involved to safeguard deposits.

The Bank Holding Company Act (BHCA) of 1956 passed. BHCA was a broadening of the GSA of 1933 for the sole purpose of keeping banks from underwriting insurance. BHCA wisely capped potential exposure to risk and upheld the integrity of the banking industry.

## The Third Stone

Fast forward to November 1999. Prosperity abounds. Wall Street is gift-wrapped in profit. Credit is easy to use. Caution is sent on a holiday. Congress decides now is the right time to repeal the Glass-Steagall Act and replace it with the establishment of the Gramm-Leach-Bliley Act (GLB).

GLB took the lid off Pandora's box. The new act did away with the conservative restrictions against affiliations between commercial and investment banks. Banks received the green light to be speculative if they chose. The old regulations were gone. It became common practice to blur the lines between commercial, investment, and insurance products by offering customers a much broader range of services. The average bank didn't waste any time becoming a one-stop financial shop. *Now your local bank, probably a branch of a huge merged national bank, will provide your business with a loan, finance your home mortgage and then package it with hundreds of others as an investment product sold by brokerage firms and mutual funds, which it may also own. The brokerage arm of your bank or insurance company will transact your stock trades, sell you a mutual fund ... loan money to your hedge fund so it can engage in leveraged derivatives transactions (so complex that banks have trouble understanding where their risk lies).*[11]

It's all one big fat financial industry today. How is less regulation working? As it turns out, less regulation is not working for the good of our economy. Playing with greater risk has pushed us into a financial crisis of huge proportions. In hindsight, yesterday's conservative regulations would have served us better.

For a business to remain financially strong, Accounting 101 teaches the importance of keeping adequate reserve funds. Our lawmakers and bankers must have forgotten this major concept.

With freedom comes added responsibility to measure the downside. A bank should not covet profits over sound banking practices. According to Timothy Geithner, current U.S. Secretary of the Treasury, a dollar in the bank should not be loaned out at more than twelve times its value. But banks pushed the credit envelope to the breaking point by overleveraging monies at thirty, forty, sixty times the capital value.

Not every financial expert was in agreement with what was happening. Some even sounded the alarm saying, "This is foolish. Stop such risky practices. Credit is getting out of control. Who's going to pay it back? Does anybody care? We could end up face down in the ditch dashed on the rocks." But the voice of wisdom was ignored.

Today our economy is in the ditch. It's deep. It's muddy. It's painful.

The practice of overleveraging carried us into the perilous land of financial instability.

It will take years to climb out of this mess. Piling more debt on top of too much toxic debt can't work. Our problems begin to be solved on the day we return to a more proven set of accounting principles. Can we work through this crisis and emerge a stronger people and nation? Yes. If we are willing to do what it takes to build up cash reserves and tear down debt.

## A Confidence Game Is Being Played

We owe it to ourselves to learn how to question what we hear. The Fed does not want the general population to lose confidence in the strength of our government. What we hear in the news often does not reflect the real story. Changing up words is an old trick. For example, instead of reporting that company XYZ is not turning a profit, the word pundits rephrase facts into more positive statements. By changing the lingo ever so slightly, a loss doesn't sound so bad anymore: XYZs first quarter earnings were better than predicted. CFOs anticipated a $1.3 million loss. Instead, there's good news. The actual figure shows a loss of only $1.1 million for the first quarter.

Bad isn't as bad so that's good. Huh? Think about it.

When does a loss stop being a loss? *Never!*

The profit is still missing!

The Federal Reserve is pumping out fairy dust, creating the illusion that things are getting better.

We are being fed psychobabble and it's time to refuse to be force-fed false information. Look at the numbers. Numbers don't lie. Exercise independent thinking before drawing a conclusion. Ask a few questions:

1. Is it really in our best interest to rescue bankrupt corporations?
2. Is it really prudent for our government to monetize debt (to print money) to pay off toxic loans and label this new practice "quantitative easing"?
3. Would we be better off if the weak companies were allowed to fail and the strong ones given opportunity to rise up? That's how true capitalism has worked until now.

Some expert economists believe America could be on the same path as Japan. The recession for them lasted twenty years and taught good and practical lessons. The Japanese people became serious about savings. They once led the world in highest savings rate per capita at twenty percent. But today Japan's financial future is quite the opposite. *The more Japan borrows, the more revenue must be devoted to paying interest. Japan's total bond issuance in fiscal 2011, including roll-over of existing bonds and the additional 44.3 trillion, is 169 trillion yen—184% of the entire annual budget. Given Japan's low birth rate and longevity, the generation which is now retiring is outsized compared to the younger generation which is supposed to fund the retirees' retirement. As globalization has eroded the old social contract of lifetime employment and high salaries, many of the younger generation earn a mere slice of their parents' wages. Predictably, Japan's savings rate has plummeted as retirees start withdrawing their savings, and many younger workers find their incomes too low to save anything.*[12]

The recent 2011 powerful earthquakes, devastating tsunami, and nuclear power plant catastrophes have added an immeasurable economic burden to the people of this island nation that was already teetering on the brink of financial ruin.

## Depression

The simplest definition of a depression is a period of low economic activity due to unemployment rising and Gross Domestic Product falling (GDP). Government spending through stimulus dollars is the only way to officially avoid being labeled in a recession or a depression. But you decide. Let the facts speak for themselves apart from political babble created by the government to keep confidence up.

The Fed can declare a recession without declaring a depression. But today, it is fair to believe both scenarios are being felt. A depression is based on the number of people out of work over three consecutive quarters in any given year. Month-after-month we are experiencing the greatest number of job losses *ever* in the history of our country (though official numbers were not kept during the Great Depression of the 1930s). Since December 2007, when the recession officially began, until February 2010, 8 million jobs were lost, bringing the total unemployed in the United States to 14.8 million people. A frightening number!

During a depression, increased unemployment is accompanied by a significant change in Gross Domestic Product (GDP). But the numbers told to the public have been stroked by those in power. The government fears the D word. People might panic, lose confidence, get depressed, and even start riots in the streets if the weakened economy was officially called a depression. There is an illusion of being in a period of recovery when stimulus packages are at work propping up the economy. Backstopping banks, and so much more, is like the work of an accomplished magician who doesn't share how the trick is being pulled off with his audience. Nonetheless, the magic surprises onlookers and is usually accepted without question.

Visions of the Great Depression of 1929-1939 might come to mind. Back then bread lines were quite common. Looking back at the facts, the Great Depression was brought about by underlying weaknesses and imbalances within the economy. Sound familiar? Like the upbeat years prior to September, 2008, the 1920's had been full of boom psychology and referred to as the Roaring Twenties.

*Prior to the Great Depression, governments traditionally took little or no action in times of business downturn, relying instead on impersonal market forces to achieve the necessary economic correction.*[13]

Legislative changes were made in the economic policy of the United States. Among the actions taken were forms of taxation, industrial regulations, public works, social insurance, social-welfare services, and the ability to deficit spend. It was during this time that the United States assumed a principal role in ensuring, *catch the word ensuring*, economic stability at home and in most industrialized nations. That sounds like Uncle Sam signed on as the watchdog over all trade markets. Interesting thought.

Thankfully, from that era in history changes were put in place to intervene early in an attempt to keep a *depression* from settling in. But, the downside of that decision was to soft-pedal serious problems. Fed talk only shares part of the bad news with the public. To tell all is considered a pill that's too big to swallow and one that runs the risk of chaos erupting in the streets. What we hear is almost always guaranteed to be less than what we really need to know.

But truth has a funny way of rising to the surface one detail at a time. News leaks happen. People in the know let pertinent facts slip out. Broadcasters dig deep for answers to national concerns and then present those facts to listening audiences.

Families in financial trouble, and those who've lost jobs, feel depression in their gut. As of December 31, 2010, more than 43 million Americans (one in seven) are receiving food stamps. Something's amiss. Hunger on the rise is a reliable barometer of tough economic times. Local food pantries are struggling to keep up with the demand for food. Oregon is listed as one of the top four "hungriest" states in the country.

## Deflation

Deflation is historically defined as a tightening up of available money that causes prices to drop.

During a deflation, cash is king and debt a terrible thing. The stuff money is owed against is no longer worth the price that was paid for it. With prices falling and jobs hard to find, fewer goods are being bought.

The housing industry is an excellent example. Deflation reduces the value of real estate (bare land, residential, and commercial properties). Home prices contract. Equity shrinks or vanishes. More than twenty million mortgages are now underwater. Millions of families are strapped to monstrous mortgages that are worth far less than their prior market value. Some homeowners, even those who can afford to stay, wonder why that stance makes sense anymore. Others try to negotiate more reasonable loans, or seek relief from a short sale, to stave off foreclosure.

The same is true for commodities (i.e. cotton, corn, wheat, rice, peas). Big fortunes were lost when prices took a sudden nosedive. Debt held on those investments now exceeds their worth in the marketplace, creating a population of insolvent people, insolvent businesses, and insolvent governments.

Every period of deflation is preceded by a sustained downturn in the stock market. Deflation prolonged over a long period of time results in a recession. And there are many indicators this is a period of recession. Deflation is here to stay until there is proof of economic recovery.

Money can be made during a deflation by those who are in a position to buy assets at bargain prices.

There is an all-out attempt to reopen credit lines to consumers. Spending keeps the wheels of commerce greased. Not spending bogs the system down. That's the reasoning behind government intervention that began with TARP (Toxic Asset Relief Program) monies and is now called "The American Recovery and Reinvestment Act." There is collusion between the government and the Federal Reserve. Their common goal is to get credit moving again. The Federal Reserve is 1) printing money in an effort to lower interest rates and 2) pumping up stocks and commodities as a ploy to inflate assets. However, consumers are already in credit trouble and banks are undercapitalized and wisely tightening lending policies. *Americans borrowed less for a 10th consecutive month in November {2009} with total credit borrowing on credit cards falling by the largest amounts on records going back nearly seven decades.*[14]

Consumers are trying to pay down debt despite what the Fed wants to see happen through stimulus packages. Paying off debt makes sense. But it also creates deflation. When people don't buy goods and services, demand shrinks and leaders in Washington D.C. are not happy. Their expectation is that we inflate ourselves out of this financial crisis. A ridiculous plan!

Stimulus money piles additional debt on top of an already oversized national debt of more than fourteen trillion dollars. Add to that number the trillions of dollars owed for off-budget expenditures on the *other* set of books. The totality of that number is unknown but is estimated to be in excess of twenty trillion dollars.

Who's stuck with paying off the national debt? Take a look in the mirror. Taxpayers (you and me) carry the burden. Our wallets fund the federal government. No wonder financial stress is daunting today. Bigger and bigger tax bites lessen the amount of take-home pay for workers.

*The American Psychological Association says that more than 80 percent of Americans are suffering money stress, and there are increasing reports of domestic violence, violent crimes and suicides. Many people are so worried about their finances that they can't function, and don't know what to do first.*[15]

The best way to keep money stress money minimal to nonexistent is to embrace the use of good financial principles at home. Those who survive deflation well do so with cash to spend and little or no debt to carry. Deflation ready people aren't caught unprepared by a surprise jolt to the economy. They already live as if a rainy day will come by keeping spending habits under control.

## Contraction

Contraction is defined as a lowered standard of living.

I recently heard a financial commentator say, "Frugal is the new chic."

Smaller homes are gaining popularity again. I grew up living in a two-bedroom home with my parents and three siblings. The six of us did family in a 900-square-foot home. I can't remember thinking it was crowded or unusual.

With contraction comes the desire to pay off debt and to grow savings. Americans are suddenly interested in saving money again.

Walmart is attracting customers who once spent their money in trendy shops.

God wired humans with powerful survival instincts that hold true in both physical and financial portions of life. That explains why sensible men and women opt to contract spending habits when financial security is under attack. Economic survival relies on how quickly a way of life is changed to accommodate current circumstances.

People in survival mode don't buy extra things. Instead, creativity kicks in and there's a newfound desire to make do. Eating at home, and packing a lunch for work or school are chosen over dining out several times a week. A new appreciation for thrift stores and clipping coupons is found. A paring down to a lower standard of living falls into place. Frugal becomes the new chic. There's no shame in being frugal. The blessing of a cozy bed to sleep in, water in the tap, and bread on the table keeps a smile on our faces. Forty dollars that might have been spent at the movies six months ago is now buying enough groceries to make it through the week. Beans, rice, and pasta go a long way when they have to.

Contraction jumps into the economy as a good teacher. Contraction passes on lessons of heightened appreciation for what we already have and pushes us to get real with living expenses. This valuable tutor, if respected and acted upon, can produce a sustainable financial strategy. Family finances will be better off in the long run.

Hard times have a profound way of setting people in a new direction. Before this financial crisis is over, there is reason to believe millions will choose to break free of the debt cycle and stay that way.

## The Bottom Line

- Recession is the result of overleveraging dollars.
- Depression is a consequence of unemployment rising and GDP falling.
- In deflation, prices fall; cash is king and debt a terrible thing.
- Contraction results in a lowered standard of living.
- Prices do not go up forever.
- The government holds back facts to keep confidence high.
- Survival skills call for the ability to change as economic circumstances shift.

## Increase the Wealth Challenge

Recap what life in a contracting economy represents. Get out a tablet and pencil. Make two columns. In the first column, list things your family spent money on before the financial crisis hit. In the second column write down those things that will help dollars stretch further (i.e. packing a lunch). The whole family should contribute ideas. Encourage the children to add artwork to the page. Later place your list in a visible place to hold each other accountable to the plan. This challenge creates family teamwork moving forward with a common goal.

## Common "Cents" Sense

*You have planted much, but have harvested little ... You earn wages, only to put them in a purse with holes in it. "Give careful thought to your ways."* [16]

## Streetwise: \ˈstrēt\ -,wīz\

Possessing the skills and attitudes necessary to survive in a difficult or dangerous situation or environment; a promising line of development or a channeling of effort ... characterized by wisdom: marked by deep understanding, keen discernment, and a capacity for sound judgment ... hinting at the possession of inside information

Merriam-Webster's Online Dictionary, 2007-2008, Merriam-Webster Incorporated

# Four

## From the Streets to Streetwise

## How a Mafia son come out a winner in the money game

*In all realms of life it takes courage to stretch your limits, express your power, and fulfill your potential; it's no different in the financial realm.*[17]
—Suze Orman

Charlie grew up in the Italian ghetto of Boston. His early experiences are a vivid picture of an only son—only child—who grew up under the influence of his Papa, a powerful man who just happened to be a capitone in the Mafia. Charlie tells the story:

When I walked with my papa down Hanover Street I felt proud. People respected him. He wore a nice suit of clothes, a tall top hat, and shiny black shoes. He carried himself like a businessman of substance, head held high, and lots of dollars in his pocket. Nobody messed with him. But, if they owed him money, which many of them did, they quickly moved to the other side of the street. I learned quickly that survival depended on exhibiting a tough exterior others could not penetrate. Weakness was not tolerated and money that could not be paid back when it was due brought terrible consequences. In my neighborhood, using intimidation and bringing fear to others was just how the game was played. I'll never forget hearing grown men scream with pain or crumple to the ground from a punch that broke an arm or rib—or worse. Owing money you couldn't pay back was a terrible thing.

### My All *Mighty* Dollar

I was groomed to believe power and money were synonymous with respect. As I grew into my teen years, my father's attitude became my attitude. Although I did not become part of the Mafia, I took this attitude into my adult life.

Let's move ahead to our marriage in 1975—a third marriage for me and a second for Maxine. Together we brought five children into this new family. Two years later, another daughter was born. Life became very challenging to say the least. My wife's experience with money was just the opposite of mine. In her childhood home, money was used to survive one month to the next, put food on the table, pay the bills, and some went in the bank.

When it was time to pay the bills at our house, Maxine was the one who wrote out the checks. She would grow a knot in her stomach every month. My angry bouts and tight hold on money was closing in on us. By 1982, we were perilously close to calling it quits. Out of desperation my wife joined Bible Study Fellowship and began applying Biblical principles to her life. To begin with, I made fun of her and even accused her of hiding behind the cross, but she stuck with it.

It wasn't long before I was deeply impressed by the peace my wife had attained. She even stopped yelling back at me and began to love me in spite of our difficulties. Forgiving me over and over again couldn't have been easy, but it certainly diffused hundreds of arguments. A few months later, I came in contact with several men who spoke about receiving Christ into their lives. They talked of knowing God personally. Their lives had been strewn with anger and broken relationships—no different than mine, only God was making a difference. I had never heard of such things before, yet their testimonies convinced me these were true changes. Two weeks later I asked Jesus into my heart not realizing I was also inviting Him to deal with my attitude about money, too.

## Walking Up a New Street

I am by trade a Certified Public Accountant. Often I was approached for financial advice from people at church. Money problems were stealing their joy and creating major problems. Our hearts were burdened. Could a Bible study be found that would teach financial principles in a practical way? Should we develop one? After much research we were led to Howard Dayton at Crown Ministries. Crown's materials met the criteria we were looking for. They were both practical and biblically based. In 1990, we led our first Crown Ministries small group study. The results were exciting as people immediately began to apply the concepts.

I accepted the position of Pacific Northwest Regional Director for Crown Ministries. Convinced that the Lord also wanted us to be debt-free, we set about that goal and in 1992 we became entirely debt-free, including our home mortgage. To describe the euphoria this kind of freedom brings isn't easy. But, if I were a mountain climber, I'd have to say having the burden of debt gone is right up there with a reaching the top of Mt. Everest kind of a high.

Over the next few years we led groups and trained leadership from many churches and many denominations. One day it became apparent the time was right to merge my thriving accounting practice with a larger firm to make more hours available for involvement in ministry. By now, speaking opportunities brought about by my position with Crown confirmed that God had gifted me to preach and teach, too.

I began to study for the pastorate. In 1995, I received my first minister's license and was ordained in 1999. My wife and I began to pray that we would be called to a church that really needed us. Our prayers were answered when we heard about a congregation of about 100 people in Eagle Point, Oregon, whose pastor, Reverend B.J., was waiting for a heart transplant. The little church was not able to pay the salaries of two ministers. Because we had no debt we were a perfect fit for their unusual set of circumstances. Because we had saved money, and were receiving ongoing monthly payments from the buyout of my business, we were in a solid position to continue to meet our living expenses whether we got a paycheck or not.

Years ago, neither one of us would have dreamed of working for nothing! This was a definite change of attitude for a money-hungry guy from the North End. The congregation was warm and accepting. Two months after beginning our pastoral position, Pastor B. J. was awakened in the wee hours of the night and jetted to Seattle where he received a new heart. My ability to oversee this church body during a difficult time meant their pastor could take the months he needed to focus on getting well.

## Why Do We Chase After Money?

Everyone needs money to survive. The lights won't stay on without money. Basic needs have to be met. The problem in wanting money comes when people of all ages love money too much. The contentment factor has all but vanished in many countries today.

Trying to get rich, or just being desirous of material things, spurs many to chase after the greenbacks. Greed could top the list. Maybe the reason to want more cash is to cover unexpected bills. And sometimes the need to feel good about ourselves is soothed momentarily by spending money. Could there be an ambitious goal to be better than the next guy and the competitive spirit is running wild?

## Grandma's Prayers

Knowing where I am today, I cannot help but reflect on my childhood years. With my history, it would have been easy to assume I would have no other choice but to pick up where my father left off. Many of my friends did just that; they followed in their fathers' footsteps. Most are dead or in jail today, but not me. I can only attribute staying out of trouble to God's grace and my secret weapon—a praying grandmother. God was listening to her prayers.

Grandma didn't want her beloved son, only 56-years-old at the time, to get cancer and die—but he did. I was angry the day Papa died, but that didn't change anything. He was gone. After my grandmother's death six months later, I was drafted into the Army. At age twenty-two, I finally realized I was free to make my own choices. Unfortunately, I did not attain God's wisdom for another eighteen years. I continued to chase money for prestige, recognition, and the fear of what would happen if I didn't have any (I'd get beaten up).

But, once I realized God had a lot to say about money, and a plan for me to spread this news, my life began to change in big ways. What amuses me most is that instead of loving money and using people, like I used to do, God is now using me to touch the lives of thousands of people with the message of hope for financial freedom. If God can give me, a guy educated in the secular world of money, a freed-up attitude about my all *mighty* dollars, He can do it for you.

### The Bottom Line
- Know the downside of debt. Owing money can get really painful.
- The desire to chase after money is fueled by many things: fear, emotional needs, greed, peer pressure, and worldly desires.
- Find contentment. Someone else will always have a bigger house, a nicer car, a more exciting vacation, a greener yard, and a bigger water bill.
- Self-worth is not measured by money and possessions.

- Focus on the primary purpose of money: to provide for our needs.
- Appreciate the things money can't buy—good health, great relationships, peace.

### Increase the Wealth Challenge

Take a long look at your attitude about money. How has money motivated your career choices? How did your childhood impact your desire to have more money? What can be done today to align your way of thinking with your assets and potential? Make a deliberate decision to put aside anything that keeps you from finding contentment and God's will for your future.

### Common "Cents" Sense

*Above everything else, guard your heart. It is where your life comes from.*[18]

## Slick Talk: slick\-,tȯk\

Characterized by subtlety or nimble wit; wily (a reputation as a *slick* operator); language that appears to be earnest and meaningful but in fact is a mixture of sense and nonsense; inflated, involved, and often deliberately ambiguous language

Merriam-Webster's Online Dictionary, 2007-2008, Merriam-Webster Incorporated

# Five

## Marketing Slick Talk Sets the Trap

### Are you tired of scams, tricks, and lies?

*Everybody loves the Wealth Effect on the way up, but they forget that it also has a reverse gear.*[19]

—Charles Hugh Smith

Tom and Heidi's financial struggles began like lots of other couples trying to live the American dream in any town, any state, from coast-to-coast. Their plans started out happy, sounded doable, but took a nasty turn into an unforeseen humorless tangle of escalating debt and threat of foreclosure.

"We married ten years ago," Heidi said. "I had been let go from my job two weeks before our wedding but found a new job a month later. Tom was fired from his job two weeks later. This was the beginning of an up-and-down roller coaster of employment. In ten years he's had eight or nine jobs—so many I lost count. His average length of employment in any one career has been about two years.

"In 1999, a year after our wedding, our first child was born. I took maternity leave with the hope of going back to work later. Sadly, the company couldn't work around my daughter's schedule and I was laid off.

"To make matters more complex, the following year we were involved in a serious car accident. The outcome in 2002 was a small settlement of $29,000. We decided to use $3,000 of that money for a down payment on our first house and put the rest in savings. The mortgage payment of $700 a month, including taxes and insurance, was manageable for us. We were very happy. Then the other shoe dropped.

"The weekend we moved into our house, Tom was in another car accident. This time there was a fatality. A pedestrian had walked directly in front of his truck, rolled up onto the hood, hit the pavement, and was instantly killed. Tom wasn't at fault but the emotional trauma brought on

Post-Traumatic Stress Disorder. His employer, Sprint, helped us get placed into the FMLA (Family Medical Leave Act) to retain his job. But weeks turned into months of missed work and we had to use a portion of what was left in savings to buy another vehicle for Tom to drive.

"Two months after settling into the house I was pregnant again. Our son was born in January 2003—four days after Tom had been fired from Sprint. In June he started working for US Cellular. It was a good job and he moved up quickly. Because of his skills with customers, he moved to a higher position in a couple months. Everything was going great for nearly a year and a half. Then, the week before Thanksgiving 2004, US Cellular let about 30 of their higher paid employees go. Tom was in that group.

"A small amount of money remained in savings and we did get unemployment checks. It was during this season of no employment that we discovered some scholarship money had been set aside from a previous job through the Jobs Plus program. One dollar for every hour of employment had gone into a scholarship fund. Almost $1,000 was assigned for Tom's use. What a great opportunity to learn a new career. The housing market was doing well so it seemed like a good idea to take the $1,000 and learn how to sell real estate. By summer 2005 Tom was selling real estate. His first year was amazing. The housing market was soaring and our income was improving so much that by early 2006 we decided the time was right to upgrade to another house. But instead of selling the house we were living in, we decided to refinance with a home equity loan and rent out the first house."

Streetwise thinking would question leveraging one home to buy an additional house. We'll talk more about the Wealth Effect that pulled them into this kind of thinking in the next chapter. First, let's hear the rest of their story to understand the rationale taking place.

"It was our belief," Heidi continued, "that we were taking the investment our home represented and using it to grow a better financial future. Now we had two houses. Some of the $120,000 equity was used to purchase the second house with only ten percent down. The rest of the borrowed money went into a savings account to help make the mortgage payments.

"The plan was to have half of the amount coming from our pockets and the other half from the savings. The new mortgage on the first house jumped from $700 to $1,200 a month. The mortgage on the second house, the one we live in, is a whopping $2,000 a month. It was not possible to rent the first house for more than $900 a month. That meant we'd need to come up with $300 each and every month just to stay current with the mortgage payments."

Oh my! The whole idea was designed in a way that showed no regard for the safety of the family budget. Let's hear more.

"We knew the housing market wouldn't continue to grow as fast as it had, but we figured, as did the rest of southern Oregon, that it would only experience a slow-down. That's not what happened. Things got much worse. Real estate took a dive a month after we moved into the second house. Tom only sold two houses between June 2006 and July 2007. It was obvious he had to find a job with steady income. He was hired. But his wages are nowhere near enough to cover what is needed to pay our bills. We've relied on credit cards to pay utilities, and because our income is low, we applied and qualified for food stamps.

"We used up all of our savings and even a small inheritance that I received from my grandfather is gone. We went in to talk to our mortgage company to see if there was anything we could do to save our home. Long story short, because we were not in default, there is nothing they can do. The type of loan we have prevents us from getting anything changed. So now, for the first time, we will not be paying our mortgage. I hate being in this position. I believe it is against what God would have us do, but we have no choice. There is no money left. Tom's income, after taxes and insurance, only brings $1,400 a month home.

"Right now we are sitting on two car loans that demand $320 a month with balances totaling $10,000. Our credit card debt is near $8,000. The amounts aren't huge, but our problem now is that we just can't pay it. We are listing our house in a short sale to see if we can avoid foreclosure. The other house will be listed as well in hopes we can use what equity we get out of it to pay down our debt. We also plan to sell my car and buy another one outright to eliminate one car payment.

"To be honest, at the time we bought the second house we really felt we were doing the right thing," said Heidi. "Up until a few weeks ago, I kept asking God why this was happening to us; now I have learned just to tell God I trust Him and ask Him to give me strength to bear this burden. I have learned to lean on God a lot more. I believe He is preparing us for something better than what we have now. But as long as I have a dishwasher, I'm going to choose to be happy."

## An Ongoing Foreclosure Crisis

Numbers coming out of the financial sectors tell a story of an America that is spending its resources well into the future. Too many of our citizens are losing their homes, relying on credit, and saddling future generations with trillions of dollars of debt to pay back.

*A record 19 million U.S. homes stood empty at the end of 2008 and homeownership fell to an eight-year low as banks seized homes faster than they could sell them.*[20] As of the first quarter of 2009, things got even worse. *The mortgage crisis is spreading and hitting new heights: Borrowers with good credit now make up the largest share of foreclosures as job losses and pay cuts exact their toll. A record 12 percent of homeowners with a mortgage were behind on their payments in the first quarter, the Mortgage Bankers Association said.*[21]

This is a disturbing problem. When *qualified* borrowers face foreclosure it's not a good sign. Lenders wrote loans in good faith not expecting to lose money on this particular group of people. A harsh lesson has been learned: Job losses and pay cuts are no respecters of persons. Everyone is vulnerable. Every loan written represents a potential risk to the lender. Many have been put in an unexpected financial bind, too. That's why it's insensitive to fault them now for wanting to tighten up lending. They know the economic climate is uncertain. Billions of dollars have already been written down. Entire mortgage departments have vanished—defunct—out of business. Foreclosures continue to bear down on families. Like locusts marching across green pasturelands, there seems to be no end in sight.

On January 11, 2011 CNBC reported: *Home values have fallen 26 percent since their peak in June 2006, worse than the 25.9-percent decline seen during the Depression years between 1928 and 1933, Zillow reported. November marked the 53rd consecutive month (4 ½ years) that home values have fallen. What's worse, it's not over yet: Home values are expected to continue to slide as inventories pile up, and likely won't recover until the job market improves.*[22]

The Federal Reserve is working hard to keep chaos from erupting around the world. Why? Because foreign investors own large quantities of our mortgage backed securities. Foreclosure in the United States spells big trouble for people beyond our shores.

Like Tom and Heidi, a growing number of families confess they are relying heavily on credit for everyday necessities like groceries, electricity, and diapers. Intuitively there is agreement that adding more debt cannot be the right answer but impulsively the pressing problem is survival. Credit fills that gap.

How is it possible to make ends meet and jump off the credit card merry-go-round at the same time? There's only one way—get streetwise about money. Set a plan in motion to stop those ever-spinning cycles of debt from pilfering the future.

## The Bottom Line

- The illusion of wealth can lead the best of us astray.
- Remember Tom and Heidi's story. Refuse to accept the get-rich-quick myth.
- Riches grow best the old-fashioned way with steady plodding over time.
- Build up a solid work resume before taking on homeownership or an investment portfolio.
- Live a content, modest lifestyle—one that respects the family's paycheck.
- Challenge slick talk. Don't hand over dollars based on hype or peer pressure.
- Prepare for the unpredictable. Jobs are lost, accidents happen, health changes.

## Increase the Wealth Challenge

Take an honest look at how the Wealth Effect has come into your own life. However this shakes down don't be too hard on yourself. Allow what you find to act as a learning curve. Figure out how to live off of the real money you earn. The goal is to no longer create a standard of living from the fount of false equity.

## Common "Cents" Sense

*Don't weary yourself trying to get rich. Why waste your time?*
*For riches can disappear as though they had the wings of a bird!*[23]

# Caught: \ˈkȯt also ˈkat\

To take hold of; to obtain through effort; to overtake unexpectedly —usually used in the passive <was *caught* in a storm>; to get entangled <*catch* a sleeve on a nail>; to become affected by; to attract and hold; to grasp by the senses or the mind <you *catch* what I mean?>

Merriam-Webster's Online Dictionary, 2007-2008, Merriam-Webster Incorporated

# Six

## What Creates a Bubble in the First Place?

## Caught up in the Wealth Effect

*Behind the temporary gains created by tech stocks like Pets.com and flipping condos like pancakes, the real driver of the wealth bubble was easy credit, cheap credit, and way-too-easy cheap credit.*[24]

—Brian J. O'Connor

Tom and Heidi got caught up in the Wealth Effect. Simply stated: the hope of gaining riches quickly. The Wealth Effect charms innocent people into believing an affluent life is within easy reach. A bubble is being created. Those originating the plan grease the idea with fancy slick talk. The appeal is to whet the appetite and part us from our money. As more and more investors are convinced the idea is a solid way to prosper, the market artificially rises up higher and higher. Yes, money can be made during this upward climb—but only for those who know the bubble won't last. Those few folks know when to get out. The majority don't have a clue. Unsuspecting investors find out too late and end up with a painful loss of capital and an enormous pile of debt. What sounded good going in revealed a sinister twist in the end.

### Living the Dream

Americans have one dream in common. On the whole, we all want to own a home. This desire is imbedded in our psyche. When the time was ripe to plant a housing bubble, the perfect soil was already in place.

Marry the desire to own a home with the perfect advocate and the gate opens wide. This Wealth Effect couldn't have found a more high-profile individual than President George W. Bush to encourage lenders and borrowers alike.

By virtue of his office, the Constitution and laws of the Unites States, Bush officially proclaimed June 2007 as National Homeownership Month and proudly wrote: *Today, nearly 70% of Americans own their own homes, and the rate of minority homeownership has climbed to above 50 percent since I took office in 2001. The American Dream Downpayment Act of 2003 is helping thousands of low to moderate income and minority families with the down payment and closing costs on their homes. I urge citizens to consider homeownership opportunities in their communities, and I applaud American homeowners for helping fuel the economy.*[25]

The President of the United States publicly voiced his seal of approval. A clarion call went forward like a giant green light. *Buy a house. Come one. Come all.* Borrowers felt like true American heroes doing their country proud by advancing the economy to greater prosperity.

In hindsight, perhaps the President and his advisors may have been shortsighted. The ideal was wonderful. Get people into homes. That's a nice thing to want to do. But the result of all those loosely structured loans pushed millions of people and our nation into dire economic straits.

Be wary. Every Wealth Effect carries another less obvious agenda into the arena. Pumping easy money into the economy is only the first part of a much bigger picture. Putting buying power in the hands of borrowers lined the pockets of lenders. Many executives became wealthy in a short period of time. The credit bubble grew to magical size. Borrowed money was the product being sold and the profit center fueling the underlying agenda to get-rich-quick. We might ask why so many highly respected economists and financial experts tossed rules of caution to the wind? We'll never fully know. Greed and profit seem obvious. Encouragement from the government made it all sound so safe.

## True Equity

True equity is determined by the difference between a purchase price and a selling price. To know how to price a home, real estate agents consult a list of other houses of comparable size, amenities, and demographics that have recently been sold.

For example, eight years ago, in 2003, the housing market was robust. A close friend purchased a home for $215,000 in a modest city on the outskirts of Seattle. Only four years later, in the spring of 2007, based on other sales in the neighborhood, that same house would have listed for $365,000! If the house had been sold right then—at the pinnacle of the housing bubble—cashed out equity landing in the bank would have been a whopping $150,000 (minus improvements and closing costs). An impressive gain.

Our friend felt it best to wait another year before trying to sell and look for a larger house. Oops. The housing bubble burst in September 2007. By 2008 the asking price of homes had taken a serious hit. Mortgages, by the thousands, were falling into default and facing foreclosure. Families were being evicted or handing the keys over to the lender in lieu of foreclosure.

The Wealth Effect had put on the brakes, shifted into reverse, and turned out the lights. The party was over.

Granted, our friend is among the fortunate. He has a small enough mortgage to still capture a profit. Many people are not so lucky. One in four mortgages is underwater. More is owed than what the property can realistically be sold for today. There is no equity.

Let's digress. Back in the 1950s, equity gained was primarily based on paying down the mortgage. When the loan reflected a payment, equity was gained. Say twelve payments of $125 a month were applied in a year's time on a thirty-year $14,000 mortgage. The loan holder paid $1,375 to the lending institution. Assume $500 accumulated as principle payments and the rest was interest. Homeowner equity increased by $500 that year.

Historically, homes never skyrocketed in value like the phenomenon we witnessed in this housing bubble. Real estate moved up at a steadier more gradual pace—one that could sustain reasonable economic growth.

## Borrowing: Then and Now

Back in the 1940s, 50s and up into the 70s most credit given out was used to help businessmen get started with new equipment for business. On an individual level, borrowers could get a home mortgage, but the rules were very stringent. Before being approved, the man or woman had to be credit-worthy, hold a steady job for several years, and have a sizeable down payment of 20–33%.

The same guidelines were true for auto loans. In those days, a lot of planning and saving was a natural part of preparing to make a major purchase. Good character traits and fiscal responsibility mattered to the lender. Not as many people qualified to borrow large sums of money.

The U.S. Census Bureau's historical report, revised November 27, 2001, reported home ownership of one-family detached homes at 55 percent in the 1950 census. By 1960, homeownership topped 60 percent due to favorable tax laws and easier mortgage financing. In 2000, ownerships exceeded 66 percent. These statistics saw a steady increase except for a dip in the 80s.

## Aunt Louise and Uncle Tom

Charlie's Aunt and Uncle bought a home in upstate New York during the 1950s. They raised their two sons in that two-bedroom clapboard house with its big front porch and oversized back yard. Together, they set about paying off the mortgage. Month-after-month year-after-year they sent in money until one day the last payment was made. Apart from the birth of their boys, there wasn't a prouder happier moment.

Tragically, the older son died in an auto accident. The younger son married and was blessed with two children. One day the home directly behind the parents' house came up for sale. The son and his wife took out a mortgage and set about paying off the loan. Back yard to back yard they raised their son and daughter.

A few years later, Grandpa died. Grandma remained in her home until she too passed away. Who got the house? The natural order of things meant the son inherited the house. He and his wife, now empty-nesters, moved across the yard into the home where he had grown up.

The second house wasn't empty for long. The couple's adult son, along with his wife and two young boys are shaping their own dreams in the house where he had grown up. They climb the same staircase, sleep in the same rooms, cook in the same kitchen (now remodeled). If the walls could talk what stories they'd tell.

To date, four generations have lived on these two properties. Call it legacy. Call it family closeness. The stability of this multi-generational picture is hard to miss.

Setting down roots to cling to is a good thing. The foresight of this couple modeled the value of a home as the centerpiece of family. From this hub, life happens. In this living room, this kitchen, this yard, memories are made.

In such a mobile society, not many of us will be able to fully emulate this kind of family dynamic. Our loved ones are scattered across the nation and around the world. Our current home is not the only home we'll live in. When opportunity knocks we'll head off in a new direction in pursuit of a better career and income. Or, perhaps we'll move closer to our adult children rather than them coming back home. Wherever life takes us, family roots must follow. Thankfully we can keep the photographs on the wall, write letters and emails, plan special visits, share vacations, and build from there.

Maybe it's time to reassess our own values. If so, take a fresh look at the whole idea of home ownership.

1. To what extent does our house represent a home more than an investment?
2. Is our time spent with family in healthy proportion to our desire to grow wealth?

Every morning delivers a fresh opportunity to move in a new direction—one that is loaded with potential to lay down a strong foundation for the next generations.

## What Went Wrong?

As the government saw fit to ease loan requirements and made credit easier and easier to acquire, mortgage lenders followed the scent of big profits. It seemed the sky was the limit. Greed was driving the economy. Everyone wanted a piece of the action.

An elusive euphoria, charged by the intoxicating scent of instant wealth, caught on. The family residence became the number one means to bankroll a great life. Slick talk of opportunity sang out loud and long, its tune like the beautiful bells that ring every hour on the hour from the National Cemetery. *This house promises to pay big bucks later*, they chimed.

Life sometimes sings off-key. Promises aren't always kept. What goes up also comes down.

The marketing psychology behind buying a home took a dramatic shift in recent years. The sales pitch to get in on the action was very convincing. All types of modern mortgages made it possible for just about anybody to purchase a home. The availability of easy loans brought expansion to the housing industry as never before in our country's history.

Boomtowns sprang up all across the land. Overnight the price of an average home rose at a ridiculous pace. The psychology of the day was "buy a house—you can't lose. Buy it now—it will cost more tomorrow."

A sense of urgency drove so many people to do whatever it took to jump in the game. This is how the Wealth Effect moves full speed ahead. More and more folks climb aboard believing this was an investment that could only continue to rise in value. This creates another problem. Momentum like this also begins to drive up the standard of living at warp speed. When we feel rich, we spend more. Or, more accurately, we put more on credit.

It was inconceivable that real estate prices would drop. This boom seemed ironclad. Buy now. Flip tomorrow. Sold on the idea that home values always increase, real estate emerged as the profit center of choice. Where else could a person hope to strike it rich so fast? From the street sweeper to the brain surgeon, bright minds joined average Americans all across the country. The hope of riches had caught us up in the Wealth Effect. Money borrowed for property was accepted as favorable debt. The end would justify the means—or so we thought.

Right about now take a deep breath and a closer look at yesteryear's financial mindset. Perhaps Papa was right: Pay as you go. Save for what you want. Borrow with the greatest of caution.

Back then being prudent was all about having a strong desire to pay off a loan fast. There was no inclination to grow the mortgage larger. The thinking was to protect the home, preserve the roof over the family's head, and clear up debt as quickly as possible. There was a proud anticipation of the day when the last payment would be made and the deed to the property held securely in hand. *Paid-in-full* stamped with an official seal on that legal document validated true ownership. This was a time to celebrate, invite the neighbors in, and pop the cork.

A whole lot about yesterday's values makes sense for today. A contracting economy is the perfect point in time to see a resurgence of streetwise thinking accompanied by smarter spending and more modest living. Children can experience the joy of growing a garden and learn to appreciate family talks around the dinner table. The uncertainty in the economy can provide an opportune time to get back to the basics at home.

## Remember the Dot.Com Crash?

The psychological nature of the Wealth Effect manipulates common sense at its core. Men and women are driven by fancy words and upbeat talk to risk plunging deep into credit with one goal in mind—the hope of becoming independently wealthy.

A Wealth Effect is not a new phenomenon. We have only to think back a few years to the dot.com heydays. Buzz words and slick market talk rallied excitement for internet stocks. There was very little substance being offered. Common folk didn't understand how to be cautious. Getting rich was the goal. Investors were caught off guard. Again, greed drove people to do what rationale might have warned against.

Hard-working men and women, bent on gaining instant profit, risked their 401(k)s and pensions and loaded up on dot.com stocks. With paychecks being funneled toward investing, amassing credit card debt to meet living expenses seemed to be a smart choice.

To make matters worse, spending increased as if the profits were already in our pockets. Sound familiar? This is the most common behavioral result of a Wealth Effect. People feel rich. Feeling rich leads to spending more borrowing more. Families ramp up lifestyle choices to live at the level of perceived wealth. Expensive clothes, European trips, bigger cars, and nice dinners out at classy restaurants became standard fare. Of course, all of this was bought with credit, not cash. Debt is growing by leaps and bounds. Nobody seems to care. The brokerage house statement tells us we have lots of money.

For a while, portfolios rose at a super fast and unusual pace. The financial markets appeared magical. Quick riches were being made—for those who knew how to get in and out of the dot.com market fast. But most investors rode the train too long. It derailed. Hopes of profit turned to loss as dot.com landed in the ditch belly-up.

Bottom line, the dot.com boon turned out to be a paper tiger. A monthly statement, ink on paper from a trusted brokerage house looked good at first. Until the unthinkable began to happen.

As it goes with all impressive Wealth Effects, the market rises for a while, people jump in, and then things go terribly wrong. The big chance to grab hold of the brass ring vanishes. No one dreams the bubble can burst. There is no reality check going on with Wealth Effect until it collapses.

Dot.com detonated with the foul smell of smoldering ashes after a wildfire. *In 2000 and 2001, countless Internet stocks fell from $50 or $100 a share to near zero in a matter of months. In 2001, Enron went from $85 to pennies a share in less than a year. These are the early casualties of debt, leverage and incautious speculation.*[26]

Enron, the big daddy of dot.com players, turned into a curse word when the real truth came out. A fake trading floor was only one piece of this slick picture. The floor fell out from under millions of investors. Lawsuits mounted from angry shareholders left with rusted out portfolios. Worthless paper. No profit to be found. Only shattered dreams, angry spirits, stressed out lives, and the hardest truth to face for the truly tapped out folks—financial ruin.

Now, in our day, with the devastating mortgage crisis, the cyclical nature of Wealth Effect has again left another tsunami behind.

## We Can't Eat Equity

Human nature is vulnerable given the right set of circumstances. And money casts its spell on too many of us. Possessing financial savvy includes the ability to accurately interpret asset values. Brokerage firms are required to send monthly reports to their clientele. Statements compare the present month's market value to the prior month's value for the securities held (i.e. stocks and bonds) within the portfolio. This point of accountability keeps individual investors informed of profit or loss over time.

Where things fall apart is when people believe the numbers printed on the monthly statement, delivered by the neighborhood mailman, are equal to cash in the bank. No one can eat equity—no matter how much salt and pepper is poured on top. Don't overlook this important point.

Paper equity is not the same as spendable dollars until the item (stock, bond, home, etc.) is sold and the cash sits in a checking or savings account at the bank. Until then, these are phantom dollars. Not everything goes up in value. No one should begin to live at the level of an increase that has not been cashed in. Unfortunately, phantom money was put to use as a ticket to an upscale lifestyle. Spending ran rampant, keeping pace with monthly statements, with little fear of the bottom falling out. The Wealth Effect became a sucker's game.

Daily, economic conditions fluctuate giving rise and fall to financial markets. At 9:30 am there is an opening bell on Wall Street. At 4:00 pm a closing bell. Five days a week this happens—just like clockwork. And, when our stock markets close, markets around the world are still at work buying and selling.

See the Wealth Effect as a coin with two sides. Heads you win, tails you lose. Unless the pockets are deep, and there is lots of money to fall back on, don't play this game. It can be a very dangerous trap. When heads flip to tails, life turns ugly—fast.

Be on guard. *By smooth talk and flattery they deceive the minds of naïve people.*[27]

Falling for get-rich-quick schemes is a sure sign of being smitten by the Wealth Effect. If slick talk wasn't profitable, there'd be no reason to worry. But it is the worm on the hook dangling temptation before us. Many bite the worm and are caught in a vulnerable financial position. Always question the risk attached. Be cautious, or run the other way.

## Consolidation Loans

The bills are piled high. The stress is awful. Arguments about money seem endless.

What's a family to do?

It might be a good time to start praying for solutions. Is an opportunity to consolidate Debt Mountain into one easy payment a smart thing to do?

Maybe not.

Every loan places the borrower in bondage. The Bible states that the borrower is servant to the lender (Proverbs 22:7). Most of us get that point. And yet, when push comes to shove, borrowing tops the list as the number one way to solve money problems.

Loans created from home equity through the refinance of a mortgage have the potential to make a tough financial spot even worse. It is never a good decision to bury a multitude of consumer purchases inside a mortgage. Not ever! When a tank of gas, a honeymoon, or a set of tires is paid for over thirty years, the cost of those items becomes astronomical. Interest over thirty years is now being added to the tank of gas, the honeymoon, and the set of tires. Equity loans are much costlier to the borrower than a credit card purchase will ever be.

Most importantly, consumer borrowing, when rolled into a home loan, attaches unsecured credit card debt to a secured home mortgage. Not a good idea. The once unsecured debt suddenly becomes secured debt locked into the life of the home mortgage. Consumer debt has been given permission to increase the mortgage. And the bigger the indebtedness, the greater possibility of default should tough times come. Unless there is a crazy desire to lay the groundwork for a lower standard of living in the future, don't consolidate debt into a home mortgage.

Instead, examine the problem carefully. Is there a real need for an equity loan? What is the goal? Is it to get rid of credit card debt, fund a vacation, pay off a car or student loan, or offset everyday household expenses like groceries and gasoline? None of these validate borrowing against the house. A medical emergency might be considered in a different light and become a right incentive.

Look for better ways to get out from under consumer debt.

1. Work with the lenders. Negotiate.
2. Sacrifice some fun to realign the budget.
3. Take a second job for a while.
4. Seek counsel.
5. Sell something.
6. Pray for solutions to be found.

Bankruptcy should not be the path of choice for borrowers. But, in some cases, like extreme medical debt, it becomes the only way to find freedom in the aftermath of a very difficult unexpected circumstance.

Student loans and taxes cannot be bankrupted out.

Once consumer credit is packaged inside a home mortgage, it morphs into a different animal. In the end, the house that shelters the family might be taken away. All the more reason to protect the home front. This is where family lives, builds memories, and comes to feel safe and secure. The best thing to do is make a goal to pay off the home mortgage rather than add to its principal.

## Proceed with Caution

Don't give the Wealth Effect permission to jeopardize the future. Television commercials purposely have a hypnotic effect on viewers. Each product being marketed is meant to sound good enough to separate us from our money. Mute commercials. Go get a drink of water.

Take a bold step and stop borrowing. Taking on more debt is not what's best for our families. Paying off debt and building up savings is a much better choice.

Wealth Effect has spurred too many of us to live at a higher standard of living than is realistic. A false sense of wealth drives spending habits. Now it's time to sort through the financial turmoil and get back on track.

All of us should proceed with caution. Stories of shattered dreams aren't hard to find. This bubble burst but it's not the end of the Wealth Effect. It won't lie dormant for long.

Use the days wisely. Make preserving capital a top priority and managing risk a main concern. We live in times of economic uncertainty. Do away with the old impulsive ways and bring forth financial wisdom and structure.

## The Bottom Line

- What goes up can also come down.
- Shop mortgage rates and only accept a fixed-rate loan.
- Know how much debt your budget can safely tolerate.
- Debt can grow large enough to place the family in jeopardy.
- Using borrowed money to repay debt is a high-priced bad idea.
- Never attach unsecured consumer debt to a home mortgage.
- Growing wealth is a good goal—chasing riches is a poor objective.

## Increase the Wealth Challenge

There is more happiness and greater peace when finances are in order. See financial freedom as an achievable goal. Starting today, brainstorm two things: 1) What one thing will help you break the debt cycle, and 2) name a group (Samaritan's Purse), or a cause (Dogs for the Deaf), or a community outreach program (Rescue Mission) that you admire and would enjoy being a part of. Now that you have decided to be a smart money manager, you'll have more time, resources, and energy freed up to pursue other interests.

## Common "Cents" Sense

*A bird in the hand is worth two in the bush; mere dreaming of nice things is foolish; its chasing the wind.*[28]

# Score: \\'skȯr\\

A number that expresses accomplishment
(as in a game or test) or excellence (as in quality)
either absolutely in points gained or by comparison to a standard

Merriam-Webster's Online Dictionary, 2007-2008, Merriam-Webster Incorporated

# Seven

## Know the Score

### What is a credit score—why is it important?

*A credit report, also known as a credit file or credit history, is unfortunately not one of life's options. You have to have one ... because it says a lot about a person's character.*[29]

—Mary Hunt

Janella Carr was feeling really upbeat about the job she'd landed through the temp agency. There were no problems with her skill levels or social attributes. She had every reason to believe this company would keep her on their payroll for years to come—until an unexpected problem arose.

"I'd found the job I really loved through a temp service. My employers were pleased with my performance and I felt this was the job I'd been waiting to land for a very long time. At the end of six months I was offered the job full time. That's when the credit check came into play. It was the policy of this company to run a credit check on everyone who was being considered for full-time employment before making a final decision to hire—even if their work on a temporary basis was highly favorable and respected. My work was great; my credit score was low. I was let go and denied full-time employment. I was devastated."

In the United States, FICO is the company that provides the most extensively used credit scoring model. FICO is an acronym for Fair Isaac Corporation. Six months of credit history is needed to establish a credit score. Our three largest credit reporting agencies are Equifax, Trans Union, and Experian. All three agencies use FICO software to determine credit scores. Each of them offers one free credit report per year. The scores (scores only) are then sold to those who underwrite car loans, mortgages, and insurance policies, as well as employers, landlords, and an unending mixed bag of credit card issuers and those extending business offers.

It is the industry norm for consumer reporting companies to report accurate negative information, even lawsuits or unpaid judgments against us, for a period of seven years, or until a statute of limitations runs out, whichever is *longer*. Bankruptcy information sticks to the report for ten years. Criminal convictions have no statute of limitations. Oddly enough, that same rule of thumb applies to reporting when a person has applied for a job that pays more than $75,000 a year or if they've tried to obtain credit or life insurance for $150,000 or more. Like diamonds, these pieces of credit history last *forever*.

Individuals can and should get a copy of their credit report at least once a year. Better yet, we should stagger our requests and get three credit reports per year. Since Equifax, Trans Union, and Experian each offer one free report per year, it's an easy task to do. Another big reason to look at credit reports every few months is to be on the lookout for identity theft against ourselves or any minor children.

Identity theft rings wreak havoc all across the world. Because Social Security numbers are assigned shortly after birth, boys and girls are vulnerable targets. Fraud that includes the stolen identity of a child may be the hottest ticket in the underground market for stolen IDs. Children are being exploited in alarming numbers and parents usually remain unaware of this crime for years. Don't wait until the child attempts to buy a car or heads off to college to guard his or her identity. Protect the child's future by checking their individual credit scores. To get the score of a child less than thirteen years of age requires filing a special request form. For those older than thirteen, the form is the same as for an adult seeking a credit report. Forms are found at www.annualcreditreport.com or by contacting the phone number or address listed below.

1. Log on to web site www.annualcreditreport.com.
2. Make a telephone call to: (877)322-8228.
3. Mail a written request to: Annual Credit Report Request Service, PO Box 105281, Atlanta, GA 30348-5281.

Other sites offer credit reports but beware. Many of these are imposter sites. The only government authorized source is www.annualcreditreport.com.

When a credit report is ordered, it will include information on where we live, how we pay our bills—on time, late or delinquent—and whether we've been sued, arrested, filed bankruptcy, have tax liens or monetary judgments filed against us. Race, sex, marital status, national origin, or religions are not factors. Age can be used.

A credit report is *not* a credit score. The credit report is free but the credit score is not usually free. Expect to pay about $15.95 from www.myfico.com or $47.85 to purchase credit scores from all three agencies. Prices could fluctuate. Since Equifax, Trans Union, and Experian operate independently of one another, each may each generate a different FICO score because they could have slightly different information recorded in the credit history.

FICO uses a numbering system between 300 and 850. Like a game of bowling the higher the individual's score, the better. Borrowers with a score above 720 are generally considered prime. For example, a mortgage of $150,000 given to a buyer with a score over 720 will qualify for the best loan available. He could pay 3% less interest over the life of the loan than someone whose credit score is below 700. The loftier the borrower's score the less interest is paid out and the smaller the monthly payment. It's very possible to see a variance of $300–$500 per month which translates to well over $100,000 to $200,000 in dollars being paid back over the life of the loan.

The graph below gives you a breakdown of credit scores across the population.

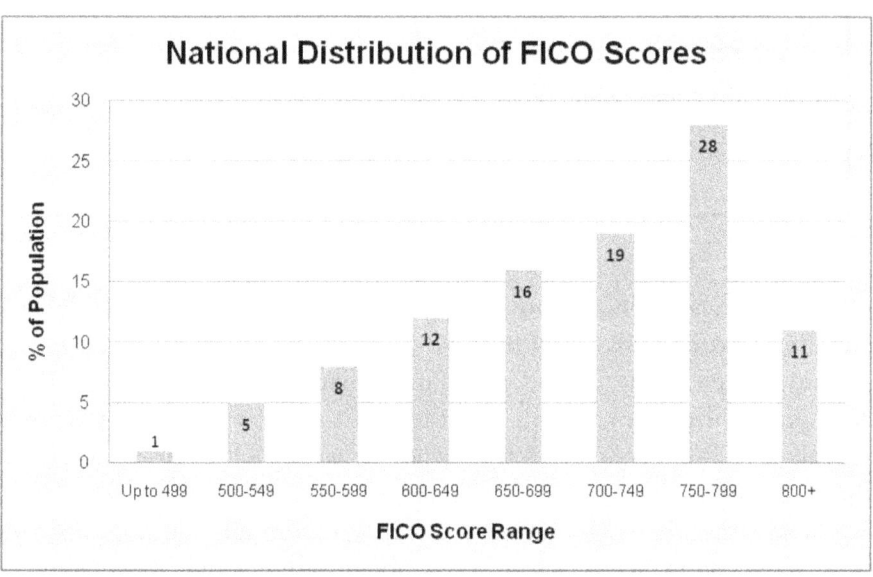

Favorable credit scores allow us to do some rate shopping. Lenders are blessed to have our business and we look for the best loan available with the smallest interest rate. Be streetwise while shopping. If the need is an auto loan, to avoid lowering your FICO score, shop rates within a two-week period of time because comparing ten different lenders becomes ten lenders all requesting a credit report on you. FICO is able to distinguish whether we are shopping around or out opening multiple credit lines if the activity stays within the 14-day time frame. Self-inquiries, or inquiries from existing creditors, don't affect a credit score. Only new credit grantors affect a FICO score. And it can affect the score by several points in the wrong direction. Ouch!

| FICO | | | |
|---|---|---|---|
| 720-850 | 5.95% | $2,386 | $458,822 |
| 700-719 | 6.08% | $2,418 | $470,401 |
| 675-699 | 6.61% | $2,557 | $520,620 |
| 620-574 | 7.75% | $2,866 | $631,932 |
| 560-619 | 8.60% | $3,103 | $717,252 |
| 500-559 | 8.94% | $3,200 | $751,928 |

Example based on 30 year fixed mortgage of $400,000

Source Data: MYFICO.com

How fast can a FICO score change? That depends. There could be mistakes in a credit report. Those mistakes, like having numbers posted wrong, can be changed rather fast and would immediately change the report. FICO rules grant thirty days from the day the credit report was initiated for individuals to contact companies that reported wrong information to correct those errors.

Most times, however, improving a FICO score takes steady plodding over time. The majority of financial problems are self-inflicted, making it necessary to commit to paying debt down, being a sensible money manager, and making payments on time.

FICO scores are divided into five unequal categories. Some portions count against us more than others: payment history (35%), amounts of money owed (30%), length of the credit history (15%), new credit (10%), and types of credit used (10%).

## Payment History = 35 percent of your score

Everything from great news to downright ugly problems dumps into our financial history. One-by-one every credit instrument used adds to the story—department stores, mortgages, installment loans, bankruptcies, liens, judgments, collection proceedings, and wage garnishments all surface. Timely payments sing beautiful melodies. Delinquent payments, as well as the amount of the delinquency, supply sour notes painful to our ratings.

## Amount of Money Owed = 30%

FICO evaluates monies owed on all outstanding accounts and the number of accounts with balances. A big piece of information found in this category is the amount of credit in use in comparison to the total amount of available credit. In other words, we do not want to max out any credit line. For instance, if we have a credit card with a $30,000 line of credit, it is in our favor to only use one-third of the available credit. It's better to increase the credit limit on the card than to use 100 percent of available credit. FICO scores will reflect high numbers when we stay within the formula range of one-third and drop when we max out an account.

Proportions of installment loan amounts still owed are compared to the original loan amount. Let's say in 2006 a $3,500 loan, over three years time, was transacted for living room furniture. A credit report is drawn two years later. The balance owed the lender shows a year's payments still owing. This is good progress. The loan is progressing at a responsible pace.

## Length of the Credit History = 15%

This category is pretty simple to understand. How long has it been since the account was opened and what activity has been seen. In 2006, I opened a new account with a department store chain. Since opening that account, I have used my charge card three times. The balance has been paid in full and there is nothing owed on the account. I could have paid only a portion of the balance due. But I didn't want interest charges added to the items I'd bought. A good rule of thumb to follow is that unless paying in full creates a true hardship, there should always be a willingness on our part to keep revolving credit accounts paid off on a monthly basis.

## New Credit = 10%

This portion of the reporting formula not only numbers the amount of recently opened accounts by number and type of account, it also takes into consideration the number of people inquiring to have a copy of our credit report. It will make a difference how long it has been since an inquiry was made and if the new credit being sought is an attempt to re-establish good credit after a poor payment history. Applying for too many retail credit cards, just to save 15% on the total bill at the checkout register might be sending the wrong message to FICO. Our FICO score could slide further in a downward direction. Be streetwise. Salesclerks are pressured by management to ask customers if they want to save money by opening an account. These offers sound smart at the time but are one more way retailers push their way deeper into our wallets.

## Types of Credit Used = 10%

In this piece of the formula, FICO examines the mix of credit being used. What is the assortment of credit cards, mortgages held, installment loans, retail accounts, and other types of borrowing? For instance, Mabel the grocery clerk has three retail accounts (Costco, Penney's, and Macy's), two mortgages, and is making installment payments on a five-year auto loan. All of these obligations factor into this part of her credit score.

Smart lenders practice sharp business sense when asking for a credit report. All of them should want answers to as many questions as possible before giving us credit. To be legal, all who make inquiries must gain our permission before running a credit check.

## How Does FICO Affect an Authorized User?

What does it mean to be an authorized user on someone else's credit? Should someone else be allowed to piggyback on another person's credit? Once upon a time adding a son or daughter as an authorized user to a parent's credit card was considered a smart teaching tool. The young adult instantly inherited the good track record of the parents. Credit was easily established. There was no need for a cosigner for the high school graduate struggling to establish a credit history—which takes a long time. Instead of begging to be trusted with credit, Kathy could easily be added in to a respectable FICO score established by her father. The benefits were huge. The same low interest rates Dad could get were now hers when she bought her first car, took a trip abroad, or headed off to college.

On the flip side, it makes no sense for a young person to become an authorized user with a parent who has lousy credit. Authorized users only benefit if there is a pristine score to piggyback onto. Otherwise the attachment becomes a harmful liability. If the mom or dad are habitually late paying or have filed bankruptcy, those irresponsible actions transfer the negative information along to the authorized user's credit report—even though the authorized user had nothing to do with the signed contracts nor was directly involved with any legal proceedings connected to the bankruptcy. In simple talk, the authorized user would be deemed just as flakey as the account holder. Guilt by association is all that stands to be gained from aligning oneself with anyone who is in financial trouble.

Our recommendation is to develop a personal credit history apart from piggybacking. A great way to start is with a secured credit card. A secured credit card provides good training ground for a young person. The parent puts a limited amount of dollars into a savings account, anywhere from $300 to $10,000, which determines the credit limit given to a son or daughter. The secured credit card requires that a cash collateral amount be deposited into the savings account. Shop around. Look for a card that does not charge an application fee plus an annual fee.

Don't turn the credit card over to your child without adding information and accountability. Knowledge paves the road to success. Streetwise parents explain the proper use of the card to the older teen/young adult who is ready to be trained in the use of credit.

- ❖ Rule number one: There is a predetermined credit limit.
- ❖ Rule number two: The balance must be paid off each month.
- ❖ Rule number three: Create a monthly spending plan.
- ❖ Rule number four: The young person's personal checking account is used to keep the account active. Have a clear understanding of *who* deposits money into this account, how much, and how often.
- ❖ Rule number five: If the card is not handled responsibly, the line of credit will be closed.

Secured credit cards are a good way to build a credit history and teach responsible financial management at home. If the user defaults on the monthly payments, the bank then takes money from the original savings account and applies those dollars to cover the balance owed. Not paying in a timely fashion destroys the purpose of having the secured credit card.

The day will come when the person working to build up a good credit history will receive offers for credit in the mail. This signals you that the bank is reporting a credit history and it's time to look for a more conventional credit card.

Choices of having no fees and good interest rates are limited on secured cards. Secured credit is meant to be in place for a short period of time only. This card is a stepping-stone leading the user to a place where unsecured credit becomes available. The specific intent is to build, establish, or improve, credit—period. If payments are made on time over a 12-month span, the individual will likely be trusted with an unsecured credit card. Be sure the banking institution is reporting the activity on the new account to the credit bureaus before doing business with them because the purpose in taking this step is to establish, or reestablish, credit.

Take FICO scores seriously. When FICO is kept in platinum territory, we'll be blessed by the most advantageous personal financial position available to man. That strong advantage point bumps us to the head of the line for borrowing money at the lowest rates, getting that dream job, being considered a good insurance risk, or being chosen over others in an apartment search. High scores open doors and result in less money spent overall.

## The Bottom Line

- Take advantage of FICO's free credit reports.
- Quickly clear up mistakes found in a credit report.
- Credit reports expose financial history and hidden money secrets.
- Credit reports are predictors of future behavior; they dog us to the grave.
- FICO numbers are influential with need-to-know parties.
- Employers often make a final decision to hire based on details in a credit report.
- FICO scores fluctuate over time and can be improved.

## Increase the Wealth Challenge

Waste no time. Get a copy of your credit report today. Analyze each item carefully. Check for accuracy. Deal swiftly with any false information you find. Make a covenant with yourself to maintain (or work toward) a platinum credit score so you'll be eligible for money-saving opportunities.

## Common "Cents" Sense

*For God did not give us a spirit of timidity, but a spirit of power, of love and of self-discipline.*[30]

# Cover: \cov·er, ˈkə-vər

To have within the range of one's guns; something that protects, shelters, or guards; a position or situation affording protection from enemy fire

Merriam-Webster's Online Dictionary, 2007-2008, Merriam-Webster Incorporated

# Eight

## Cover Your Backside

## The super amazing benefits of savings

*Americans' personal savings rate jumped to 5.7% in April, the highest since February 1995, according to government data released earlier this week. The level of saving—$620.2 billion—was the most on records dating to January 1959.*[31]
—Martin Crutsinger

Growing up in the streets of Boston meant watching your backside. Discernment and smart maneuvers were known to make the difference between survival and a trip to jail or the morgue. Early on Charlie learned to be alert. Nothing else made sure a guy didn't end up face down in the back alley.

"Be smart in the streets—pay attention. Know your friends," Papa would say. "Know your enemies all the more. Find out who the players are. Hang onto some cash. Money is your leverage. And if you think you're being followed, go with your gut. Do what it takes to ditch the rat."

The habit of looking over his shoulder became second nature to Charlie throughout life. No different than a beloved nursery rhyme, the teachings of those early years droned on—imprinted deep, like a bald eagle on a silver dollar: *Make sure some money is socked away. Money is power. People without money lose. Money puts me in the driver's seat.* From this powerful soundtrack came the habit of saving money and a career as a Certified Public Accountant.

Charlie will never willingly spend every dollar he makes. With the tenacity of a pit bull, he won't let go of those smart money concepts that have served him well and kept him miles away from financial ruin.

## Lessons Caught

History is an excellent teacher—*if* one generation passes the lessons along to the next. Otherwise, like in the financial crisis today, people brushed off yesterday's lessons as outdated and lose sight of some very important principles. Fortunately, many of the old streetwise teachings are now making a comeback.

Not many of us would willingly choose to experience a reoccurrence of the historic Great Depression of 1929–1939, but financial forecasters are making serious comparisons between then and now. Back then, the catastrophic collapse of stock prices on the New York Stock Exchange began three years of stock price declines until the value of the market by late 1932 had dropped to a mere 20 percent of its worth in 1929. An incredible 80 percent decline in asset values strained banks, individual investors, and financial institutions here in the United States and abroad. By 1933 almost half of the country's 25,000 banks had failed. Times were tough. Bread lines were long.

Contraction naturally accompanied the extreme economic drop. People spent less. Manufacturing slowed. More and more jobs were lost until 25–30 percent of the work force was unemployed. This is beginning to sound like current news.

Talk to an elderly senior citizen, someone 80 or more years young. She'll tell a story of how hard things were—some stood in bread lines; people took any kind of work they could get. Social programs didn't exist. Family after family found themselves in dire straits. Hope ran low. Needs ran high. Suicide was on the rise.

The generation that survived—perhaps our grandparents, mothers, fathers, aunts and uncles—learned a big lesson. People with savings fared better. They could still put food on the table, keep a roof over their heads, and help a neighbor. The thought of a day without money to fall back on struck a chord of fear.

My father came out of this era. He was a farmer, ranch hand, journeyman carpenter, and later a mill worker. Because he knew famine firsthand, he always … always … always saved money. His wages were average, not out of the ordinary, but he always … always … always saved money and felt compelled to do so. He'd suffered hardship. Some years, when drought hit the Saskatchewan prairie, no choice remained except to pack up and head for the Dakotas as a migrant worker.

Living frugally was considered smart back then. The idea is back in vogue now. Having money to fall back on beats being broke any day of the week.

## In Times of Affluence

*The savings rate in the United States dipped to zero in 2005, and has fallen into negative territory {June 2007} the first time since the Great Depression. ... These days, a lot more people probably wish they had a bigger savings account instead of a bigger house.*[32]

Over the decades, since the Great Depression gave way to growth and expansion, the lion's share of our population lost touch with why it's so important to save money for a rainy day. By 2007 the timeless principle of saving had been traded for a lifestyle of consumerism and credit buying.

Beware the danger associated with affluence. In times of prosperity we are in the greatest danger of letting down our guard and forgetting to watch our backside. Instead, we spend more money and plunge deeper into debt. We demand more, consume more, and believe the good times will last forever. History reveals life happens in cyclical patterns. Good years and bad years down through the ages. Every good economic period one day comes to an end. If some of the proceeds gained during a series of profitable years go unprotected, the lean times that follow will be much worse.

A lack of concern for the rapid increase in consumer debt reveals attitudes as foul smelling as the steam belching uncontrollably from deep cracks in the earth's crust near Kilauea's crater. The gasses are hot and toxic. Although interesting to look at, nothing of real value grows nearby.

This is a good time to take inventory. Perhaps our spending habits also stink. Is the aroma a good one or a rotten stench that spreads far and wide? Spending too much on discretionary items reeks of wanting to live for today, spending tomorrow's paycheck, enjoying the spoils of now, and distancing ourselves from future concerns. According to history, this is stinking thinking.

Many financial experts say this current recession/depression is going to be worse than what was experienced in the days of the Great Depression. If they are right we should want to be as ready as possible to face what life dishes out. A pity party won't pay the bills. A good nest egg will. Practice a little sacrificial living. Forego some spontaneous spending. Lay the money aside for tomorrow's use. None of us should expect to live indefinitely on borrowed money. A day of reckoning comes. A financial crisis strikes. Peace is forfeited. Stress escalates.

Streetwise money managers agree that it's best to keep debt to a minimum and stay way ahead of the creditors.

## Find a Mentor

Twenty percent of people do save money. These folks are pacesetters for the rest of us. In the midst of economic uncertainty American's have once again started to save. The savings rate has climbed back from negative territory in 2007, when the housing bubble burst, to 6.7% in June of 2009. That's huge! Well deserving of applause.

The trend to save is hanging around according to the Commerce Department. *The Commerce Department's broader measure of personal saving has risen to 5.8% of disposable income in 2010 from a low point of 1.4% in 2005. That's in large part because it counts reductions in personal debt, such as mortgages and credit-card balances, as savings. For example, paying down a credit card with a 20% interest rate is a better way to save money than taking out a bank CD yielding 1%. But defaults, rather than saving, have driven much of the decrease in debt.*

Whatever the driving force behind saving money, this might be the right time to ask a long-time saver to be a personal mentor. Success is more attainable when we hold ourselves accountable to another human being. A good mentor serves as our advocate championing our goals until the day comes when we can hold tight to the brass ring. Then don't forget to celebrate the victory.

## Five Ways to Start Saving

For those who haven't cared about saving money until right now, or don't think it's possible, give it a try anyway. Dismiss *"I can't"* attitudes. Lean into the idea that the keys to our financial future belong to us. Change does happen. Get creative. Change is not held hostage by yesterday's decisions. Show up with a passionate *"I can"* effort. Our families all deserve a chance at a bright financial future.

Anyone ready to be a saver gets serious about lifestyle choices. The next five steps are a good place to begin.

1. Have a desire to save money. Don't entertain apathy. To be apathetic is to be indifferent, lacking concern or emotional energy to pursue the goal.
2. Study pay stubs for money leaks. How much tax is being withheld? It is common for personal exemptions to be understated. For instance, a family of four might claim only two exemptions. A single person might claim zero. Underreporting results in too much money being withheld from the paycheck so a sizable refund check comes back from the government each April. This is silly thinking.

The tax system should not be used as a savings account. Of course Uncle Sam will keep taking our money, but we'll earn no interest. The same holds true for state governments. And if the governments carry too big a debt load, too, like California, the money might not be returned as expected. California issued IOUs instead of refunds in 2009. If underreporting of dependents is happening, fill out a new W-4 form at work. Don't continue to let the government act as a banker. Redirect those found monies into living expenses and true savings.

3. Savings works best when the habit is practiced year round. Make sure the money is deposited in an FDIC-insured bank that pays a fair rate of interest. We should treat ourselves as a financial priority and pay ourselves first. After knowing how much can be realistically worked into a savings plan, stick to the arrangement—99 % of the time—no matter what! The one percent miss only happens in an emergency.
4. Determine to eliminate debt as fast as possible. Debt is not our friend. Debt bleeds away hard-earned dollars! To be in good financial health, the hemorrhaging has to stop. Then all the money wasted on interest paid out can be redistributed into more beneficial places. Start with the smallest bill and get it paid. Then apply the money that was going to pay that bill to the next bill and get it paid and so on.
5. Stop depending on credit cards unless the bill can be paid in full each month. Charge only what is in agreement with the family's spending plan—or try to do without. Use a cash system perhaps. Pulling dollars out of a wallet is a good way to train ourselves to be wise spenders. Statistics show that people who spend cash are more frugal than those who use credit cards. A psychological connection occurs when the fingers touch the dollars. Try it. See if it really is more painful to part with the green stuff. By making it harder to let go of our money, it is easier to stick to a spending plan.

## Freedom from Debt Feels Good

Being free of debt is possible. Don't think it isn't.

Our debt-free day came in 1992. We need to give Crown Ministries some credit here. It wasn't until 1990, after we got involved in financial ministry, that we understood God's best for us was to live without debt.

We forged an aggressive plan to eliminate all debt within five years. But God had a different idea. We prayed and steadily put extra money onto the bills. More money than we thought would be available somehow started coming into our hands. We sold the boat. A minor accident brought in a small insurance settlement of $4,000. All windfall dollars went to paying off the mortgage. *Stay the course. Don't deviate*, we told ourselves. Every unexpected dollar pushed us closer to our final goal. We labeled found money the *God factor*. Between our faithfulness and the *God factor*, to our amazement two years and four months later, everything owed was paid, the deed to our house was in our hands, and we were debt-free. What an amazing feeling! Now we could go where the Lord directed us to go—serve where He wanted us to serve without financial stress.

The first month without a mortgage payment felt pretty strange. We'd written those checks for years and years. Now we had to say out loud: *Hey*, we *don't owe that bank any more money*. Thankful isn't adequate enough to describe how good it feels to be free of debt. Appreciative, humble, unbound, and emancipated might be better.

A new spending plan had to be made to take into consideration the extra money that was once being spent to pay the mortgage. We were able to fund lots of things: college tuition for our children, retirement accounts, evangelism, charity, and paying our own expenses while giving personal time to ministry work.

Believe it or not, we're not such an unusual couple. Many other people have chosen to get out of debt. In 2008, from our close circle of friends, four families paid off their home mortgages. They also love the freedom they found. There's a sense of gratitude when dollars are no longer owed for interest and payments.

The tables have turned. The banks now pay interest *to* these smart freed-up customers.

## Why Don't People Save?

We were curious. Why don't people save money? The most common answers are:
1. "I have too many bills."
2. "I don't make enough money."
3. "I have a good cash flow."
4. "The government will take care of me."
5. "I only have one life to live."

6. "I'm too young to be worried about savings."
7. "I'm too old to be worried about savings."
8. "Savings accounts pay so little they can't keep up with inflation."
9. "I need to keep up with the Joneses."
10. "I don't like reading bank statements."
11. "I have a credit card for all the extra stuff."
12. "I'm a spender."

There are enough lame excuses to keep us financially illiterate for a lifetime. None of them are streetwise. In order to master money the excuses have to go.

Below is a list of four distinct lifestyles. This is meant to be a personal assessment first, then a household assessment. Highlight the one that best describes how you personally manage money, and then use another color to pinpoint the predominant money style of the family unit.

1. Live above my means. Looking good is the rule of thumb: big house, cars, fancy clothes, vacationing in style, massive amount of consumer debt.
2. Live at my means. No savings and spending everything down to the last penny.
3. Live within my means. Spending plan, some savings and retirement money is amassing, bills are current and life seems comfortable.
4. Live below my means. Saving money, ignoring the distractions of materialism, feeling content, and having little or no financial stress. I am debt-free or close to that position.

Fiscal independence is only a reality for people who either live within their means (lifestyle three) or those who live below their means (lifestyle four). Lifestyles one and two describe people who choose to live with economic vulnerability from day-to-day.

Apply common sense. Make a conscious decision to add power to personal finances. Saved money works for—not against us. Save some money. Choose to live on the positive side of the ledger—in the black. The other side—the icky red ink—is loaded with one problem after the next chasing us through the streets of life nipping at our heels.

Saving money shows appreciation for our paycheck. Work isn't easy for most people. It's toilsome. Even if we like what we do, we still work hard for our dollars and will continue to labor most of our lives to support our families. Not saving money shows disrespect for the family's financial stability. Continuing in the red means our existence will be one of just barely scraping by day-to-day, month-to-month, year-to-year. The wolf will always be right outside the door.

## Time Is Money

Charlie has a favorite saying: "Time is money." Envision time as creations masterpiece—a priceless commodity. Money put away over time earns more money. Money makes money while we sleep if it's saved or wisely invested. Let time be a good friend. This friend blesses us with profits as wealth, over time, builds.

Do we still need a little more motivation? Charlie tells us how he created incentive to make socking away money more like a game than a chore.

"I found ways to encourage myself. One thing I did was to make a savings box at home. A drawer, jar, envelope, old shoe, or whatever works just as well. It doesn't matter what the container looks like. I even read a story of a guy who took a worn out basketball and put a slit in the top. Week after week he threw in his loose change until the ball was full. He then made a trip to the bank. Only then did he open the basketball wide enough to take his money out. He had enough to open a sizable savings account. My simple little savings box accomplished the same thing. I liked seeing it fill up and get heavy. That made me happy. By the time I was old enough to drive, I had enough money to pay for my first car."

## Value Delayed Gratification

Delayed gratification used to be the norm. Putting money away for a future purchase meant we'd enjoy the item "later." Waiting while saving cash to buy a bicycle, a washer and dryer, or a pretty dress, used to be a common practice. Most department stores worked off the theory of delayed gratification by offering layaway plans to their customers. If a customer wanted to buy a $75 dress from The Dress Cottage, she would fill out a simple form (name, address, phone number) and give the clerk $20 perhaps—enough to hold the dress in layaway. The customer was given a layaway ticket and came back at regular intervals to pay money toward the full price of the dress. Only when the final dollar was paid could the lady take home the dress and enjoy what she'd bought. There is a drastic difference between layaway plans and credit card purchases. Delayed gratification keeps us from going into debt. What we take home we actually own.

Too bad true lay away plans went the way of the dinosaur when credit cards grew in popularity and abundance. *Borrowers were only too happy to bury* themselves in debt during an era of instant gratification not seen perhaps since the waning days of the Roman Empire.[34]

Credit deposited plastic buying power into the hands of the people and we loved it. Delayed gratification was dismissed to the sideline. Consumer debt grew and grew and grew.

Human nature is an interesting phenomenon to study. Most of us want what we want and we want it now. Smart marketers know instant gratification is impulse driven. They are carefully trained to play into a customer's emotional vulnerability. The last thing the seller wants is for the buyer to wait to save money before making a purchase. From their perspective, the quicker the sale is made the better for their company's bottom line. Salesmen are trained to talk up the product that's caught our eye, convince us it's a great buy, and woo us to the checkout counter.

Hasty decisions get people into financial trouble. Be ready to encounter marketing tricks before going into the store. Otherwise temptation can easily rise above common sense. Never shop with an "I deserve this item now" attitude. First give deliberate thought to making the purchase. Is it streetwise? Does it fit into the spending plan? Why do I want it?

A customer should not give any sales rep the opportunity to convince him he needs to make a particular purchase. That responsibility belongs to the buyer. If we're streetwise, we won't fall for a marketer's schemes.

Never make emotional purchases. Only shop when emotionally unattached from the merchandise and with the budget in mind. Then, if the decision to buy falls in line with our financial goals, the item is bought out of sound reasoning and not reckless spontaneity.

In March 2011 I discovered a reappearance of layaway plans in a Sears advertisement. But as I read the fine print, I became uneasy. The set of rules that govern their layaway convenience are full of disclaimers and fees and not at all like the layaway plans I had been accustomed to: *All fees nonrefundable. Cancellation fees apply. Not available at all Sears stores. 12 week layaway option available on purchases of more than $400. Exclusions apply.* Don't get suckered into a payment plan that is designed to sound good but in reality cost the consumer plenty.

## A Realistic Cash Reserve

Financial planners who counsel families suggest storing up a cash reserve equivalent to six months of housing expenses. Yes, that's a lot of money and it will take time to amass, but the end result is worth going after. Six months of cash reserves provides a generous cushion to tide a family over should a job be lost, an accident happen, or death take a wage earner.

With money in the bank, a leaky roof can be replaced, a vacation can be enjoyed, or a job layoff endured. Without an emergency fund there is no safety net. We will be quick to accumulate more debt to solve immediate problems. This creates a greater risk that when hard times hit we could even end up homeless on the streets.

In Portland, Oregon alone, 16,000 people were reported as homeless during January 2007's winter cold spell. A great number of these folks (families with children, too) didn't plan to be street people. They are middle-class citizens, just like us, our co-workers and neighbors, who fell on dreadful times with no money to bail them out. The rainy day took them down hard. Everything that stood for stability was gone. It will take a long time to get back on their feet financially.

Southern California is coming to grips with more and more middle class people being added to the homeless population. In May of 2008, CNN news reported how parking lots opened in Santa Barbara, California for homeless middle class people to live in their cars. *There are 12 parking lots across Santa Barbara that have been set up to accommodate the growing middle-class homelessness. These lots are believed to be part of the first program of its kind in the United States, according to organizers.*[35]

Layoffs from jobs, out-of-control debt, and unpredictable patterns of life are why it is so important to be streetwise about money. The reason to save is the same reason to have a spending plan. It's for our own good! The sole purpose of managing our money well is to have enough to go around. Knowing how to live within our means month-to-month and year-to-year prepares us to face both the ordinary cost of living and unexpected expenditures. Don't misunderstand. Nobody likes to be hit with an unexpected bill but everyone, at some time, experiences the reality of paying for interruptive extras.

Charlie went to the dentist a few months back only to be told he would need $10,000 of dental work done or risk a worse problem in the near future. A second opinion confirmed he really did need to get the dental work taken care of. Fortunately, we had savings put aside to draw from. Although inconvenient and unplanned this additional dental bill was still manageable for us.

## Put Money to Work for Us

Every dollar saved works for us—and not against us. Smart lenders understand this formula. Profit comes from using depositors' monies to make more money. It sounds pretty simple. Lenders loan out cash and charge interest for using customer deposits. Our deposits become bank capital.

A savings account earns interest on the dollars in the account. The bank pays us a small amount of interest for the privilege of using our money. We are like junior partners with the lenders when we have a savings account and earn interest.

Albert Einstein brilliantly said, "Compound interest is the eighth wonder of the world." Deposited dollars put the magic of compound interest into action. The simplest way to understand the phenomenon of compounding interest is to think of money making money twenty-four hours a day—even while we sleep. Accumulated interest adds back to the principal so that interest is being earned on interest all the time. The only way to stop the compounding of interest is to withdraw the money.

The earlier a person begins to save, the greater their wealth at age 65. The sooner money begins to be socked away the smaller the amount of money needed to meet the targeted goal because the time value of money is at work. This means a million dollars doesn't have to be put in the account to have a million dollars in the future. This motivated us to achieve our goal. Let's use Frank for an example. At age 20 Frank started putting away $43.28 a week with a rate of return of 8% and ended up with a million dollars at age 65. Over 45 years, his contribution to savings was a grand total of $101,275.20. That number is nowhere near a million dollars! But Frank's portfolio grew to $1,000,383.34 as a direct result of growing wealth from compounding interest over a great span of time. At retirement age, he had nearly ten times more money than he had physically put into savings account. $899,108.10 was Frank's increase through the years.

Now think about saving with a 6% return on the money. At 6% Frank's weekly contribution to his savings account increases to $83.22 in order to achieve the *same* million dollar goal at retirement. He must put more money in himself—$194,734.80 over the same 45 years. His return is still impressive. A major point being made is that people don't have to earn excessive salaries to arrive at the outcome goal. Interest made on saved money over time is fittingly called the eighth wonder of the world.

In contrast, Harold didn't think much about saving for the future when he was Frank's age. He didn't start to put $2,000 a year into savings until his 35$^{\text{th}}$ birthday; a full fifteen years after Frank had begun. To even dream of having a million dollars at age 65 he would have had to put $99 a week away, which just wasn't possible based on his wages as a mechanic. But he could manage to put away $2,000 each year. At age 65 Harold had a nice $352,427 in savings. Not bad at all. But he accumulated much less than Frank because he had less time on his side.

It behooves us to look around for the best investments, not the highest interest rates available, to safely maximize yield and minimize risk. We should know what our risk tolerance level is and only put money where we respect that exposure. A general rule of thumb to remember is the greater the amount of interest paid, the higher the risk involved and the greater the chance of losing money. Most of us should not plunge into risky investments. The safest thing to do is practice steady plodding. Put money away at moderate interest rates and stick with a conservative investment plan.

Consider seeking the counsel of a trustworthy financial advisor when the time comes to branch out beyond the familiar savings accounts or certificate of deposit.

The time value of money is a very powerful advocate. Compound interest is a wealth building blessing we should not want to miss out on. Copy Frank's example. All of us can do what he did:
- Start with a plan
- Open a savings account
- Add to the account monthly

Commit to save what money we can and be consistent. The magic of compound interest takes care of the rest.

## Where Should We Save?

A local bank or credit union is the most logical place to open a savings account or get a certificate of deposit (CD). Shop around, however. Interest rates can vary from one place to another. The most popular savings accounts offer a minimum deposit with no maintenance fees. Plan to eventually link the regular checking account with a money market account. Money Market accounts pay more interest on a daily basis than do most regular savings accounts. Having both accounts allows us to move money from savings to checking as it is needed and without hassle. Most certificates of deposit require the depositor to wait a certain length of time before withdrawing the funds without a penalty. This could be three months, four months, one year or more. The idea of the two accounts is to earn more interest on the parked money while waiting to use it later in the year to cover bills (like auto insurance) that come due in future months. The length of time selected for the CD is determined when the spending plan is created. Then the money can be parked where it receives the best yield.

Money that isn't needed for a year or more can be put away for a longer period of time. For example, Bank of America, Wells Fargo, Chase and most banks have special deals online. There will be rules to follow. You might have to meet a minimum, like $5,000, to start the account. Entry offers entice depositors to open accounts and keep the money deposited without withdrawal for a set period of time—say four months. Be aware of the special deals. Make sure—make sure, make sure—*all* monies put away in any institution are FDIC-insured. FDIC stands for Federal Deposit Insurance Corporation and is insurance backed by the United States government to protect account balances. Don't be naïve. Not *all* monies deposited with financial institutions fall under the protection of the FDIC insurance. Most are FDIC-insured, however. The rules have changed recently. *Deposits at FDIC-insured institutions are now insured up to at least $250,000 per depositor through December 31, 2013. On January 1, 2014, the standard insurance amount will return to $100,000 per depositor for all account categories except for IRAs and other certain retirement accounts which will remain at $250,000 per depositor.*[36]

Money contributed to 401(k) plans is not the same as saving for a rainy day. 401(k) plans are set aside for long-term growth with retirement goals in mind. Do not tap into this money as one would a passbook savings account meant to meet ongoing needs. Dollars in a 401(k) are put away for retirement and can't be tapped into for today's needs without paying big penalties for early withdrawal and income tax on the amount taken out. We will talk more about 401(k)s and long-term investments in another chapter.

### The Bottom Line
- Fire up an intentional desire to save money.
- Make no excuses for not saving money.
- Living within or below our means is smart money management.
- Living at or above our income level is risky behavior.

- Don't miss the big blessing of compound interest.
- Not *all* banks are FDIC-insured.
- Only put money in accounts backed by FDIC insurance.

### Increase the Wealth Challenge

Do away with excuses. Start saving—even $5 a week adds up. And, if saving is already a habit, can more money be tucked away? If so, how much? $_____ Research where your savings are deposited to know for sure that these monies are backed by the FDIC. Banks do fail. If you discover you are in a vulnerable position, move the money to a secure location. Research interest rates at the same time. Could you get a better interest rate elsewhere? Don't move money without thinking through the tax ramifications first.

### Common "Cents" Sense

*In the house of the wise are stores of choice food and oil, but a foolish man devours all he has.*[37]

# Count: \ˈkaůnt

To include in a tallying and reckoning: the total number of individual things in a given unit or sample obtained by counting all or a subsample of them: to deserve to be regarded or considered

Merriam-Webster's Online Dictionary, 2007-2008, Merriam-Webster Incorporated

# Nine

## Count the Costs

### What is the true cost of spending?

*Face the situation squarely. Don't hide from your money troubles, identify them. That means making lists of all of your debts and bills and making a realistic assessment of your cash flow.*[38]

—Linda Stern

Gloria Califf, while a school bus driver in Washington State, found herself in an unexpected tight spot.

"I was really looking forward to the end of the month and payday because this month I was getting a larger than normal check. I couldn't wait! I had even charged a couple of extra things, knowing this was a good time to do it. But when I opened my pay envelope I was shocked. The check was not right. It was terribly wrong! My pay was only one-third of what I was expecting. I plummeted from elation to exasperation in a matter of seconds. I immediately phoned payroll. The recorded message let me know the payroll person was out on vacation for a week. This was horrible news."

"What did you do next?" I asked.

"I spoke to our secretary and my supervisor. After some research, it was discovered that my time card with all my extra work had not been turned in to payroll. I still hoped for a miracle, but a week later when Charlene returned from vacation, she was swamped with work and I was told she didn't have time to pay me until the end of the next month."

"Yikes! Were you angry?"

"Yes, but I swallowed my disappointment and tried to remind myself that this was only an inconvenience. I wasn't planning to dig into my savings until Christmas, but now I needed to. Taking the money out early was hard, but once I made the decision to use it I felt better. I was so thankful the savings account was there for me to use. That money made all the difference between a huge problem and a mere inconvenience."

Gloria wasn't happy when her paycheck was shorted. None of us would be. But her good habit of putting money aside on a regular basis allowed life to move forward uninterrupted—despite the curve ball she was thrown.

Savings acts as a shelter covering the family in time of need. To spend every dollar, and put nothing away, is akin to economic suicide leaving the family exposed to the storms. If putting money aside means eating beans and rice more often, instead of pork chops and cheesecake, change the menu a couple of times a week. Keep a portion of those earnings building a bankroll for future goals, times of scarcity, or a sudden emergency.

## Examine Your Monthly Needs

Good financial managers know how much money it takes to operate for an entire year. Consider the home similar to a business entity. Just as a business plan is necessary for success, a home spending plan is even more essential to the family's success.

Set about studying the family's income and expenses. Constant expenses can be recapped for a twelve-month total and then divide that number by twelve to arrive at a real monthly cost. To acquire a true picture of how much is spent, write down every expenditure for one full month.

Have a tablet and pencil handy. At the beginning of the month, and for thirty consecutive days write down every dollar that comes in—every penny that goes out. Even a 69¢ candy bar is an important purchase to record. At the end of thirty days, tally it all up. How much is being spent for utilities, rent or mortgage, food, gasoline, clothing, pets, medical, travel, entertainment, gifts, and so on? Most people are surprised at the frivolous spending that is going on.

Next take into consideration other expenses that occur during the year on a non-monthly basis. Perhaps that list will include home or automobile insurance, property taxes, vacations, private schooling, retirement goals, medical matters, Christmas, birthday gifts, basketball tickets, or burial expenses. Even though semi-annual, quarterly, or bi-monthly bills aren't paid in monthly increments (like the phone bill is), break them down into monthly amounts to arrive at a realistic annual budget projection. The goal is to eliminate as many surprise cash outlays as possible.

One way to soften stress associated with bill paying is to consider all bills as they add to the total incurred in a calendar year (or fiscal year) end. Find a total for twelve months worth of bills. Each individual payment represents one-twelfth of the annual bill. Now we've arrived at the monthly number. For us, the auto insurance on our two cars runs $704 every six months. Charlie and I need to double that amount to work a year's total. We need $1,408 to cover the cost of automobile insurance. When dividing $1,408 by twelve, we realize $117.33 needs to be put aside every month. Instead of a bombshell when the bill comes, we are all set to write the check without hesitation.

Simplify when possible. For instance, the day our mailman delivered a $390 gas bill to our door was the day we became serious about equal-payment plans. A couple of phone calls took care of the problem. We started equal-pay with our electric and natural gas companies to avoid getting any more budget-busting bills a few months out of the year. Without equal-pay, it was too easy to falsify the reality of our monthly budget during the unusually low months. We love having every month the same. No more fooling ourselves into feeling rich in August when the natural gas bill is $23 and impulsively spending money on a beach trip when it should be set aside for January's heat bill. Constant numbers make us a whole lot happier and create a more constant sense of security.

Families who choose to participate in equal-payment plans minimize unexpected budget shortfalls. Numbers that don't fluctuate help us stick with our spending plan. Once a year equal pay plans reset based on the prior year's actual usage. Some years the amount goes up; some years it goes down a few bucks. The adjustment is quite trivial compared to uncontrollable seasonal fluctuations.

Take control today. There is no better time than right now to start counting the costs.

Smart money managers are also realists who want to know how much money it takes to make ends meet. They get it that the only way to conquer financial stress is to figure out where the dollars are going in order to arrive at honest and helpful bottom-line numbers.

The simple "Spending Plan Worksheet" and "Budget Summary" on the next two pages can help you begin your journey to financial stability.

## Spending Plan Worksheet

**Monthly Income:**

| | |
|---|---|
| Wages | $_____.___ |
| Wages (spouse) | _____.___ |
| Social Security | _____.___ |
| Retirement | _____.___ |
| Alimony | _____.___ |
| Child Support | _____.___ |
| Rentals Income | _____.___ |
| Investments | _____.___ |
| Interest Income | _____.___ |
| Unemployment | _____.___ |
| Other _____ | _____.___ |
| Other _____ | _____.___ |

**Total Income** $_____.___

**Secured Debt:**

| | |
|---|---|
| Home Mortgage | $_____.___ |
| Rent | _____.___ |
| Auto Loans | _____.___ |
| Student Loans | _____.___ |
| Tax Lien | _____.___ |
| Recreational Vehicles | _____.___ |
| Other _____ | _____.___ |
| Other _____ | _____.___ |

**Total Secured Debt** $_____.___

**Monthly Expenses:**

| | |
|---|---|
| Tithe/Contributions | $_____.___ |
| Taxes: Federal | _____.___ |
| State | _____.___ |
| Property | _____.___ |
| Child Support | _____.___ |
| Alimony | _____.___ |
| Child Care | _____.___ |
| *No Nag* Personal $ | _____.___ |
| Savings: Long-term | _____.___ |
| Savings: Short-term | _____.___ |
| Clothing | _____.___ |
| Food | _____.___ |
| Medical/Dental | _____.___ |
| Auto: Gas | _____.___ |
| Repair | _____.___ |
| Utilities: Electric | _____.___ |
| Natural Gas | _____.___ |
| Telephone | _____.___ |
| Cell Phone (s) | _____.___ |
| Garbage | _____.___ |
| Water & Sewer | _____.___ |
| Security System | _____.___ |
| Home Maintenance | _____.___ |
| Insurance: Auto | _____.___ |
| Homeowner's | _____.___ |
| Life/Disability | _____.___ |
| Health | _____.___ |
| Education/School | _____.___ |

## Monthly Expenses: (continued)

| Unsecured Debt: | | | | |
|---|---|---|---|---|
| | | Personal Care | _____.\_\_\_ | |
| | | Entertainment | _____.\_\_\_ | |
| Credit Card | $_____.\_\_\_ | Travel/Vacation | _____.\_\_\_ | |
| Credit Card | _____.\_\_\_ | Dues/Memberships | _____.\_\_\_ | |
| Credit Card | _____.\_\_\_ | Miscellaneous | _____.\_\_\_ | |
| Credit Card | _____.\_\_\_ | Subscriptions | _____.\_\_\_ | |
| Credit Card | _____.\_\_\_ | Gifts | _____.\_\_\_ | |
| Personal Loan | _____.\_\_\_ | Other _____ | _____.\_\_\_ | |

**Total Unsecured Debt**     **Total Monthly Expenses**
$_____.\_\_\_                         $_____.\_\_\_

## Spending Plan Summary:

| | |
|---|---|
| Total Household Income | $_____.\_\_\_ |
| (-) Total Monthly Expenses | _____.\_\_\_ |
| (-) Total Monthly Secured Debt | _____.\_\_\_ |
| (-) Total Monthly Unsecured Debt | _____.\_\_\_ |
| **Total Monthly Disposable Income** | $_____.\_\_\_ |

# Summarize the Spending Plan

How did you do? Is there money leftover at the end of the month or are you operating in the red with more going out than coming in? _____

Did you squeeze "no nag" personal money into the budget? _____ How much? $_____ We all need some nag free money for a cup of coffee, lunch with friends, or a trip to the nail salon even if it's only $10 a month.

When spending outpaces income, two choices are available.
1. Find ways to cut expenses.
2. Figure out how to produce more income.

Sometimes the best way out of a budget shortfall is to integrate both options. Remember: Sacrifices made today reap great blessings tomorrow.

## Plenty of Ways to Save a Buck

1. *Create a game with loose* change—Charlie uses dollar bills to pay for a $1.50 cup of coffee at a local café. He gets 50 cents back. Then he goes to buy a 35-cent candy bar at the grocery store. Even though he has the 50 cents still in his pocket, he takes out another dollar bill to pay for the candy bar. When he comes home, Charlie has a $1.15 to put in the savings jar. He plays this game whenever he shops. It is a good habit that encourages him to save. From this loose change game, Charlie saves $200–$300 a year.

2. *Use an Impulse List*—Larry Burkett, founder of Christian Financial Concepts and Co-founder of Crown Financial Ministries, taught the world the value of delayed gratification with his simple, yet brilliant, impulse list. If you are thinking of buying a new tool or kitchen gadget, first write it down on the impulse list. Be patient. Wait 30 days. If in 30 days you still believe you need the item, okay. You're now ready to move ahead with the purchase and have had time to shop around for the best price. What often happens is that after 30 days, the desire is gone. What we thought we needed is no longer a lingering desire. The idea proved to be emotional and fleeting. Using the impulse list makes the difference between purchasing based on a whim or buying an item that will be put to good use.

3. *Cut back on the extras*—if you purchase a fancy coffee drink every day, cut back to every other day. Three coffee mochas a week at $3.50 each add up to $42 a month gained for savings. Eat at home more often—don't give up restaurants altogether, just cut back and have a plan in place before reading the menu or seeing the dessert tray. Share a meal, order water with lemon instead of soda pop, wine, or lemonade. This benefits both the pocketbook and your health. Take a long look at other spending leaks like cable TV, gym memberships or movies. Examine where the dollars are really going. You can redirect some cash flow into savings.

4. *Put it in the bank*—once the savings jar begins to accumulate a few dollars, go to the bank and open a savings account. Deposit the saved money and start earning interest. Now the money is making money while we sleep.

5. ***Give up a habit***—cigarettes, alcohol, Big Gulps, lottery tickets, office football pools, online poker, or any other optional behaviors that may or may not be a good health choice, rethink these habits. Something as simple as a lottery ticket bought everyday at a neighborhood convenience store can prevent us from maximizing our savings potential. Start a new habit. Toss those reclaimed dollars in the savings jar instead. One couple in our circle of friends labels their jar the "Maui Jar." They designate this particular accumulation of savings for vacation fun.

6. ***Use coupons***—they add up to big savings. Get savvy with newspaper and online discount coupons. Anything from groceries to books to electronics often has a coupon offer lurking about. Those who are internet savvy can check online for lots of discount offers. It's up to us to search them out. A couple times a month I find a $10-off coupon for a grocery market near me. By spending $50 I get $10 off at the register. That's a $10 savings on my grocery bill every time I remember to clip that coupon from the paper.

7. ***Buy in quantity***—compare the cost of smaller portioned items with larger family-sized ones. Put the difference between buying the costlier smaller amount and the bulk size into savings. A few zippered plastic bags make it easy to split up larger quantities for multiple meals. For instance, one head of romaine lettuce at Safeway costs $1.79, but the same lettuce in a 6-pack at Costco costs $3.29. The price per head of lettuce came down to around 55 cents. I've just saved $7.45 on lettuce alone! Romaine lettuce holds up exceptionally well so I'm not concerned that I have bought too much or it won't keep. We'll use it within a week or two. I admit there will be times when it's not possible to use up a large container of food before it starts to go bad. It's important to have a backup plan to avoid waste. Try to find someone else who's interested in having some of the apples or plan to make applesauce to store in the freezer for future use. The same buy-in-quantity principle holds true for beans, rice, soup, toilet paper, coffee, cereal, and hundreds of other items.

8. ***Share with family or neighbors***—everyone does not need to own a personal leaf blower or power washer or a ten-foot tall ladder just because we can find one to buy. Some people in the family or neighborhood will

likely have these items sitting in their garage. For instance, we share our power washer with our son two or three times a year. Explore using "free" from someone else's stash of stuff if possible. Of course, be considerate of the item borrowed and return it in good shape. Repair any damages.

9. *Live a raise behind*—employees typically spend a raise in pay before we get a raise in pay. We spend based on the knowledge of the increase in wages before it ever happens. Turn over a new leaf. Be delighted that an increase in pay is coming but continue on the old spending plan so the "raise" can be saved for future needs.

10. *Look at phone plans and utility bills*—make sure the cost is cost-effective. Landlines and cell phone bills should be evaluated to discover how money is being spent. Don't miss out on the best deal. Realize phone companies offer new plans often, and at substantial savings over older plans. The question of whether to drop unused minutes should be assessed. And is the landline even necessary any longer? The electric company has energy experts willing to help find those wasteful energy leaks and offer ways to cut down heating and cooling costs. The garbage company is another place to look for some extra cash. Can the family do with a smaller refuse bin? Can the service be bought with less frequent pick-ups?

11. *Tune in to classified ads and yard, garage or estate sales*—what's being sold by private parties can be bought at a fraction of the cost of buying new. From curio cabinets to wall hangings, drill bits to stepladders, lawnmowers to patio furniture; search long enough and we're likely to find just what we're looking for at a great price.

12. *Use thrift stores*—aisles are teeming with good clothing and household items at a fraction of the cost. Shop one to two seasons ahead and great bargains can be found. The only problem we might need to work through is what size our child will be next summer or winter. Value Village or Goodwill Industries are loaded with good merchandise. Many things on the racks are either new or like new. Ross, Tuesday Morning, and T.J. Maxx are excellent stores where discounted prices are the norm. Product lines are very extensive and include clothing, bedding, dishes, children's toys, face creams, jewelry, exercise gear, purses, tables, suitcases, and lots more. Great

shopping and not hard on most budgets. Incredible amounts of money can be saved on ordinary items and it's even possible to find some name brands.

13. *Eat before grocery shopping*—hungry shoppers hunger for a taste of everything. We'll be prone to buy more than we left the house to get. Snack before going to the market. Shop from a list. Stick to the list unless a necessity like milk, bread, or eggs was inadvertently left off the list. Buy according to need and not to gratify a craving for treats.

14. *Join the gleaners*—gleaners are a significant part of many counties and communities. Community gleaners offer better local food options than do county-run programs. For a few volunteer hours (2–4 hours) each month, the volunteer shares in a variety of collected foodstuffs and household products: fresh fruit and vegetables, breads, toilet paper, paper towels, hair-care items, frozen foods, pumpkin pies, hamburger helpers, tortillas and much more. Gleaning is time well spent but take only what you can store or use. Gleaners set aside a big chunk of time to process what they bring home. For instance, coming home with two whole salmon means taking the time to cut the fish into serving portions, and either cooking, canning, or putting much of it in the freezer for future use.

15. *Stretch food dollars*—Create menus around the local supermarket's weekly specials. Perhaps chicken this week and hamburger next week. Potatoes and corn on the cob might be priced right today, watermelon or apples another day. Frequent local growers' markets or produce stands. Learn how to can, or freeze, fruits and vegetables that are in season for use in the off-season. Come mid-winter, the taste of corn, shucked from the field, blanched and frozen months before, will bring smiles.

16. *Find free entertainment*—indulging in theatre events, sporting venues, or symphony tickets more than a few times a year can strain a budget. Look for free concerts and entertainment to attend. Local parks often provide family friendly fun during the summer months like free concerts in the park and a movie night once a week. Or, invite friends over for a game night. Pop some popcorn. Hike a nature

trail and take a sack lunch and a camera along. Libraries and state parks also host fun and educational activities. Look for a listing of events online or in the entertainment guide of the local newspaper. Every organization that receives state or government money is required to offer one free day a month to the public. All you need to do is call and find out what day it is.

## The Bottom Line

- Know what it costs to run the household each month.
- Appreciate living within a spending plan.
- Savings safeguards the family.
- Activate equal-pay plans with as many monthly bills as possible.
- Be on the lookout for money-saving ideas.
- Bargain shop (online or newspapers) before going out to buy.
- Discipline daily spending habits. A mocha three times a week, instead of six, frees up $10 to meet other needs or to grow savings. ($10 x 52 = $520 per year)

## Increase the Wealth Challenge

Create an honest bare-bones household spending plan. Find out if there is a surplus or a deficit to work with. Take a couple things from the "Plenty of Ways to Save a Buck" list and just do them! Then put the *found* money in savings so you can experience the happy gratification that comes when money is put to work growing more money while you sleep.

## Common "Cents" Sense

*Be sure you know the condition of your flocks, give careful attention to your herds.*[39]

# Chance: \ˈchan(t)s\

Something that happens unpredictably without discernible human intention or observable cause

Merriam-Webster's Online Dictionary, 2007-2008, Merriam-Webster Incorporated

# Ten

## Why Games of Chance Are a Poor Bet

## Do you want the real truth about the Gaming industry?

*America accounts for around 48 percent of the total world gambling market of approximately $260 billion annually.*[40]

—Gambling Watch Global

How will the bills get paid when Dad or Mom gambles away their paycheck? Terry found out the hard way that trying to make a family man out of a gambler was a pretty poor bet.

## Terry's Story

Growing up I didn't see anything wrong with gambling. Much of my parents' free time was spent heading for Las Vegas for rest and recreation away from their five kids. They had a thirst for dice, cards, and the slots. For them these games were just a fun time. I didn't know there was any danger in gambling.

Tom was always a gentleman to me and not pushy in any way. He was a nice guy from a good family. After high school, he joined the Air Force, like his father before him, and ended up at Edwards AFB, about an hour away from me. Later that year, I graduated from high school and after spending no more than a couple of days together a couple of times each month, we decided to get married in a ceremony at March AFB. After a honeymoon from Reno to San Francisco, our married life began in a little apartment back at Edwards AFB. The problems began immediately. I had not spent enough time with Tom to know that most of his spare time was spent drinking at the base NCO club. He would drag in at 2 o'clock in the morning, sleep, and be at work at 7am. Many nights and weekends would be set aside for poker parties, some at our apartment. I didn't play, but I didn't really mind either. Gambling was harmless—or so I thought—and at least he was with me when they played at our house. It was only penny-ante poker. The stakes weren't high. Or were they?

The first time in our married life gambling cost us real money was when Tom took a $350 loan out at the base credit union. Tom had come up with the wonderful idea of turning a Volkswagen Beetle into a dune buggy for me to ride through the desert. I remember that Friday like it was yesterday. I'd spent the morning at the bowling alley doing my best to break 150 when a phone call came in for me. I eagerly walked to the desk thinking we'd soon be picking up the VW. I was ready to feel like Mario Andretti in the sand, the wind dancing wildly through my long hair. Soon I'd have freedom and speed!

"Hello," I said into the phone.

Tom's voice was excited alright! "Mae and Donny want to know if we want to go to Vegas for the weekend. What do you think?"

Needless to say, I never felt the wind dance through my hair. We didn't get the VW. We had a weekend in Las Vegas with our friends. Unfortunately, I didn't see much of Tom that weekend. Gambling is really a solitary sport.

Our first daughter arrived two years later. Two weeks after her birth, Tom was shipped out to Japan. We weren't able to join him for six months. During that time, he continued to enjoy poker and beer nights with the boys. Except for our two and one-half years together in Japan, I felt like a single parent despite my wedding ring.

One day, after we'd moved to Oregon, I met a retired schoolteacher named Geraldine. She invited me to her church. I started attending with her and taking our daughter to the children's program. Before long I decided to accept Christ as my Savior. When I told Tom what I had done, he said he thought that was good, but that he hoped I wouldn't become a fanatic. Eventually Tom met Geraldine and it wasn't long before he'd also accepted the Lord. Life was pretty good for our family. We attended Bible studies, made new friends, and added a second daughter to our family.

Alcoholics and gamblers can also be Christians. The day came when my husband resumed his poker nights. This was a lifestyle, not a once in a while thing. For a while he would come home by eight or nine at night, which left little or no quality time to interact with our family. But after my anger kicked in, he stayed out later and later, stopping at a bar on the way home.

The first time we split up, our youngest daughter was two years old. I took the girls and drove to Texas to stay with my sisters for six weeks. Tom finally called, "When are you and the girls coming home?"

"I don't know if I'll ever be coming home!" I answered.

Tom was more than surprised. He didn't get it. I had told him over and over and over again how his neglect was affecting me and the girls. Even though we had fought over this stuff so many times, he didn't have a clue why I wanted to stay in Texas. The talks went on and on. When he agreed to go to counseling, I agreed to come home. The idea of counseling simply became another thing to fight about.

During the 1980s, the State of Oregon legalized open gambling establishments. Instead of going to Reno or Las Vegas a few times a year, now all anyone had to do was drive to the nearby Gold Hill Hotel. It wasn't a hotel any longer; just an old building with a few poker tables and a lot of suckers bellying up to the bar. Tom became a regular. If we had a fight, I knew where I could find him. We were not rich. Here he was gambling our money away instead of paying the bills. He might as well have flushed it down the toilet. My anger at Tom's addictions and my rage at my own inability to leave choked out any desire to read my Bible. I doubted my salvation and grew resentful toward God. On the surface, I continued to smile and tried to protect my children from the truth. The more I pretended, the angrier I became. The day I found out that Tom had gambled part of our mortgage payment was the day I finally said, "Enough!"

Tom moved out of our house and into a small trailer in a friend's yard. This time we were separated for almost three years. One day the phone rang again. It was my husband.

"I've stopped drinking and returned to the Lord," he said.

I was happy for him—happy and angry at the same time. Now that I was getting my life together, he wanted our life back. Instead of insisting Tom move back to the valley and live his changed life on his own for a while so I could observe how he was doing, I let him move back in. Our 24$^{th}$ anniversary came around. I waited for an invitation to dinner or a bouquet of flowers. None came. The next day he apologized. He was at a poker game and forgot.

Soon I learned my husband was deep in credit card debt due to his relentless gambling addiction. I no longer trusted him. I could not relax my hold on *my* money. I always kept something back from my paycheck and never told him what I made. How do you live with someone you no longer trust to take care of you? And how hard it must have been for him to know I didn't trust him.

A year later we found out Tom's mom had cancer. This news ushered in the next big downward slide. Stress escalated. Old behaviors returned. "Just one beer—just two," he'd say. And the wheels go round and round. At the end of our marriage, Tom was gambling over $1,500 a month and had grown a hankering for the big casino, a two-hour drive from our home. I found evidence that he was dabbling with internet gaming, also. The Lord only knows how much money was actually lost.

## Gambling Is Big Business

So how much betting is really going on? As reported by Sports Betting Facts and Stats: *Seven of ten adults in the United States placed some sort of wager in the last year. The online gambling industry generated $12 billion in revenue in 2005. $600 billion changed hands {2007} worldwide. Online sports' betting is estimated to be 5 times bigger than Las Vegas sports betting. Illegal sports betting (bar room bookies) is estimated to be 35 times bigger than Nevada's. Over 20 gambling companies are listed on non-U.S. stock exchanges. The biggest poker company has a market value of almost $9 billion. The biggest sports betting company has a market value of almost $3 billion.*[41]

Do we have a problem? For sure! Gambling is big business today. Money that should help families make ends meet is being thrown away on games of chance. Casinos and all kinds of betting are allowed in every state except Utah and Hawaii because state governments smelled an income stream and wanted a piece of the action. Greedy legislators set about legalizing what was once illegal. They convinced the voting public a gambling industry would improve our lives by creating jobs and filling the states' coffers with spendable resources. A dribble of the proceeds would be funneled into education. And the casinos themselves would link financial support to community places like the Washington Park Zoo in Portland, Oregon.

The marketing worked. What was a few years back typecast as dirty money is now a force to be reckoned with. The profits are big. But what price is being paid?

Gambling's dark side is taking a toll on family life. Games of chance are not sending the right message into the home. Most of us don't have any room for financial blunders to skim off household money; yet we accept these games without much hesitation. By the millions, patrons (most of us with modest incomes), including military men and women on overseas assignments are pulling money out of pockets in search of entertainment and the hope of grabbing some quick cash. Sadly, entire paychecks have vanished in less time than it would take to walk the dog.

## Who Is at Risk?

Players beware! Gambling is a quick way to get financially whacked by an industry whose job it is to prey on the vulnerability of its customers. Bright lights and flashy billboards lure us into the fun zone. The ka-ching of 500 one-armed bandits is music to our ears. Adrenaline begins to pump. The thought of winning a fast dollar builds excitement and overtakes common sense.

Gamblers Anonymous wouldn't even exist if all this fun didn't become a serious addictive cycle for a whole lot of people. When the rush to play gets in our blood it's tough to shut it down and walk away unscathed. Every time the bet is placed, the handle is pulled, or the card is drawn, and we tell ourselves, *I feel lucky; maybe this time the jackpot is mine*, look out.

One truth to remember: The house always wins. Any chance of winning is extremely miniscule compared to how much money is almost guaranteed to be lost—money that most times people cannot afford to lose. Added to financial ruin, unpaid rent and electric bills, is the greater destruction to the family unit. Many marriages fall apart, as Terry's did. Cycles of disrespect set in at home.

A gambling habit shakes a family's sense of economic security at its core. Emotions rise and fall like a roller coaster as promises to stop playing are broken over and over again. Anger and denial become common. The betrayer is no longer seen as an advocate for the family but as a destroyer who can no longer be trusted. Fear of how the family will survive dominates daily life. The non-gambling partner needs to set clear boundaries in place to protect the family's money. It's advisable for the responsible person to be proactive. Close the joint account and open another bank account in his or her name only. Don't allow the gamer access to this account—no matter what! The destroyer is only given a modest allowance.

Perhaps someone reading this chapter knows this kind of pain firsthand but isn't really sure if the fun has turned into a serious problem. This list of ten questions might help uncover that answer.

1. Do I, or someone I love, think about gambling daily?
2. Do I, or someone I love, argue with loved ones or close friends over money spent on gambling?

3. Do I, or someone I love, have a compulsion to chase my losses?
4. Do I, or someone I love, borrow money, use credit cards, or sell stuff to gamble?
5. Do I, or someone I love, feel depressed or experience mood swings because of my/their gambling?
6. Do I, or someone I love, hide or deny the gambling with people I/they are closest to?
7. Do I, or someone I love, gamble until everything, down to the last dollar, is gone?
8. Do I, or someone I love, let household bills go unpaid because the money's been spent on gambling?
9. Do I, or someone I love, cash in retirement accounts or insurance policies in order to gamble?
10. Do I, or someone I love, ever feel self-destructive or suicidal because of gambling?

Answering yes to any of these questions is a symptom of a serious problem. It would be wise to recognize the problem and get help. To find Gamblers Anonymous meetings near you go to www.gamblersanonymous.org or call 1-888-424-3577 toll free. To get help in a particular state the hotline for the National Council on Problem Gambling is 1-800-522-4700 or visit their website at www.ncpgambling.org/state_affiliates/.

Even church leaders can fall prey. In March 2007, members of a Portland, Oregon church were stunned to find their trusted pastor had taken at least $30,000 of church money that had been earmarked to help parishioners with rent, bills and food, to finance his gambling addiction. Of course, he has been removed from the pulpit and pleaded with his flock to find it within themselves to forgive him. The board did let compassion win out. They chose to offer grace and a generous severance package to help the pastor pay for his treatment.

There are no get-rich-quick schemes worth our time and hard-earned dollars. Believing games of chance are just for fun is the gotcha clause the industry wants us to grab hold of. Think twice. This is risky entertainment and a huge drain on the family's wallet.

When it comes to making a dollar, the old-fashioned way is still the best. Save and invest smartly. Find happier family-inclusive kinds of fun. Play games (no betting), take a walk in the park, eat ice cream cones, watch a movie, or build a sand castle.

Learn from Terry's story. Playing with games of chance has the momentum to take us where we don't want to end up. In the end, the entire family suffers needlessly from one person's self-serving lack of good judgment.

## Charlie Learned Early

Thirty or forty years ago gambling was easy for me to do. If I missed five nights out of a hundred at the dog track that was a lot. Gambling was part of my childhood in Boston. My father ran an after-hours' nightclub in the same way the speakeasies had operated from 1920–1933 during the Prohibition era when banning alcohol didn't stop its use. Bars just operated underground. A speakeasy was an unlicensed establishment dispensing alcoholic beverages when alcohol was officially illegal. To get in you had to be a trusted customer or know someone who was, have a password, or show a card. For instance you might show up at one o'clock in the morning. The door was kept locked until the doorman checked you out through a narrow slot. If you said something like, "Paulo sent me," and they knew Paulo, you would be let in.

There was no longer Prohibition, but the Blue Laws in Massachusetts made it illegal to operate a business after midnight on Saturday and all day Sunday. This didn't stop the games from taking place. As during Prohibition, the floating card and dice games went underground. My father catered to the folks who wanted to keep drinking and playing dice and card games. The location of the game after closing time was known by only a couple of people. As a boy, it was my job to wait on the corner and lead the players through a maze of streets and back allies to the secret place. If the cops caught on, the game moved. Many times the police and city officials were bribed to overlook the activity taking place.

I was taught young how the house always wins. Players don't understand what takes place in the back room. Think about it. Gambling parlors are not in business to lose money. When $100 is put into play (by five people with $20 each), the house immediately takes five percent of the pot. This is called *raking* the pot. Only $95 is in play. The house cuts 5% off the top of each pot. The average player might sit through 200 hands of cards in the course of a night with an average pot of $10. Fifty cents per pot is raked for the house each time.

There's no way for a player to get his or her money back. If one person stays long enough at the tables, he will go broke because the house keeps raking the pot. Get streetwise. All games of chance are designed to take money from us, not give money to us. The ploy is for the public to continue to believe gambling plays a positive role in our communities. Its entertainment masquerades in rhythm to our senses and we love it. But those dazzling lights robed in get-rich-quick schemes conceal a more sinister conspiracy—to profit big from our losses. For this reason, casinos will continue to come up with fresh ways to draw us in. Be leery. Offering incentives is a marketing ploy.

## Targeting the Youth and the Elderly

What about the youth population? More kids today gamble than are involved with drugs, smoking or drinking, according to Jeff Derevensky, a psychology professor at McGill University in Montreal. One reason: They're growing up with a message that wagering is acceptable. "Today's 10-year-old will spend their entire life in a world in which gambling is sanctioned and owned by the government," he says. The addiction rate among youths is two to four times that of the population at large.[42]

What about seniors? Psychologist Dennis McNeilly began studying the effects of gambling on seniors and found that casinos tailor their marketing to attract an older crowd. The Station Casino in St. Charles, Missouri, for instance, has a Golden Opportunities Club for people 55 and older where they can earn credits toward meals and gambling chips. The casino also offers free valet parking and $1 lunches to seniors, and some of its slot machines are based on detective stories from the 1940s. Some casinos run shuttle buses from retirement homes. McNeilly found one casino that featured former stars of Lawrence Welk's TV show. The industry even has a term, "third-of-the-month club," to describe gamblers whose casino trips coincide with the arrival of Social Security checks. This is tragic!

"The senior population is getting destroyed by gambling," says Ed Looney, the executive director of the Council on Compulsive Gambling of New Jersey. He cites the fact that in 1997, gamblers 60 and older accounted for 65% of the $3.7 billion Atlantic City took in. "You have a right to market your product, but there's a line you need to draw," Looney says. He points out research that shows seniors get to the crisis stage of gambling faster, and don't have the time to rebuild their finances when they get in trouble. "There's no way they can recover," he says.[43]

Cascadia Behavioral Healthcare, a Portland, Oregon nonprofit counseling service believes payday loans are a big part of the problem. If payday lenders weren't in business, problem gamblers would hit bottom much faster. Video lottery happens to be the game of choice for most problem gamblers. When players run out of money, they are told to go to the payday lenders who in turn give them more money to burn on video lottery. Over the past seven years the number of payday loans in Oregon tripled to 841,000 while annual video lottery revenue increased by 82 percent to $733 million.[44]

## What Are People Really Looking For?

Once the door to temptation opens, there's a euphoria attached that is similar to white-water rafting for the thrill seeker. Living through a class 4 rapid on the Deschutes River in central Oregon sets a lot of people up to go back and try it again. Winning a poker hand ushers in the same possibility of success or failure in a very short period of time. Failing to win only makes the gambler believe *next* time will be different. Keep plunging. Luck will change. It has to! Blinded by the adrenaline rush the next pull of the handle, roll of the dice, or race card purchased only heightens the experience.

Social gamblers might not act compulsively or ever become addicted. But is the money being put to good use? Does gambling honor the family's budget? Will our participation in these games cause someone else to stumble into addiction? In January of 2007 the Mayo Clinic staff wrote a piece on compulsive gambling. Most people who wager don't have a problem with compulsive gambling. But an estimated 2 million American adults do become compulsive gamblers at some point in their lifetimes. In males, compulsive gambling typically starts in adolescence, while it's later for females.[45]

Two million adults who become compulsive gamblers is certainly a conservative number. The estimate doesn't include every adult with a gambling problem. What about people like Tom? He doesn't show up in this number. He isn't alone.

*Nightline* aired a segment on gambling on May 3, 2007. What they found was: Twenty years ago, only a handful of women sought treatment for gambling addiction across the United States. Today, of the estimated 6–8 million gambling addicts in the United States, half are women.

A lot of gambling is very subtle and done from the convenience of home or office. Sports' betting is a common occurrence in lots of workplace lunchrooms. Billions of dollars alone were bet on the Super Bowl last year. And day-traders are playing the stock market from behind a desk. Many have lost big bucks in the blink of an eye.

Gambling isn't an industry we should be eager to support. So what drives such a large number of us to happily drop money on a game of chance when we wouldn't give it as quickly to charity? What might we be looking for? There are several possibilities.

    A. A chance to get-rich-quick
    B. The thrill of taking a risk
    C. A way to stave off boredom
    D. Fun and entertainment
    E. A way to fill an unidentified emotional void

Professional counselors and therapists suggest the latter. Finding out why someone makes a poor choice rather than a good one requires knowing some information about the individual's life story. What events shaped their behaviors? Trauma, abandonment, fear, injury, loss, as well as other possibilities exist.

A good counselor coaches her clientele to know themselves from the inside out. Over time, the true void becomes obvious. At that point old destructive patterns are exchanged for new constructive behaviors.

Therapy isn't always the step to take. Charlie, once a gambling man fond of dice games, black jack, and the dog track, is no longer interested in games of chance. You might ask, *How did this transition take place?* Without a doubt, the biggest change factor came in understanding God's love, accepting forgiveness in Jesus Christ, and realizing God had a better plan for his life. The more biblical truth he applied, the more he understood and enjoyed living life to the fullest from God's perspective. Now, when Charlie looks in the mirror, he sees a man who's forgiven and happy in his own skin. You couldn't pay him enough to go back to those old ways. That chapter is closed.

You can find victory in the same way. God's mercies are new every morning and His promises are meant to be taken personally. God doesn't slumber and He's never too busy to hear you call out to Him. His faithfulness endures for all generations. Anyone who is tired of the status quo, and who is looking for fresh hope, can grab hold of God's will and begin to shape a better life for themselves.

## The Bottom Line

- Games of chance are a poor bet; family and financial ruin can await.
- What starts out looking like fun with penny-ante poker, an office football pool, or lottery tickets, is no different than an entry drug like marijuana to a drug addict.

- Young people and the elderly are targeted specifically by the gaming industry.
- Question whether it is wise to support any games of chance that benefit the gaming industry.
- Gambling addiction is a real and growing concern.
- Lights, sounds, and jackpots are all designed to appeal to the lust of our eyes and our desire to get rich.
- Replace gambling hours with honorable family fun; hike a nature trail, ride a zip line, plant a garden, go bowling.

## Increase the Wealth Challenge

Take this chapter's list of ten questions to heart. Highlight any of them that apply to you or a loved one. If money is being gambled, pledge to stop that costly habit; even if it means getting professional help. Smile as you redistribute money once recklessly put at risk, whether socially or otherwise, to a better good. One formula is to use 70% of those recaptured dollars for living expenses, 20% for happy agreed-upon family fun, and the remaining 10% to fatten up the savings account. Smile, laugh, and enjoy how good it feels to make good decisions with your time and money.

## Common "Cents" Sense

*Good planning and hard work lead to prosperity, but hasty shortcuts lead to poverty.*[46]

# Merge: \mərj\

To cause to combine, unite, or coalesce;
to blend gradually by stages that blur distinctions

Merriam-Webster's Online Dictionary, 2007-2008, Merriam-Webster Incorporated

# Eleven

## Families That Blend—Should the Money Merge?

## Stepfamilies and their unique money issues

*Research indicates that only about 20 percent of remarried couples discuss their finances prior to marriage and almost none seek professional help for assistance in considering financial issues.*[47]

—Sharon Leigh and Janet A. Clark

Sharla and Rolf are a remarried-with-children couple.

"His, mine and ours is a brief description of our blended family," said Sharla. "Rolf has a boy, age 13, who he pays child support for. I have a boy, age 13, who receives Social Security. Then there is our son, age 6. The financial aspect for us has been challenging but that is not uncommon."

"What do you mean?" I asked.

"We both have the same goals of not having debt and paying cash for whatever we can. We have one credit card which we do our best to maintain a zero balance on. I am the spender; he is the saver. Early on in our marriage I learned that we needed to have a written plan spelling out our assets and debts (Rolf's idea). We meet with our financial advisor each year and are honest about our *needs and wants*. Our views are very different about what is important and what is not when it comes to purchases so we do our best to allot a dollar amount and then it is not open for discussion (my idea)," said Sharla.

"We both honor the system of buying on sale, using coupons or selling something to buy something. We live on one income. We are able to keep our home because we have met with the manager at the bank to settle our differences and stay open to the end goal of not having debt. It isn't easy but watching the homes sell in our area keeps me motivated to maintaining the agreement with my husband by really paying attention to my love for shopping. Since I am the spender, I have learned to use my debit card as it holds me accountable to my husband. We are putting away the maximum in his 401(k) and setting aside money monthly in small increments for the children's college fund.

"And what about Rolf's ex, your stepson's mom?" I asked.

"Regarding the other bio parent, we do our best to live by the parenting plan. It helps all involved to avoid any potential arguments. Unfortunately life is not perfect and the differences still occur. The children all have chores and receive money for these chores so it helps them learn different habits of spending and saving as well. When they want something they purchase it themselves—or at least a portion of it," she said.

"You are already training your children to be responsible spenders with their money, but what happens on those rare occasions when the two of you disagree over spending or parenting?"

"We've been married seven years and can still have disagreements but we choose to live by the rules of good communication. That means we don't bring up old issues; we're open to listening to new ideas; we respect each other's wants; and we remember to save, save, save," Sharla answered.

## Conveying Respect

This couple is facing life's issues with a practical, productive plan for their family's money. This husband and wife are a good example of positive communication. They gather new ideas, grant respect, and save for future needs. Despite stepfamily challenges, Rolf and Sharla are determined to forge a solid path forward. I have no doubt that their diligence will pay off.

One big thing to take away from this story is the respect being conveyed for the co-parenting relationship taking place with Rolf's son's mother. Growing up in two homes is never easy. Smart couples know kids make adjustments best when a cooperative parenting style between Dad, Mom, and the stepparent(s) is carried out. The two boys who live with Rolf and Sharla all the time are also blessed by the harmony displayed amongst their brother's parenting figures. The boys are learning that blended families can get along when they want to. The best gift a parent can give his or her child is to model the maturity that accompanies healthy relationships.

Sadly, most stepfamilies find the act of co-parenting quite difficult. They fall short of the mark when it comes to co-parenting in positive ways. Instead, these moms and dads openly display contentious relationship skills toward an ex within earshot of the children. And who suffers the most? The young ones who have no voice in the matter—the innocent children.

Treating an ex as a rival combatant needs to stop. Show the children it's possible to share parenting and negotiate problems with grace.

## A More Complex Family

Blended families are naturally a more complex financial unit than a biological family would be. While most previously married people are eager to join our lives to a second or third spouse, we might not be as ready to hook together the money. And, should we? The simplest answer to that question is: not always.

Unless there is full disclosure by both parties about financial matters, and a layout of each credit report, don't open a joint account. Ugly money secrets have been known to surface after the enjoyment of the honeymoon is over. Then the sparks begin to fly. A spouse who was formerly in a positive financial position suddenly realizes she's tied to a deadbeat lover and is not the least bit amused. Story after story are told of women who've been swindled out of an entire life's savings, a divorce settlement, or an inheritance by a silver-tongued guy whose real need is to be rescued from the depths of debt, freed from IRS trouble, or eager to find a wealthy sugar mama. Men can also fall prey to pretty talking ladies. It's just not as common.

Nasty little secrets shatter trust and threaten the survival of a new marriage. These avoidable issues usher in a financial crisis that could have been avoided by not comingling finances until the facts were known.

We all need to be streetwise lovers. Get rid of the rose-colored glasses. Talk about money before the wedding day if you're not married right now. Bless each other with honesty. Don't walk the aisle until financial matters are disclosed on both sides.

For those already married, make up for lost time. Print out credit reports. Reveal all assets and liabilities. This information is of utmost importance to the family's financial future. Full exposure about our money allows a marriage to get off to an impressive start where relationships can be the focus.

## Why Blended Family Finances Are Different

Money is the most common source of conflict in all families. But tempers flare much faster in remarried homes for several specific reasons.

1. Dollars are generally spread thinner. Child support, perhaps spousal support, and piles of icky sticky debt are a common downside for stepfamily life. Of course, there are exceptions.

2. With a larger family come added medical costs, more extracurricular activities, and additional educational expectations. It's all part of raising children. Each one of these add-on expenses stresses the pocketbook and impacts family goals. Some things may have to be put on hold. That thought doesn't always sit well with the adults in charge. We often get mad. But anger is a lousy companion for money problems. Keep anger in check and make a plan to cope with the extras. Delaying the purchase of a flat screen TV or a pizza party is far better than frightening the family. Plan in advance to make sudden compromises when the unexpected extra costs come along.
3. One partner, or both, demands a prenuptial agreement to prevent personal assets accumulated before the marriage (and limiting those amassed during the marriage) from benefiting the spouse or stepchildren. Trusts and prenups can create a safety net or become uncooperative. For individuals who marry again, after the children are grown, and with inheritance issues at stake, prenups are often a smart solution. Every family should address this issue—the sooner the better. A Family Trust or Last Will and Testament should be on the agenda. But for those who are in the child-rearing years, a self-serving stingy attitude with money can be extremely detrimental. Pooling our money is often the better choice. Comingling dollars works well for most families. There's a feeling of belonging to a family that is moving forward as a team to achieve goals and make the most of opportunities. Thoughts of favoritism aren't a problem. All heirs stand on equal ground.

## One Question

A divorced man ready to remarry asked Charlie this question. "I have a daughter and a son from my first marriage that I want to be the beneficiaries of my IRA account upon my death. If I do get married again, does my next wife have to sign a waiver allowing my children to get 100% of these funds when I die?"

"The answer is simple," Charlie said. "In community property states, the federal law requires that a spouse consent to the naming of someone other than herself as the beneficiary of your retirement account. All retirement accounts: IRA, 401k, 403b, Defined Benefit and all types of pension funds fall into this category.

"The best way to make sure your children inherit these monies is to have a prenuptial agreement signed before the wedding that includes this kind of consent.

"There are other beneficiary documents to consider," Charlie said, "with different rules. Life insurance policies, stocks or trusts held in individual names, or automobiles held jointly, must have the beneficiary formally changed in writing. Contact the issuer of the documents. Visit the Motor Vehicle Department to take care of business. Otherwise, upon death the person named as beneficiary or in joint ownership, in most cases an ex-spouse, gets the asset. Make sure new beneficiary forms are signed and title changes are made."

## Life Between Two Homes

Absorbing the impact of two or three outside homes affecting life under our roof isn't easy to put up with and it is a unique dynamic that no biological family ever experiences. With a great measure of tact, we are cornered into considering all the people involved—like it or not. Disagreements always center on either children or money.

Schedule conflicts, court-ordered support, and shared expenses head up the drama list. Tempers lessen when seen through a crystal clear lens. What's normal for blended families to encounter?

1. Children belonging to two families are loved in both homes and need their parents to respectfully accommodate the back and forth schedules.
2. Boys and girls didn't create the problems; adults did by divorce, cohabitation, or death.
3. It takes money to raise children. Child support is one way the courts attempt to provide for children's needs.
4. It's likely other expenses will be shared as the children grow: medical, education, or clothing.

Blended families attempt to balance three differing agendas. His son comes to our house; her children go to their dad's house. And we have plans to take the family to the water slide park for the weekend. At eight o'clock Friday night the phone rings. The boy's mom sent him to his friend's paintball birthday party instead. The balance is challenged.

The first reaction from most parents and stepparents is to get out of sorts when things don't go as expected, or an added expense comes along. A good day can be ruined in less than a minute's time unless we anticipate absorbing moments of disappointment. Remember the rest of the family is ready to go. Swimsuits are packed.

## Be Sensitive

Eleven-year-old Kenny's dentist recommended braces for his teeth. His mom wasn't going to address the problem because braces cost too much money. In her mind this news meant adding one more bill to an already thin wallet.

Kenny's dad, Jim, now remarried, lives in another city but sees his son every couple of weeks. He's worked hard to keep a good father and son relationship intact and regularly talks with Kenny on the phone several times a week. When he heard his son needed braces, he talked it over with his wife. Together they agreed that this expense wasn't frivolous. It was important enough to add to their budget.

Yes, Jim pays child support. Yes, it would be great to get some help from Kenny's mother. No, they expect things will not turn out that way. The orthodontist was contacted and arrangements made for the bill to be sent to Dad's house.

For the child's sake, financial sacrifice is sometimes the right choice to make. Braces are both helpful and important for Kenny. Jim and his wife did what was best to cover the need for their son without getting into a heated discussion with Kenny's mom.

Parenting adults are smart to keep bad attitudes at bay. Arguments with the other biological parent don't help. Any unfinished business from the past marriage is in the past. Those old battles have no place in the new family.

Bless the family by lessening the tension between homes—especially over money. Negotiate financial arrangements in ways that create win-win outcomes for the children. When parents do this, boys and girls will not feel like an unwanted expense. Of course there will plenty of times when it is not wise to pay for a requested item or funds are not available. It's okay for a youngster to work for a skateboard rather than be given one. Know the difference between a real need and a want.

Three questions can be taken to heart before responding to any unexpected expense.

1. What is the upside for my son or daughter if I take on this expense?
2. What is the downside for my child if this expense is ignored?
3. Would I absorb this cost if my child lived with me year round?

## Court Decrees and Other Surprising Truths

A couple of nasty truths might come as a surprise. Creditors do not honor divorce decrees. If our name is on a loan with an ex-spouse, we are still responsible for that debt until the ex pays off what is owed or takes out a new loan in his/her name only. A judge might decree that one party pay a particular debt, but the judge does not have the legal jurisdiction to remove a borrower's name from a contractual obligation. He or she can only rule that one of us is responsible to get the debt paid. In reality, as powerful as a judge might be, his ruling does not make it so. The integrity of the individual must be relied upon.

If we marry a person whose credit score is higher or lower than ours, that number affects our ability to get joint credit. Let's say spouse A has a platinum 800 score. Spouse B a low 500. The *joint* credit score falls between the two numbers and drags the platinum number down to a less than desirable place when applying for joint credit.

On the other hand, if we are seeking credit individually, our own personal credit rating prevails. Our partner's score only affects ours when applying for *joint* credit.

## Residual Attitudes Can Act Out

If we've been burned over dollars the first time around, the second marriage could easily start with trust issues on the front burner and at least one partner with a very tight hold on the purse strings.

It's not unusual for at least one remarried spouse to have money problems hanging over his head. Sometimes the issue might not have been one of his choosing, but his name is on the loan one line above his ex. The lender has every right to expect to be paid and will hold both parties accountable.

Quite often both partners say "I do" with unresolved debt or financial liens. Rightfully so, a prior negative experience creates a guarded mind-set within the new marriage. Managed correctly, this is not such a bad thing.

Residual attitudes send both good and bad vibes. The old adage—once burned shame on you, twice burned shame on me—is a worthy statement.

Start by weighing the facts. A cynical bitterness is bad. Why am I cynical? Clear caution is good. Why am I feeling cautious? None of us should want to be swindled a second time, or manipulated. A stubborn demand for accountability with every dollar is horrible while accountability to a spending plan is acceptable.

## Dividing Household Expenses

Just how household expenses should be divided is confusing. Who holds the checkbook? One answer doesn't fit all. Each family develops a unique dance with the dollars. Some boogie. Others tango.

Fairness is important when figuring out who pays for what. All financial systems require honesty, cooperative communication, and consideration of the family's lifestyle. Major adjustments to spending habits might have to be entertained.

First, write out nonnegotiable expenses:
1. Child support and spousal support
2. Rent or mortgage
3. Auto payments
4. Food
5. Gasoline
6. Medications
7. Utilities
8. Consumer debt

This is a sample list that can be easily divided with or without a joint account. The goal is to make sure there is enough money deposited to cover the bills. The partner with the more substantial income is able to contribute more to the family's budget than a spouse who works for minimum wages. Both work hard but compensation differs. Teamwork is the picture we are painting.

Don't undermine the family. Two become one in marriage. Marriage imposes our partner's financial story upon us—good or bad. Accept the financial obligations that are attached to a spouse's children. Fussing over what can't be changed is ridiculous. Work together. Show real concern. Placing blame is as silly as holding selfishly to *our* money when it can be used to meet the family's needs.

## We Are Predisposed to Be Different

Individual personalities and predisposed thinking make us different from one another. Our differences show up in many ways—money included. Different isn't right or wrong—just not the same. While our original worldview is shaped before we leave high school, its perspective can be flawed. All of us can discover areas that would profit from change.

Many couples find it easier to get on the same page by enlisting an outside source of counsel. This could be a financial class, a book written on the subject by a credible author, or a seminar. Crown Financial Ministries is one resource we don't hesitate to recommend. Visit www.crown.org to look at their list of teaching solutions.

Fifty-fifty plans create tension and build resentment. To insist that expenses be split right down the middle is destined to fail particularly if one spouse earns more money than the other, has less debt, has more children, is a saver instead of a spender, or is a spender rather than a saver.

There is a right approach and a wrong approach when it comes to blended family finances.

*Wrong* approach: I didn't create that bill. Don't expect me to pay it.

*Right* approach: It's our problem. With my help we have enough resources to wipe out this debt in two years.

*Wrong* approach: He's your child. It's not my responsibility to pay for his college education.

*Right* approach: This is our family; I'll help. Together we can find ways to fund his education and give my stepson a shot at a college degree, too.

The children need to know what's happening with the family's money. Let them participate. Give everyone a voice—even the eight-year-old. How else will they learn to manage their finances?

Hold family meetings once or twice a month. Explain all the bills. And give thanks for all the good times the family has been able to enjoy because there was money enough to play or dine out or go to the movies.

Adopt flexibility as a motto and unselfishness as the lingering melody at home. When we honor one another with word and deed and dollar, blended families shape a resilient future.

The years go by. Children grow up. They leave home. Think forward. What will our marriage look like when we are empty-nesters? Will we be lovers? The decisions we make today are guaranteed to shape tomorrow.

## The Do's and Don'ts of a Prenuptial Agreement

Prenups are a touchy area for most couples.

Cheri carefully contemplated a prenuptial agreement before marrying her second husband. Both of them entered into the relationship with comparable assets. Each owned a home.

Cheri came to the conclusion that a signed prenup can create a safety net, but it is first and foremost a business contract.

"So how did you decide whether to Prenup or not?" I asked.

"For myself," Cheri said, "I needed to listen to the Lord for wisdom. From that prayerful listening came the logic to have a heart-to-heart discussion about finances with my boyfriend. I needed to know his financial picture upfront and disclose mine to him."

"Did the conversation go well?"

"Much to my amazement he became very transparent and real with me," Cheri continued. "Without hesitation he explained his situation and the debt he'd accumulated over the last six years. I appreciated hearing how the Lord had graced him with the ability to be a responsible father —one who continued to pay child support—while he learned a new career that would get him back on his feet financially."

"I admire the openness that took place before the rings were exchanged. How did you proceed to the final decision?" I asked. "And, what was that decision?"

"I educated myself about different kinds of prenup agreements and even talked with my attorney at length. He emailed me a couple of samples. After looking them over," Cheri said as she placed her coffee cup back on the table, "I knew it wasn't the right answer for us. A new Living Trust and Pour-Over Will written to protect our survivors was a better plan. Hubby-to-be agreed. There was enough trust between us to nix prenup thoughts and follow our hearts into this new relationship."

Communication and honesty led to a comfortable protective decision for Cheri and her husband. That's not the case for every couple. Let's talk about another prenup that didn't end as happily.

Companionship and sex without guilt motivated this next couple to get married. Both were in favor of a prenup before the wedding. Louise and Carl had been dating for a long time. Their circumstances were similar in some ways. Each had lost a previous spouse. Both had grown children and grandchildren. Louise had two houses. Carl had three.

Carl, a sharp businessman and adamant about a prenup, was a man of many assets and ample wealth. Louise was a woman of modest means. She wanted to retain what was hers—the title to her two homes. They represented the only security she'd have to fall back on. She'd done well enough on a clerk's salary.

Carl made an appointment with his attorney to draw up the agreement. Sometimes one can be too trusting, and love does prove blind. Carl and Louise retained their individual homes and assets. However, another directive was included in this prenup. Carl granted his adult children total control over everything he owned. They had the power to care for his and his wife's financial needs should he be unable to make those decisions.

Louise didn't catch on to the significance of this binding arrangement that day. Getting married was on her mind. Long after saying "I do," she found out just how difficult it was to be under the control of the children.

"Carl's children had no respect for me," Louise said. "I tried so hard to be their friend but it didn't work. And Carl didn't make things any easier."

"Tell me about the good times," I requested.

"Sure. Carl and I took many wonderful vacations here and abroad. We ate at wonderful restaurants and enjoyed the theatre. He knew how to sweep me off my feet and be so romantic," Louise said, smiling as her mind drifted back to those carefree days walking hand-in-hand in Paris and the accordion music filling the air as the gondola carried them through the canals of Venice.

"So what went wrong?" I asked.

"Being a stubborn Italian man, his concept of family was fixed. Family meant blood relatives—his offspring—not stepfamily. His children made sure Dad didn't undermine their inheritance. The prenup was intended to address their financial concerns. Carl had no problem handing his checkbook to them."

"Those three didn't like it that their dad wanted to travel here and there but humored his wishes while he was capable of making decisions. That all changed after our seventh anniversary. Carl got sick. One day the doctor gave us the bad news. My husband had inoperable brain cancer."

"I'm so sorry," I said. "This had to usher in the worst-case scenario."

"Yes. I was forced to go to his daughter every time I needed a dollar. I couldn't pay the light bill without begging for money and explaining why. I felt like a vulnerable child bowing to the rule of his family's whims.

"I cared for him at home as long as I could manage it. When Carl needed more specialized care he went into a nursing home. I spent hours at his bedside—right up to the day he passed away. Not once did I get a thank you from my stepchildren."

Upon Carl's death, the prenup dissolved. Prenups are only meant to protect assets or minor children in the event of divorce and not death.

The wording of Carl's Last Will and Testament now takes precedent.

"Did Carl make arrangements for you in the will?" I asked.

"Yes. He set aside $2,000 a month for me, the surviving spouse. And it stipulated that I could continue to live indefinitely in the house we once shared.

"Of course those arrangements didn't please Carl's kids," Louise said with a look of disgust. "They continued to make my life a living hell. Weekly I was told I should move out of their dad's house. My husband was dead. I was exhausted. Why couldn't they find a small amount of compassion? I questioned how I'd ever gotten into such a mess."

"Three years have passed. How do things stand today?" I asked.

"I had to hire an attorney to stick up for me. A year ago I moved back into my own home," Louise answered. "I agreed to accept a settlement from Carl's estate. At last I feel free to move on with my life."

## A Word about Cohabitation

As popular as this loosely-tied lifestyle is today, it has no true support system in place for the partner or the children to rely on. Cohabitation is not as problem-free an arrangement as it might appear to be.

The majority of these families prove to be more temporary in nature. There is less chance of success for couples who choose to live together without the legal protection of marriage. When things don't work out, and feelings of love vanish, and one partner walks out, cohabitating adults often run into unexpected financial concerns, especially if property or children are involved and one paycheck was never intended to be enough to cover all the expenses.

Reporter Greg Stiles, on staff with the *Mail Tribune* in Medford, Oregon, wrote a story that demonstrates this point well.

Cathy, a 41-year-old part-time teacher and mother of three, invested a $30,000 "nest egg" from a divorce settlement into her house. Her boyfriend's name was not on the mortgage or house documents, but he paid half of the $2,600 monthly mortgage payments.

"If we broke up in less than two years, our contingency was to sell and pay the capital gains or at least break even," Cathy recalls.

But even that assumption was based on a rising market. When her boyfriend walked, Cathy knew she was in trouble. She could handle $1,300 a month, but $2,600 was a crushing blow. Getting into the house was "a huge stretch made with the assumption that things would continue to go up," Cathy says.

While foreclosure doesn't necessarily lead to a bankruptcy, it will in Cathy's case. If she simply had a first mortgage on the property, she could have signed the deed over to her primary lender. However, GMAC held the second mortgage and once the property goes back to the primary lender, the second-mortgage holder could go after her personal possessions if she didn't file for bankruptcy.

"Foreclosure looks so irresponsible," Cathy says. "As someone who had always worked hard, paid bills in full and made-every-payment-on-time, what kills me is that I just couldn't find a way out. I could not find an option. It's really hard to swallow—foreclosure and bankruptcy and I've yet to live through the whole effect of that." [48]

On the bright side, difficult circumstances impart wisdom. They teach us a lot about being gullible and not placing trust in the wrong places. Let's take off the rose-colored glasses and summarize what's taken place in this cohabiting relationship and use its lessons as a foundational set of truths.

1. Living together, trusting a lover will not walk out is foolish.
2. Contributing an entire nest egg for a down payment, knowing there's no way to make the payments *if* he doesn't stick around, is careless money management. No reserve funds are waiting in the wings to cover lean times. The family becomes vulnerable.
3. To accept total responsibility for a loan intended to be repaid by two individuals, one whose name never appears on the legal documents, means accepting total responsibility for the financial obligation. Unless the borrower's salary is adequate to keep payments current, this proves to be short-sighted irresponsible behavior.
4. Lenders can be part of the problem. Greed to make profits from borrowers got in the way of smart business practices. The borrower was in a risky position from the moment this loan was drawn up. Don't overextend yourself for anyone!
5. Housing markets don't always go up. Some years they head down.
6. A partner who avoids responsibility is already a loser. This sweet-talking guy's name wasn't on anything! No skin off his nose. No dog in the fight. All losses, all trouble, came crashing down around her shoulders.

## The Better Choice—Choose Marriage

God's plan for men and women is to create a family within the confines of marriage for a very simple reason. Families grow best emotionally and financially when couples choose marriage. Those who shun this commitment experience more disillusionment and dissatisfaction over time than do married couples.

Consider the children. They are the innocent victims who have no choice but to tag along into the life a mom or dad chooses. Apart from marriage, two lovers can only hope their family unit will last. Growing up in cohabiting homes places boys and girls at a greater disadvantage than in a stable committed home. Since live-in couples can opt out easily, many boys and girls come to see home as a place where multiple parenting figures drift in and out of their lives. *Churning* (the label given to this lifestyle) imbeds feelings of insecurity as children learn early on that loved family members don't stick around forever. Commitment becomes a vague virtue not easily grasped. And, all too often, abandonment issues take root in young lives that leave scars for a lifetime.

Concerned parents put their needs aside to care enough to guard their boys and girls from repetitive cycles of grief. Childhood should not be robbed of its innocence and sweet joy.

Life shared with a partner is best modeled through marriage. Vows and rings make it harder to call it quits. A team forms—the two become one. This sacred union between a man and a woman is meant to endure both good and bad times. Under this protective umbrella, children sense security and the unspoken promise of belonging in a place that stays together.

This chapter is speaking to blended families. Like us, many of you are already part of a remarriage. For more resources visit our web site: www.rebuildingfamilies.net. Be the best team you can be. Children should be able to trust Mom and Dad, stepmom and stepdad, to be attentive to their needs. That's a reasonable expectation.

## A Sobering Thought

Everyone knows not every married couple lives happily ever after. Divorce happens. Hearts break. But the odds still favor marriage. Through this institution a family's financial needs are attended to with the least amount of upheaval. And, if the couple encounters irreconcilable differences and wants to dissolve the union, the courts are able to make rulings that take into consideration the best interests of the children and distribute assets with unbiased fairness.

When it comes to merging money, know the facts and be cautious. But when it comes to raising children be willing to first show unconditional love, but also contribute financially when it matters most. A sobering thought comes to mind. Children grow up. One day the little ones God has given us to nurture will parent our grandchildren. It seems wise for all of us to look to the future and set a good example.

### The Bottom Line
- Convey respect for co-parenting relationships in and between homes.
- Respect court-ordered support rulings—without whining.
- Insist on full disclosure of financial information before merging money or assets.
- Be sensitive to the children's needs; plan ahead for some extra expenses.
- Prenups aren't for everyone. Seek expert counsel, apart from your intended spouse, to gather enough independent information to make an informed decision.
- Lenders do not respect a divorce court's ruling. Both names will likely remain on the loan until it is paid.
- It's typical for *all* boys and girls to ask parents for the stuff they want—stepparents included. Weigh the request. The right response is not always, "Yes." Sometimes it's better to say, "No."

### Increase the Wealth Challenge

Find a quiet place to talk. Listen well. Full financial disclosure from both partners is absolutely necessary in marriage. Choose to be open, honest, and vulnerable—not defensive. Let all the secrets come forth. Trust grows when yesterday's closeted stuff has no room to become a surprise pain in the rear, or pocketbook, tomorrow. Take time to discuss individual goals and begin to brainstorm how those objectives can someday be met. The trick will be to keep in mind a positive financial direction for the *entire* family.

## Common "Cents" Sense

*You are to allot it as an inheritance for yourselves and for the aliens who have settled among you and who have children. You are to consider them as native-born Israelites; along with you they are to be allotted an inheritance among the tribes of Israel.*[49]

## Sharks: \shärks\

Are typically active predators sometimes dangerous to humans

Merriam Webster's Online Dictionary, 2007-2008, Merriam Webster Incorporated

# Twelve

### Sharks in the Shadows

## Wising up to hidden fees, scams, and malicious fraud

*Switzerland knocked the United States off the position as the world's most competitive economy as the crash of the U.S. banking system left it more exposed to some longstanding weaknesses according to the World Economic Forum's global competitiveness report 2009/2010.*[50]

—World Economic Forum

"Don't trust those banks with your money," Grandma Grazoisa would say to Charlie in a stern voice. "In 1928, I begged Lena not to put her money in the bank. She didn't listen. She gave those bankers her money for safekeeping. They gave her a deposit book and a promise to pay interest. Foolish woman! Two years later the big-shot bank was gone. Lena's book wasn't worth a plug nickel. She lost everything. Crooks—all of them! They steal money from good people."

Charlie's caution about banks is understandable when Grazoisa's remarks are seen in their historical context. Banks were hit hard during the Great Depression that began in 1929. The stock market crashed in a horrific way. Over the course of Hoover's presidency, roughly 1,500 banks collapsed each year. Banks still in business weren't always open. They could close days at a time for bank holidays. No government programs existed to rescue failing banks. The FDIC had not yet been created. People had no insurance protection on deposited funds and no welfare programs to go to for assistance. Families made do as best they could. Suicide rates were high and breadlines long. Neighbors and churches helped if they could.

Charlie's father was a young man, just twenty-two, when the Great Depression hit. Under Mama Grazoisa's upbringing, her son was taught to only put money where he'd be sure to find it later—in an old pair of shoes, a coffee can, a slit in the mattress, a jacket pocket, an empty cigar box. The fear of bank failures was as reality-based as the instinct to survive was strong.

In the same way that gold represents an infallible asset to today's investors, stashing cash provided assurance of financial security back then. During this tumultuous period of history, thousands of people found more comfort in keeping their money out of the banks.

It wasn't until late 1933, under newly elected President Roosevelt, that Congress passed the Glass-Steagall Banking Reform Act to protect savings deposits, which in turn created the Federal Deposit Insurance Corporation, the FDIC we know today.

Charlie was born in 1939. Before his third birthday, his parents divorced, his mother moved to Alaska, and he was in the care of his grandmother and father. The nervousness about banks was passed on to him as a natural part of his upbringing.

## The Bank Today

Do banks still fail? Yes! The credit crisis caught too many banks undercapitalized and in deep financial trouble. In August 2009 Colonial Bank joined the list of big banks going bust. Eleven months earlier the public looked on in disbelief as Washington Mutual and Wachovia could not avoid the inevitable and found themselves on the growing list of bank failures.

*On January 28, 2011 the Associated Press reported that regulators on Friday had closed banks in Colorado, New Mexico, Oklahoma and Wisconsin, lifting to 11 the number of bank failures in 2011, following the previous year's toll of 157 taken down by the weak economy and piles of soured loans. The 157 bank closures nationwide in 2010 topped the 140 shuttered in 2009. It was the most in a year since the savings-and-loan crisis two decades ago.*[51]

The big question: Should we trust today's banks? Yes. The risk doesn't compare with that of the Great Depression. The safety net of FDIC insurance stands behind our deposits up to $250,000 per account if we are careful to choose a bank insured under the Federal Deposit Insurance Corporation. Contrary to popular belief, *not all banks* are insured.

Ask the right questions before opening an account. Websites are an easy way to check things out.

1. Is the bank covered by FDIC insurance?
2. What is the current interest rate being paid on passbook savings accounts?
3. What hidden fees are found in the fine print?
4. What types of checking or savings accounts are offered? Do some require a minimum balance to be maintained?

Banks serve a very important role in our culture. We need banks and banks need to attract customers. But be aware that money, like blood, attracts sharks. Be shrewd enough to see every bank as a predator planning to take advantage of every opportunity available to feed on our dollars. Bank fees provide shark food and fatten up the bottom line. The shocking truth is banks make more money on fees collected than from lending money out.

A bank's capital has only one source: its customer base. Well-paid strategists constantly look for new ways to pick customers' pockets. Desperate times lead to more creative measures and a whole bunch more fine print most of us will never read.

Think about it. The average bank is more customer friendly than ever before. Courteous banks appear to look the other way when customer accounts are overdrawn; but only for as long as it is financially beneficial to the bottom line.

As recent as the 1980s and early 90s, writing hot checks spelled trouble with a capital T. The person who wrote the checks was considered a thief stealing from the bank—a criminal kiting checks. If the matter wasn't quickly resolved, the deadbeat customer was deemed unworthy of doing business with that bank and lived in fear of arrest and prosecution. Having nonsufficient funds was a serious matter!

Somewhere between then and now a host of new rules, more financially punitive for the customer base, but far more profitable for banks, was adopted. No successful business operates to lose money and banks are no different. They must stay lucrative to keep their doors open. Creating multiple fees is how the game is played. But the customer base doesn't have to make it so easy for the bank sharks to dip into our cash. Feeding sharks becomes a costly habit. Overdraft protection sounds like a positive thing. But, overdraft protection comes at a cost, too.

Millions of people pay no attention to their own bank accounts. If that's you, get rid of the "so what" attitude. Become actively involved with your family's finances. Look at those bank statements with a scrutinizing eye.

Make it a habit to balance your checkbook every month. Question all fees that pop up and don't assume the charges are correct. Banks make mistakes, too. Verify everything before falling into agreement with the bank's conclusions.

## Credit Cards and Sharks

Lenders might appear to possess a lackadaisical concern for an individual's ability to pay or take their time before rushing to collect a payment. But in an article I read, there was a different reason given: *You can argue that's the democratization of credit, but it's in the interest of credit-card companies to keep people under the yoke. We've just swapped loan sharks for legitimate loan sharks This whole business of giving more credit than a person can service is not only foolish, but if you tried to do that 200 or 300 years ago, it would have been considered immoral as well. We don't think that way anymore, but essentially it is, because that person is going to be in debt forever.*[52]

Wow! Do you really want to be in debt forever? Isn't it time to find our way back to being a people who respect the use of A+ credit basics? Since the bubble burst, and so much financial chaos came on the scene, the pendulum looks like it's trying to swing back in the direction of more cautious lending practices and more fees.

A tricky ruling that caught lots of people off guard was the surprise lowering of an existing credit limit without advance notice. This practice not only incited anger, it loaded accounts with unavoidable fees that in turn created a domino reaction instantaneously bumping interest rates in some cases to maximum levels. The only explanation for this sneak attack is cash flow. The bottom line needed pumping up.

In June 2008, the *New York Times* printed an article empathizing with financial institutions: *A common practice for lenders is to lower a customer's limit as the debt is being paid down—a technique known in the industry as "chasing the balance." This way, they are on the hook for less money if borrowers default.*[53]

Realize "over limit" is a big revenue center for the card issuers. While marketing experts encourage people to spend, it's easy to go beyond a credit limit. Exceeding this boundary not only slaps on a bloody fee, it also hikes up the cardholder's interest rate. This painful bite is usually felt later as a delayed reaction on the day the billing statement is retrieved from the mailbox. The new federal credit card act, signed into law by President

Obama in May 2009, created a new ruling meant to curb this practice. Effective February 22, 2010, customers can only exceed their credit limit if they agree in advance to pay a penalty fee. Unless a cardholder is delinquent for more than 60 days, interest-rate increases will affect only new purchases, not existing balances.

Under that same new federal credit card act, as of August 20, 2009, card companies are required to review a customer's interest rate every six months. Consumers are now given the right to tell a credit-card company that they don't accept a change of terms in their card agreement. Opting out of the change, however, requires the company to close the account and allow the customer to pay off the balance under the old terms. To fully understand the new credit card rulings take a peek at: http://www.creditcards.com/credit-card-news/help/what-the-new-credit-card-rules-mean-6000.php.

The card issuer does whatever it takes to be less vulnerable to the risk of default and more proactive about profit. (Remember, banks do fail.) Don't be fooled by expensive brick and marble buildings. The same credit crisis that resulted in job losses on Main Street left lending institutions with serious problems, too. When Main Street can't repay loans, toxic assets end up on the bank's books. The shark's appetite is not satisfied. He grows hungrier and goes in search of blood to keep business operations humming along. There's only one food suitable to a financial shark's appetite: money. The customer base is the target. These moves are regarded as smart business decisions—nothing more. *Faced with mounting account delinquencies, major U.S. banks are penalizing credit-card customers late on payments by hiking their accounts to maximum default interest rates of 30% and more—even those with good credit records.*[54]

What can the average credit card user do? Lots! Exercise discipline with the use of credit and the power of choice. Careless spending habits need to be brought under the microscope. Point the finger in a personal direction. Decide that you will stop being a sloppy money manager.

A sad part of this financial crisis is that way too many families have fallen on hard times and now rely on credit cards as a means to buy basics like groceries, medicine, and gas. As balances grow larger, so does this group's vulnerability to bank fees and the eventual loss of available credit. The poor become poorer. If this is your situation, don't lose heart. Go in search of other solutions.

## Debit Cards

On August 15, 2010, the rules for debit cards changed. *If you'd like your bank to authorize debit-card or ATM transactions even if you don't have money in your checking account, then you'll need to make arrangements ahead of time with your bank. That is, make a conscious decision to opt-in to an overdraft agreement. If you opt-in, note that the bank has your approval but is not required to authorize a payment if you don't have the funds at the precise moment of the transaction.*[55]

Debit cards have gained popularity. Respect them as you would a checking account or credit card. Debit cards are also susceptible to over limit fees. The Center for Responsible Lending, a consumer organization ready to educate the public, found consumers are confused and the bank is preying on that debit card naiveté.

A debit card looks like a credit card, but it's different. Debit cards function like checking accounts except there is no need for checks to clear the bank. Debit card purchases are electronically subtracted from the checking account at the point of sale. Because this card relies on a checking account for funding, it is always treated as a substitute check and not as a credit card. Yes, it's made of plastic just like Visa and MasterCard but don't confuse the two. A billing statement won't show up in the mailbox for a debit card. These transactions show up on the monthly bank statement.

Too many users are not keeping a close eye on debit card purchases; often forgetting to record their purchased items. This common mistake makes it easy to spend dangerously beyond an existing balance's ability to cover the expenditures. Say you have a balance of $225 in your checking account. Your daughter is getting ready for prom. The dress she chose, and you paid for with a debit card, cost $98. The bank balance falls to $127. Off you go to the shoe store where another transaction of $68 brings home the perfect white heels. Account balance drops to $59. On the way home, you make one more stop at the grocery store. Again, you use the debit card to pay the $76.43 bill. Oops! The account is now in the red—overdrawn. The bank quietly thanks you for their stroke of good fortune at your expense. This mistake will cost you $34 or more. Check with your own bank to verify the exact fee that accompanies the opting-in to overdraft protection choice.

Be smart with debit card purchases. Write each transaction in the check register at the point of purchase and subtract that dollar amount from the checkbook balance when the card is used. This ten-second inconvenience will help to keep the sharks out of your cash. Nothing ticks me off more than to realize my money was wasted on a fee and not on a good time for me. Don't let a lunch stop at McDonalds for a $5 value meal turn into an extra $34 hit to your bank account. For $34 you can buy more than half a tank of gas, an oil change, an anniversary dinner at a nice restaurant with linen tablecloths and candlelight.

## Inside the Bank's Head

Alert, responsible customers are not necessarily the banks most lucrative patrons. Oh, don't get me wrong. Banks don't want account holders who are real flakes; they're happy with people prone to messing up once in a while. Customer carelessness is a productive cash cow for banks.

One of the nastier more profit-centered tricks banks began to practice was to change the order in which checks cleared the bank so it worked in their favor to impose multiple fees. Several small checks might not overdraft an account but one large check could. By changing the order of these checks, and clearing the bigger check first, the smaller ones could all become checks with nonsufficient funds. Now it became possible for more than one fee to be assessed. Internal manipulation always tips the scales in the bank's favor—not the account holder's.

Banks are more than willing to take on losses from a small percentage of negligent patrons because the number of bad accounts is more than offset by the majority of dependable customers who always pay on time or are only late or overdraw once in a while.

## Universal Default Clause

Before February 22, 2010, when a customer was late making a credit card payment bank sharks had the right to impose up to $39 in fees plus raise the interest rate on that account to its maximum allowable percentage on the spot—APR equal to the prime rate plus 21.99% no discussion needed. This course of action was commonly referred to as the Universal Default Clause and could be found in the issuer's fine print. Most customers were oblivious to this dagger of a clause until it stabbed them squarely in the wallet. Once enacted, the default rate remained in effect for a minimum of twelve consecutive billing periods beginning with the current cycle.

After February 22, 2010, the New Credit Card Accountability Act went into effect. Politicians imposed new rules on card issuers hoping to protect all of us from so many fees. But, sharks are masters at finding loopholes. Under the new rules, the Universal Default Clause is gone. The bank can no longer raise rates indiscriminately, as they had been able to do before. That sounds kind of good. But wait a minute. Interest rates can adjust *if* the bank defines when they will change. Already the list of new rulings is quite extensive and hard to keep track of.

- Variable rates: Credit card companies, now hamstrung by new rules for fixed rates, prefer issuing variable rate cards today. Variable means purchases made are not all processed at the same interest rate. This method promises to be a big income producer for banks.
- Late payments: Be 60 days late and the interest rates can be bumped up.

Look for fees to be more costly and for several new ones to be added. Late charges could cost more as time marches on. Expect to see more card issuers resorting to annual fees or charging a few dollars to deliver the monthly statement to a physical mailbox. Never underestimate hungry-for-profit sharks.

The card issuer also pulls information from credit reports to determine the credit worthiness of its customers, regardless of past performance on this particular account. At the discretion of the card issuer, a customer may be considered in default if the amount of overall debt carried leads the card companies to conclude the individual is a poor credit risk.

One good rule of thumb is to *never* use more than 30–60 percent of available credit. Don't exceed, or even get close to, credit limits—unless you find it amusing to do the bank a big favor. A wide margin helps keep the sharks from capturing the cash. The card holder is rewarded in a couple ways:

1) More money in his pocket by not paying expensive fees
2) A platinum credit score

## Read the Fine Print

Credit can become an expensive privilege. Unless a credit card balance can be paid off each month, serious consideration should be given to scaling back credit card purchases.

Even responsible folks, like Jack and Carol, who always pay their bills on time got caught off guard when sorting through a stack of magazines one evening. To their horror they found the Visa bill had somehow gotten tucked under the pile and not been paid. Now it was overdue.

It didn't seem like such a big deal at the time. Their prior history for the past eight years was platinum. A phone call to explain should resolve everything. Wrong. No sympathy from those *courteous* sharks could be found. In fact, the customer service manager reminded them that the policy was fully explained in their credit agreement.

Just one delinquent payment cost Jack and Carol a big late fee and resulted in a dramatic hike to the interest rate on their Visa account.

In December 2009, Elizabeth Warren, the Leo Gottlieb Professor of Law at Harvard and Chair of the Congressional Oversight Panel wrote: *Boring banking has given way to creative banking, and the industry has generated tens of billions of dollars annually in fees made possible by deceptive and dangerous terms buried in the fine print of opaque, incomprehensible, and largely unregulated contracts.*[56]

Be honest. Reading a credit agreement is something most of us don't do. Pages of fine print look overwhelming—like a tangled web of words meant for the legal experts to interpret. It's simpler to dismiss with the reading in order to expedite the process and get about the shopping.

But, being ignorant of the teeny tiny print is not in your best interest. It's important to know the rules that govern the credit game you're playing in order to know what to expect should you mess up or not. Grab a magnifying glass and discover the true cost of borrowing. A lack of understanding becomes your problem, not the bank's. Crying won't help. You'll be expected to pay the additional charges, as to your utter disgust, the card balance grows bigger and bigger.

As an example of what to expect in the fine print, here's what I found printed in an offer I received from Southwest Airlines for a Rapid Rewards Visa through Chase Bank in January 2010. If I signed up for this card, I would be agreeing to:

1. APR (Annual Percentage Rate) for purchases or Balance Transfers starts at 0% for the first 6 billing cycles and then shoots up to 15.24%.
2. APR for Cash Advances is 19.24% variable.
3. APR for Default is up to 29.99% variable.
4. APR for Overdraft Advance is at 19.24% variable but not available in some states.
5. Variable rate information explanation: APR may vary monthly based on the Prime Rate published in the Money Rates column of *The Wall Street Journal* two business days before the Closing Date on the statement for each billing period. Variable Purchase and Balance Transfer APR = Prime Rate + 11.99% for outstanding and

new balances after the introductory period. Variable Cash Advance APR = Prime Rate + 15.99%. Variable Default APR = Prime Rate + up to 26.99% but not more than 29.99%. Variable Overdraft Advance APR = Prime Rate + 15.99%.

6. A Grace period of at least 20 days for repayment of purchase balances is allowed.
7. Method of computing the Balance for Purchases: The Average Daily Balance method is used including new purchases.
8. There is an Annual Fee of $59.
9. The Minimum Finance charge is $1.50.
10. The Transaction fee for balance transfers is 3% of the amount of each transaction, but not less than $5.
11. The Transaction fee for Cash Advances is 3% of the amount of the transaction, but not less than $10.
12. The Late Payment Fee is $15 on balances of $1–$99; $29 on balances of $100–$249; and $39 on balances over $250.
13. There is no Over-the Credit-Limit fee (a good sign the bank encourages customers not to worry about carrying big balances).
14. International Transaction fees of 3% of the U.S. dollar amount are charged whether originally made in U.S. dollars or converted from a foreign currency.

Is your mind spinning after reading this list? Mine is. To make matters worse, some card issuers routinely add a sneaker fee (a percentage of the outstanding balance) to customer accounts for granting the privilege of carrying a balance.

The only way to nullify most of the rules and regulations stated in the fine print is to pay off credit card balances every month. Credit is big business. Use it wisely. Banks are first and foremost in business to make a profit.

And, if cards are already maxed out, don't lose heart. Get proactive. Closing account(s) is known to lower credit scores. But paying on time, and paying more than the minimum, is the best way to unleash upward correction to credit scores.

The key is to do something to break a dependence on credit. As an alternative to closing the account, shred the card(s), freeze "weapons of debt" in a blocks of ice, or bury the plastic culprits deep beneath a garden rock. Choose to be credit card savvy and come out a winner. Any move to a healthier financial condition blesses your family in amazing ways.

## Move toward Success

Personal finances are meant to be managed like a successful business entity. Families should be looking for profit, too. Profit is measured by economic sustainability that includes sufficient savings in the bank.

Moving toward success requires taking inventory of the family's income and expenses. If there's a surplus, finances are moving in the right direction. If not, you're operating in the red. Too much month left at the end of the money is not a good thing. Something's wrong. Red is a great color for a favorite shirt, but not for a family's financial picture. Living hand-to-mouth won't bring about the results that are needed for you to win the game and be streetwise. Unless families operating in the red implement change and begin to manage money in new ways, the future forecast remains that of extreme vulnerability.

It doesn't matter whether purchases are made by credit card, debit card, checks, online banking, or cash. What matters is how well a family creates a reasonable cash cushion to act as a buffer zone. This layer of protection makes it hard for sneaky fees to snatch dollars set aside for greater purposes.

Be watchful. Love yourself enough to verify account balances a minimum of two or three times a week. And always remember to record those debit card purchases as soon as the receipt is in hand.

Before heading to the supermarket or department store, know why this trip is necessary and how much money can be spent. A quick peek at the family spending plan is a good idea. Be honest about why you shop. Is this a disciplined pursuit or an emotional pastime? Spontaneous shoppers are often compulsive buyers looking to find happiness in material things when the real need is to resolve emotional hurts. It's much cheaper to pay for therapy than to spend a lifetime masking a search for love, stuffing feelings of abandonment, or not facing the truth about your deepest fears.

Never treat the ATM machine like a personal bookkeeper. Just because the receipt has a dollar amount printed on it doesn't mean that number is an accurate representation of the account's balance. Some checks or online bills might still be pending and not yet cleared through the account. Overdraft protection doesn't mean things are okay. Let's say the ATM receipt reported a $250 balance. Perhaps $200 of the $250 is already tapping into the overdraft courtesy. When $60 is withdrawn, the bank's system automatically kicks in a $39 overdraft fee. The bank doesn't mind giving its customers the opportunity to spend more. Good for the bank—bad for you the customer. The $60 expenditure morphed into a $99 strike against the account.

What a ridiculous waste of hard-earned cash! Setting up online alerts in advance could have warned against this kind of shark attack.

How clever financial institutions are today—clever enough to stay one step ahead of their account base through a wide web of manipulative maneuvers programmed to grab profit. These specialists count on the majority of us not paying attention to what's happening on the other side of the drive-up window but things don't have to remain the status quo. People are created with the clear ability to change bad habits into good ones. Becoming a smart money manager is fully possible for anyone who wants to keep more of their own money for their own use. Are you ready?

## Get Beyond the Blame Game

There's plenty of blame to go around.

Too bad more loan officers weren't thinking streetwise back when mortgages were being given to anyone with a pulse—even illegal immigrants. Those loose lending practices, a big chunk now labeled *liar* loans, is how we all got into this current financial trouble—borrowers and lenders alike. Greed led the way.

While it's fair to place part of the blame on the hungry lenders, a disturbing question remains: Why did so many good people of average intelligence (or above) fall into an obvious financial trap in the first place? A few thoughts come to mind:

- A false concept that the house was an investment that could always be sold at a profit.
- There was a desire to grow wealth fast by "flipping" houses.
- Fulfilling a lifelong dream of homeownership.
- The temptation for material goods outweighed common sense.
- An attitude of entitlement was part of the rationale.
- People gave themselves permission to spend, spend, and spend with no worry of tomorrow. Tapping into home equity made a live-for-today lifestyle possible. Easy credit gave people a false sense of "I've earned this. Why would they give it to me if I wasn't a good risk?"
- Lots of men and women were gullible! Marketers, working for the lenders, really were able to sell parachutes to scuba divers.

Honestly, no one makes anyone else buy something that's not wanted. The choice to live beyond our means is ours alone. The blame rests on our shoulders. The decision to buy more stuff exceeded our earning ability.

A sound financial lifestyle is built on a balance between take-home pay and cost of living. Economic chaos is conquered by implementing discipline with personal finances. Correct any habits that cause imbalance. For instance, if too much money is shelled out on golf each week, back off. Honor the spending plan by limiting that recreational expense. Instead of playing twice a week, play once a week.

All excuses have to stop. Actions prove that what was said in words is being practiced; both are working in tandem to achieve financial success.

## Set Alerts

Take advantage of the good things banks offer. At the top of the list is to provide customers with a lot of security options. In this electronic age, it's easy to stay on top of the money by phone, email, or text message. Bank customers can choose to know details about an account from a series of alerts that are easily activated. Some things you might want to know are:

1. When the account has insufficient funds
2. The account balance on a daily or weekly basis
3. When a payment is made
4. Confirmation when an automatic deposit has arrived
5. When a transaction originates outside the United States the foreign activity alert will send a notice
6. Awareness of checks or ATM withdrawals over a minimum of $100
7. When the account balance falls below a set amount; i.e. $500

Fall in love with these electronic watchmen. These 24/7 protectors trigger warning systems. Their job is to stand vigilant—to keep your money serving you well.

If, on a particular day, you see that there is very little money left in the account, you are able to make a good decision not to take money out or to transfer funds to replenish the account. Alerts are simple safe ways to add layers of protection capable of keeping hungry sharks from feasting from your cash trough.

## About Deposits

Q: When does a deposit become real spendable money?

A: This question requires a two-part answer: 1) Only after a check clears the bank on which it is drawn, or 2) immediately if the deposit is in the form of a cashier's check, money order, cash, or an electronic deposit.

But don't spend so fast with second-party checks. In haste, and because you have bills to pay, the money is often spent too soon after the check from a second party is received. No thought is given to the possibility that it might take time for the other person's check to clear or not clear their bank, or that the bank might have another reason why the delay of available funds occurs. You simply begin to write checks of your own which rely heavily on the newly deposited monies. A deposit might not become spendable for several days, and up to a week or two, depending on where the check originated.

Bank of America informs customers that the availability of funds could be delayed up to eleven business days if:

Deposits totaling more than $5,000 are made in a single day.

A check is re-deposited that was returned unpaid.

The bank believes a check we have deposited will not be paid.

You've repeatedly overdrawn the account in the past six months.

The bank is experiencing an equipment failure.

Operate from a point of caution. Write no checks and make no electronic payments until first verifying a pending deposit has been activated to a sure deposit. This is easily done with online services or telephone banking. Spending too soon after making a deposit can be an expensive lesson profitable only to the bank sharks or scam artists.

If the money is urgently needed or there is reason to worry, and the originating bank is nearby, go to that bank and swap the original check for a cashier's check before making the deposit. Yes, you will pay a fee for this exchange, but you'll also walk away fully confident the money is yours to spend. Any chance of insufficient funds, or surprise bank fees, has been avoided. A cashier's check is the same as cash deposited into the account.

## Zero Interest

What about zero interest offers? Chase and Bank of America have no cap on transfers from a higher interest credit card to one with zero interest. But is zero interest really a *free* move to make? Maybe. Maybe not. Look for transfer fees. There may be little to gain and the card will not remain at zero indefinitely. Typically, this is a limited introductory offer.

What appears to be a good financial decision could even play a dirty trick with credit scores. Most zero percent loans are written up through finance companies and not the retailer. Finance companies are not seen in as favorable light as a bank or retailer. An article appearing in the *Chicago*

*Tribune* said: Credit-scoring firms look at finance companies as lenders of last resort, where desperate people go when they can't receive cheaper financing elsewhere. So by taking money from a finance company, your credit score receives a major blemish, perhaps shedding 40 points.[57]

Lenders are in business to make a profit. It works to their advantage when we are not savvy about the rules of the game. From their perspective, customers should continue to juggle credit card balances between lenders. The profit margin is built in. Once you are late with even one payment, the zero percent goes away. Overnight, the interest rate jumps well above twenty-one percent and you're out shopping for the next sweet deal.

The dollars lost add up fast. Be attentive; not gullible. Guard the financial front. Sweet deals do backfire. Go into any transfer of accounts with eyes wide open. There could even be a fee charged from both sides of the transaction. Find the gimmicks hidden in the fine print. Then, if the move makes sense, press for an automatic transfer if possible.

## Minimum Payments Take How Long to Repay?

*Almost 90% of Americans do not know how long it will take to pay off a credit card bill making minimum payments. The survey showed that 55% of respondents thought minimum payments would get the job done in less than seven to eight years.*[58]

Let's do some credit card math. Suppose a flat screen TV is bought for $2,000. Let's figure out just how long it would take to pay off a $2,000 balance making minimum payments.

| Credit Issuer | Interest Rate | Minimum % payment | Total Interest | Years to Pay |
|---|---|---|---|---|
| Chase | 19.8 % | 2.00% | $7,636. | 41.8 |
| Discover | 12.5% | 3.50% | $781. | 9.4 |
| Bank of America | 8.9% | 2.80% | $651. | 10.4 |

Gulp! Most of us are doing a fine job feeding sharks. It will take a long time to pay off $2,000. Why do we choose to put ourselves in bondage for so long?

The interest rate and the percentage of the required minimum payment vary from one issuer to another. Minimum payments are factored by the lender. The smaller the payment required each month, the longer the consumer, who buys into making minimum payments as an okay way to live, stays in debt. This choice of debt repayment creates a big profit center for the credit issuer. Lenders love borrowers who remain in debt forever! They rake in the dollars while the borrower pays two or three times the original cost of the television. More money is made on interest and fees than was spent to purchase the item. One big streetwise rule of thumb is to *never* ever pay only the minimum. Always pay more. Pay as much as possible; if doable, pay off the balance each month.

Consumers have power. Your financial future will go in the direction you launch it.

While most couples press forward as a team to shape financial goals, it is equally important to offer helps to those husbands and wives who struggle to make ends meet because they are married to a financially out of control spouse. One partner longs for financial stability—the other recklessly undermines every attempt to succeed. Something has to change to rescue a family like this from financial suicide. The best solutions come wrapped in "tough love" boundaries meant to restrict unruly behaviors.

Hope for these conflicted families is found when the responsible spouse no longer enables the wild spending to continue. Instead, he or she does whatever it takes to press on toward an upbeat financial future. Some smart "tough love" moves are to:

- Close all joint accounts
- Provide a limited allowance
- Hold credit cards in individual names
- Seek expert counsel
- Push for intervention

Whether the one using credit is responsible or not, lenders don't give a rip if overspending happens. Why should they? Fees kick in and they smile. The user weeps and pays.

Credit is a privilege that should come with a disclaimer that says: "Caution: This card could be hazardous to your pocketbook. Exercise self control or suffer the consequences."

## Malicious International Fraud

Bank accounts can be hit on by scam artists from inside the country and outside our borders. Fraud is big business. Our own bank account was scammed twice! Two personal friends had their Facebook accounts hijacked and contact lists and credit card information stolen. Soon after, everyone on the contact list received a letter we were supposed to believe came from our friend. The Subject: Help!!

> *Please i really don't feel like disturbing with my little problem but i don't have any other options rather than seeking for help from you, please try to understand, I am stuck in England and we need help getting back home, we were robbed at gun while on vacation here, my bags, cash, cards and cell phone were stolen at GUN POINT. It such a crazy experience down here, right now we just need help flying back home, the authorities aren't being 100% supportive. good thing is i still have my passport, just don't have enough money to get my tickets, I am sending you this e-mail from the city Library, I will appreciate what so ever you can afford to send me for now but what i really need is 1,500$ you can get it to me through western union, please i need you to understand how urgent i need this help from you, I promise to pay back your money as soon as i return home. Get back to me asap.*

Lots of international fraud takes place and most scams originate in Nigeria or other faraway countries. The above example was an emotional appeal. Unfortunately, for those who get caught up in these scams, the end result is typically lost money and/or identity theft.

Learn to nip this game in the bud. First, attempt to make contact with the person you know. Is she at home? If your friend or family member can't be located, make other phone calls to mutual friends and ask questions.

Some things about this letter raised a red flag real fast.
1. My friend wouldn't use such bad grammar. (She's a writer!)
2. The story is farfetched and plays on emotions for an immediate response.
3. England is a country where the English language is spoken fluently and police are likely to be sympathetic to Americans in need.
4. The city library, though a place where computers can be used by the public, is a generic location and not to be believed.
5. The money asked for is an exact amount and most likely not the cost of two airline tickets.
6. And the dollars requested are written with the $ after the numbers.

As for this friend, she spent a lot of time reconstructing what she had. She built a new address book and informed the rest of us that if anything goes wrong on her upcoming trip to Africa, she will not be sending a general email like this one. She and her uncle will be calling family members direct.

## Compromised Bank Accounts

Our personal situation was a different scam. Our bank account was compromised, the account number stolen and new checks written with the exact information as the real ones and the numbering sequence perfectly orchestrated. This particular overseas ring goes about its business by posing as an international company legitimately hiring employees. People are told they will get paid on commissions and have the potential of earning big bucks.

This kind of fraud doesn't play on emotions as much as it preys on those who really need a job or a second job. The internet is how they recruit workers. In this economy, a whole lot of people are looking for work. GET Security, Inc. is the bogus business that got our bank account information. The qualifications for hire:

> IMPORTANT to be over 21 and a US CITIZEN and have a BANK ACCOUNT. You can earn from $50,000 up to $200,000 (depends on software sales) and more after one year working with us. Our company can guarantee $5,500 every month in your first year of work. We have stores in Spain and all Europe and we are looking for US representatives to handle US payments. We are selling various products (security systems) in US and Canada and we need YOU to process all the payments for these products because here in Europe the money orders and cashier checks are cleared within two weeks or more and is not reliable for our sales. 90% from US buyers don't have the knowledge to pay with bank to bank transfers. You can intermediate our sales (process payments) and you will be paid with 10% for every payment that you have to process. You will have your commission in hand same day because you will deduct your money from every payment that you receive after the bank or check cashing store clears the payment.

The language is polished. All of it sounds pretty good to those desperate for work. But, the truth is these swindlers are looking for gullible men and women who will act as a go-between. In the end the go-between is the one up against criminal charges. The real crooks can't be found or brought to justice. The "employee" is not only charged with fraud, but because he exchanged falsified checks for good funds from his personal account, he winds up with an empty bank account, too.

We were fortunate. Those who hired on (we learned about three) had second thoughts once the boss sent them a check for $2,450 to process, written out *to* them *from* us, they got nervous. They began to question GET Security, Inc.

Since our phone number is also written on our personal checks, these concerned people felt compelled to call us to find out if we'd made a recent purchase overseas. No! We were shocked and then very grateful to have been told what was happening. All three of our informants sent us the checks they'd been asked to launder. We wasted no time closing the account and turned the evidence over to the police department.

Realizing we were caught up in a theft ring was very surreal and unsettling. A new checking account was opened, but within a year another problem arose. This time the bad guys played with our online bill pay. One day, while recording some payments, I noticed a couple new payee accounts had been added to our list. Amounts and dates to be paid were all set in motion as if I'd authorized them. Not! I didn't recognize the payee names. Someone had gained access to our new account and planted another scam. Again, the bank was notified. The add-ins were deleted. Nothing was lost except our confidence in this bank to protect our money. Our next move was to change banks entirely. We were convinced that two episodes of fraud with the same bank might mean an inside job was going on.

A lot of thievery slips under the radar because a great number of people don't pay attention to their own bank accounts. The extortionist thinks, *Two new payee accounts with small pay outs could slip through without notice—couldn't they?* Not on our watch.

What can be done to guard a bank account? Plenty!
1. Keep an exclusive PIN for banking purposes and keep it private.
2. Change the PIN number every couple months.
3. Change security questions once in a while.
4. Be a watchful customer. Look at the account several times a week.
5. Look at bill pay activity regularly.
6. Report fraud to the bank.
7. Report fraud to the police.

There are all kinds of sharks in the shadows—the friendly ones and the dark and dangerous types. Be prepared. Another personal friend told me how she and her husband got scammed while enjoying a vacation. All they did was pay for a meal at an airport while waiting to change planes. They bought the meal with a credit card. Two weeks later, after returning home, they discovered an address change had been submitted for their credit card. Had it not been for the bank sending a thank you for the change of address, this scam could have gone on undetected much longer.

In this world where greed is common, it's up to you to protect your family's finances. Don't unnecessarily feed the sharks. Instead, be on top of your game and alert.

### The Bottom Line
- Take advantage of electronic alerts (whenever possible) on all financial accounts
- Consider debit and credit cards a convenience that's on par with cash.
- Pay early—at least a week ahead of the due date.
- Pay more than the minimum amount required to get rid of debt as fast as you can.
- Track charges and balances on accounts via internet or telephone several times a week.
- Examine all fees for accuracy. Question those that look unusual.
- Assume fraud can happen; do what you can to avoid becoming a victim.

### Increase the Wealth Challenge

Sit down with those bank statements. Understand the fees you are paying. Next, scrutinize credit card statements carefully before paying those bills.

Verify every purchase made with credit. And always be sure to question any fees or purchases that cannot be confirmed.

## Common "Cents" Sense

*Who is wise and understanding among you? Let him show it by his good life, by deeds done in the humility that comes from wisdom.*[59]

# World: \ˈwər(-ə)ld\

Involving or applying to part of or the whole world; internationally recognized

Merriam-Webster's Online Dictionary, 2007-2008, Merriam-Webster Incorporated

# Thirteen

## All Eyes on a World Economy

## What does it mean to live in a global marketplace?

*The credit crisis has now dramatically affected the world economy. All of a sudden the actions of the little people matter. If more people had been doing what I do, if we'd cared enough to keep little people out of debt they couldn't handle, the global economy wouldn't be in the mess it's in.*[60]

—Suze Orman

Andrea and her family are Americans living in Europe. They receive financial support in U.S. dollars from ministry partners here in the United States and exchange that money for Euros to cover living expenses. Twenty years ago, when they moved overseas, the dollar was very strong—worth much more than the majority of European currencies, which were not unified into the Euro until 2002. Because of a robust U.S. dollar, Andrea's family enjoyed the advantage of extra buying power for many years. All that has changed. In the last eight years, the Euro exchange rate has surpassed the dollar by up to 60% and is currently about 41% higher than the US dollar. The "rounding upward" of prices with the unification of the Euro along with the weak dollar have reduced their buying power drastically. Today, every dollar received requires an additional 41 cents just to maintain the same lifestyle. When asked how declining dollars and appreciating Euros were affecting her family, Andrea gave a clear example.

"Some of our biggest shockers came in the cost of milk jumping from .79 to 1.10 Euro per liter (similar to a quart), and the rising price of gasoline to 1.28 Euro per liter. Multiply liter price times four and the approximate per gallon price of fresh milk is now $4.40 and $5.12 for gasoline. In the last four years our dollar buying power decreased between 35 and 60%. What used to be our fun money to fund trips to the U.S. or a small vacation now goes to our monthly expenses, and there's still a gap. Thankfully, we have been able to work part-time here translating and teaching to keep our monthly budget afloat. The whole idea of sending people overseas is in large part based on a strong dollar, though no one stopped to think about it much. At this point, it is not very feasible to be in many areas of the world without some source of *local* income in the local currency."

## World Markets

The fiscal soundness of the United States—or lack thereof—reverberates around the globe. What happens here does not stay within our borders. The USA is only one player in a great big world economy.

*On August 1, 2008, two Bear Stearns hedge funds that were heavily invested in mortgage-backed bonds filed for bankruptcy, and another had its assets frozen following mortgage-related losses. Within a week, Luxembourg's Sal. Oppenheim, one of Europe's largest private banks, announced it had temporarily closed a $750 million asset-backed securities fund it managed for Austrian investment foundation Hypo KAG. On August 9, BNP Paribas (BNPP.PA), France's biggest bank, followed suit by freezing $2.2 billion worth of funds exposed to the subprime mortgage market and Dutch merchant bank NIBC canceled a flotation plan after revealing a $188.6 million loss from U.S. asset-backed securities. It was becoming apparent that many of the mortgage-backed securities that had been used to pump billions of dollars into the global economy were considerably overvalued. Lenders around the world were getting very nervous, very fast.* [61]

How unfortunate the subprime lending crisis birthed here spread catastrophic problems far and wide. There is legitimate concern around the globe that a financial crisis of epic proportion could happen in the United States of America. And if the economy continues to worsen here, other countries will either share the pain or take advantage of the USA's weakened financial condition. One small remote seaport town with major losses to report is Narvik, Norway. This town, along with three other Norwegian municipalities, lost about $64 million, and stands to lose even more in complex securities investments that went sour. Their community no longer has money for things that matter, like schools or care for their elderly. *Norway's unlucky towns are perhaps the least likely victims so far of the credit crisis that began in the American subprime mortgage market. However, they are clearly an example of the fear that has been spread into the global economy from subprime loans. The residents of Narvik want to know how their close-knit community of 18,000 could have mortgaged its future—built on the revenue from a hydroelectric plant on a nearby fjord—by dabbling in what many view as the black arts of investment bankers in distant places. Citigroup created the investments bought by Narvik and the other towns through a Norwegian broker.*[62]

Credit card debt, like mortgage debt, gets bundled, securitized, and sold off by banks. *Citigroup, one of America's largest credit card lenders, reported that it lost $176 million in the second quarter of 2008 through securitizing such debt. The buyers of those securities observe rising delinquency rates and rising interest rates, and decide the debt is worth less than Citi thought.*[63]

Money crisscrosses borders twenty-four hours a day seven days a week via a wide array of investment vehicles such as stocks, bonds, currencies, and commodities. The world was not braced for the impact the real estate slump would have on the financial industry.

*Like a ticking time bomb, the national debt is an explosion waiting to happen. It's expanding by about $1.4 billion a day or nearly $1 million a minute.* [64] The world has every right to feel uneasy about the United States economy. Our national debt is a frightening (and growing) multi-trillion dollar problem. Despite that news, we are still the world's largest economy and rank fifteenth overall in debtor nation statistics. England is the forerunner in first place.

In 2010, Greece erupted in serious financial trouble. Riots broke out in the streets. Many experts tell the rest of us to pay close attention. Greece could be a glimpse into our own future.

*Not since the Depression have so many countries faced so much trouble at once. The financial crisis has gone global, like a virus mutating in the face of every experimental cure.*[65]

PiiGS is an acronym given to five European nations in deep debt trouble: Portugal, Ireland, Italy, Greece, and Spain. While BRIC represents four strong emerging economies: Brazil, Russia, India and China. One country's misfortune often becomes a total contrast to what's happening in another part of the world where there is fiscal solvency.

## NORAD: North American Aerospace Defense Command

It is not trivial that NORAD is being spoken of in this book. It is inserted to open your mind to how the government determines economic policy. First, let's understand the role of the North American Aerospace Defense Command. The definition taken from their website (http://www.norad.mil/Home.html) is: NORAD is a United States and Canada bi-national organization charged with the missions of aerospace warning and aerospace control for North America. Aerospace warning includes the monitoring of man-made objects in space, and the detection, validation, and warning of attack against North America whether by aircraft, missiles, or space vehicles, through mutual support arrangements with other commands.

NORAD's vital warning system is prepared to protect citizens and ward off threats to national security. In a like manner, a financial NORAD is in place, too. Its purpose is to keep financial conditions in check from day-to-day. Deep in the basement of the Treasury Building in Washington D.C. sits a staff of workers whose job is to monitor global financial conditions. We will refer to this operation as the "NORAD of finance." Under the direction of Michael Pedroni, daily reports are prepared to report interest rates, derivatives, municipal bonds, credit markets, and a multitude of other financial news happening around the world. At 5 o'clock every evening the Secretary of Treasury and the President of the United States are given a report. From that report, discussions take place that factor in financial markets and determine how the economy is controlled. Almost nothing happens by chance or free market coincidence. Out of sight there is a great deal of economic manipulation going on.

## The Government Steps In

September 2008 was added proof of the shakiness of the American economy. During the second week of September, the United States government took over private industry mortgage giants Freddie Mac and Fannie Mae. These two companies alone issued half of all mortgages in the United States—or $5.6 trillion. The federal bailout, in layman's language, means that half of all mortgages in America are now nationalized and under the government's direct control.

Nationalization is not a word the government wants to toss about loosely in the public sector. It has a negative connotation—one that smacks of socialism. Still nationalization is the impending truth we need to be wary of.

In his *Communist Manifesto*, published in 1848, Karl Marx proposed ten measures. Proposal Number Five was to bring about the "centralization of credit in the banks of the state, by means of a national bank with state capital and an exclusive monopoly."[66] Are the people of the United States being led down this same path? Maybe. Freedoms once seen as the bulwark of American society are slipping away repositioned by leaders who want more control than our forefathers deemed constitutional. Free enterprise takes another nudge toward the back of the bus when legislators inflict new rules that disregard the voice of the people and promote big government's intrusive move into the more popular front seats. "Cash for Clunkers" and the rescue of General Motors are prime examples.

Americans must remember the core values our founding fathers clung to. Two things made America the greatest nation on earth:
1. Godly principles
2. Free enterprise

Don't we owe it to ourselves and our children to defend these strong foundational values? Isn't it best to limit government involvement, as the forefathers wisely did, and not create a socialistic America?

## Bailouts and Band-Aids

To further inject US dollars into global markets as a means to clean up the current financial crisis is risky economic policy. Borrowing (by printing more money) to dump even more money on top of an already blown-apart credit mess only adds to the problem. Liken this practice to assessing an invisible tax meant to redistribute resources among a bunch of debtors who chose to make unwise investments or an alcoholic who decides one more drink will be the answer leading to sobriety. Nonsense!

"We must reverse the drift and complacency which has slowed down our growth at home and permitted our prestige to decline abroad. Let's get America moving again."[67] Those famous words were spoken to the nation in 1960 by President John F. Kennedy. Can you hear an echo of preemptive truth for today? I can!

Government bailouts and quantitative easing are Band-Aids covering an open sore and ensuring the cost of a real cure grows more expensive. Bailouts are not free money. Taxpayers foot the bill. And judging by the size of our national debt, it's obvious the plan is not going to be the best solution for us, our children, or our grandchildren.

Capitalism is meant to rise and fall on its own merit. Government intervention is interfering with the rules that guide true capitalistic principles. When a businessman steps up to open a storefront, he understands he does so at his own risk of success or failure. A capitalistic society does not include government backing or bailing out business ventures.

In a republic like America, grown men and women make their own work-related decisions—whether good or bad—and accept the outcome, whether profitable or disastrous. No company should ever be considered too big to fail. If a company suffers a loss, that responsibility, including the financial burden, falls squarely on the shoulders of the entrepreneur who must figure out how to bounce back without help from the government.

## A Scramble to Build Confidence

Ideology is sometimes flawed. To believe government is looking out for the public's best interests might not be a trustworthy assumption. Given the current economic circumstances, the Fed scrambles for answers that build confidence at home and with world markets.

The operable word here is *confidence*. When the economy is believed to be buoyant, people are at ease. They spend money. On the flip side, when optimism is shaken by fear of economic disaster, people buy less. Bad news can also trigger extreme behaviors. No one wants a run on the banks or riots in the streets—especially the Fed.

Take a minute to contemplate why a government would choose to dump the accumulated cost of uncollectible bad debts that originated in the private sector onto the backs of taxpayers. Only one thing comes to mind: The United States is at a critical economic crossroads. TARP, the Toxic Asset Relief Program, is a word we've grown accustomed to. Its purpose is to hide all kinds of toxic financial problems out of sight—no different than tying a canvas tarp over the back end of a pick-up truck piled high with rubbish and destined for the city dump. The contents stink and would be no more than trash along the roadside should the cover give way. The only way to extract salvage dollars from this mess is to ingeniously portray what's hidden in a more gainful light and market the contents to trusting buyers.

Economic history is being written as the world looks on. How far will legislators go to bring a soft landing to this global crisis? Or will the day come when the marketplace is allowed to chart its own path to recovery? This question can't be answered right now. But one day, somewhere in the future, that outcome will be obvious.

## The Borrower is a Servant to the Lender

The battlefield for world power is no longer dependent on military prowess. Today's super powers exercise more muscle with money than with weapons. That's not so good for nations like America who have an insatiable need to borrow money. This dependency signals a fall from the heights of economic power onto the rocky shores of fiscal imbalance—a very problematic place to be.

A common practice today is to sell off substantial portions of prized American companies and government-backed securities to foreign investors whose lifestyle and governmental values are not in sync with the freedoms that depict the United States of America. Money talks. Our need to find immediate dollars throws caution to the wind. The type of currency doesn't matter. Any country possessing financial liquidity is welcome to step through an open door of opportunity, buy up US dollars, foreclosed properties, and portions of American companies. This amounts to a stroke of good fortunate for them that could weaken the United State's role as a world power.

China and Dubai top the list of eager investors. Both have deep enough pockets to buy a formidable presence within the United States at a crucial point in history when our hand is extended to all comers.

Secretary of State Hillary Clinton believes the national deficit is sending the wrong message internationally. On September 8, 2010, Clinton addressed the deficit problem, saying: "It poses a national security threat in two ways: It undermines our capacity to act in our own interest, and it does constrain us where constraint may be undesirable."

As we place more and more dependency on foreign investors to resolve credit problems here at home, two problems must be addressed . . .

1. Who will pay back the borrowed money?
2. Looking ahead, how will this practice compromise our country's decision-making processes and safety? The Bible warns us that the borrower is always servant to the lender (Proverbs 22:7).

## Take It Personal on the Home Front

People and governments are inseparable. Each one of us holds a vested interest in our country's future and in global affairs. It is our personal responsibility as citizens to speak up about fiscal responsibility. Nothing is gained by falling in lockstep with illogical government decisions. Only puppets remain silent. Every voice matters.

Passion is a forerunner for change. Passion ignites action. For the sake of the generations to come, can this generation determine to lay down solid economic policies within our nation, our communities, and our homes?

Some of us might choose to participate in civil government, run for public office, speak out in public places, or sponsor important events.

We should all be model citizens—a people adequately acquainted with the affairs of government. People who grasp the core values held by those sitting in positions of authority and who satisfactorily understand the laws governing daily life. With this information on board, the election process serves us as it should—our representatives will be men and women of outstanding character and trustworthy ambition.

## Real Budgets Have Sinking Funds

Charlie made it a habit to educate accounting clients on the importance of maintaining adequate sinking funds. *Sinking fund* is a routine accounting term given marginal respect today. This once popular practice, relevant to the survival of a business operation, deserves to be reintroduced into our culture.

A sinking fund is equally important to a large corporation, a sole proprietor, or the average family. This budgeted item represents money put aside for future maintenance and the replacement of aging equipment. Liken money in this account to a piggy bank collecting dollars for specific needs (i.e. water heater, painting the house, dishwasher).

Years ago all companies were required to provide sufficient proof of available sinking funds. Otherwise, bankers wouldn't loan them money. The borrower had to be in a strong enough financial position to ensure long-term operation of the business. Shrewd entrepreneurs were the ones who gained respect with bankers.

A case in point is our friend Tod who is a long-haul truck driver. Every so many highway miles, maintenance is required to keep his big rig running in tip-top condition on the road. Smart long-haul owner-operators also know all trucks have a life expectancy. In Tod's case, the old truck needs to be replaced every six years. To be ready for that day, each month a percentage of earnings, determined over the seventy-two-month life of the truck, is put in the "Purchase a New Truck" sinking fund. Six years later, when the road-weary rig has done its job, the replacement is bought without piling on outlandish debt. Tod's use of a sinking fund to meet a future need makes it possible to be back on the road without a hitch. The old truck is exchanged for a shiny new one and it's business as usual.

With a little discipline, all families can begin to reap the benefits of sinking funds.

## Government Preparedness

This whole sinking funds conversation brings up another interesting question. Why don't most governments develop budgets that make use of this protective practice? Instead, like most households, finding any federal, county, or municipal budgets with administrators wise enough to consider an allowance for ongoing maintenance and replacement are few and far between.

Ninety-eight percent of governments do not provide for expenses they *know* will happen in the future. The majority of families operate the same. Postponing maintenance, and lacking a proper plan to replace what will wear out, creates a state of premeditated vulnerability. On purpose, there is no preparation for an emergency. Then, when disaster hits, there's no debt-free way to meet the immediate need. Using credit cards or seeking public funds becomes the first go-to option.

The bridges across America are one significant example of why sinking funds are so important. *The entire span of an interstate bridge broke into sections and collapsed into the Mississippi River during evening bumper-to-bumper traffic Wednesday, sending vehicles, concrete and twisted metal crashing into the water.*[68]

Only after this worn-out bridge near downtown Minneapolis, Minnesota, collapsed August 1, 2007, and many lives were lost were we told a startling truth. One third of America's bridges should be condemned! Why? These key structures aren't up to safety standards for one reason: The cost to maintain and repair bridges has not been part of the budget base. What an appalling truth! Maintenance of bridges is an inescapable reality as necessary to operations as air is to breathing.

Some of our elected officials are speaking out. *"The push to repair bridges and our country's infrastructure has become a victim of the bad economy," said Pennsylvania Governor Edward G. Rendell. If we don't put money into our roads and bridges and infrastructure, our economy will get even worse. We won't be able to transport anything across this country."*[69]

All of us should be concerned. In the city of Portland, Oregon, eight bridges connect east to west across the Willamette River. Commerce in the metro area depends on the integrity of these massive viaducts. No one passing through the metro area should have to worry about the reliability of these important structures. Being safe while crossing to the other side of the river is not a negotiable matter.

Realistic budgets count the *entire* cost of operations: The routine upkeep, carpet cleaning, furnace repair, snow removal, vehicle replacement and so on.

Another great benefit of sinking funds is the peace of mind they provide. Everyone knows money is put aside. The *surprise* expense will be manageable and not result in a major threat to safety or operations.

## Still Leading the World

Currently, despite debt in excess of 14 trillion dollars, the United States leads the world when it comes to the size of its economy. But a 2011 report from PricewaterhouseCoopers believes China could overtake the USA as the largest economy in the world by 2020 and that India's growing economy will likely be in first place by 2050.

As of the last week of March 2011, it appears that China did surpass the United States in manufacturing. But things are not quite as promising as they sound. China's zeal to be number one could be another bubble that will burst. The people cannot afford to live in the new cities being built.

*"It's estimated that 10 new cities are being built every year," Australian news program SBS Dateline says. Many of the cities remain vacant. Even though China has become the leader in development, it's adopted the idea that "If you build it they will come." There's just one problem: They're not coming. And so China has a problem—ghost cities. According to Business Insider, some estimates say that nearly 64 million properties are vacant in China. The country is plagued with empty homes, malls, and businesses.*[70]

The United States is the current economic superpower with far-reaching global influence. It is the duty of the American people to weigh economic decisions thoroughly and look to the future with a dual sense of purpose that:

1. Acts with fiscal responsibility and level-headedness for what happens on our soil.
2. Stays informed and ready to proceed with balanced decisions in global affairs.

The voice of the citizens counts. Vote! Elect leaders who respect family, walk humbly, and pledge to guard the safety of individual communities and the United States of America.

Make it a matter of personal choice not to bend to unfavorable foreign influence because of a financial crisis. The temptation to take easy money is strongest when cash is in short supply. But a quick fix might not be the right answer to ongoing financial problems. Consider all options carefully. Austerity could well be the perfect choice. It might be better to eat less expensive and simpler meals, give up a few movie nights, carpool with neighbors, chisel away at the mountain of debt, and keep all eyes on world developments rather than risk compromising the America our children will inherit.

### The Bottom Line

- Not all nations want to see the United States remain a strong world leader.
- Cash is king. People and nations flush with cash fare well in a credit crisis.
- Debt poses a threat to national security.
- Today's superpowers exercise more muscle with money than with weapons.
- Sinking funds set aside money for future maintenance and replacement of worn equipment.
- Only informed voters can cast well thought-out votes.
- The United States was established on principles of capitalism—not the dictates of socialism.

### Increase the Wealth Challenge

Does your family have sinking funds included in the family's spending plan? If not, begin a sinking fund today. Next, take an active interest in global affairs. At least once a week learn three new things about what's happening beyond our borders. Websites, news programs, newspapers, and magazines are loaded with information. Lastly, remember: Your vote counts.

## Common "Cents" Sense

*You have shaken the land and torn it open; mend its fractures, for it is quaking.*[71]

# Invest: \in-ˈvest\

To commit (money) in order to earn a financial return;
to make use of for future benefits or advantages

Merriam-Webster's Online Dictionary, 2007-2008, Merriam-Webster Incorporated

# Fourteen

## Invest Beyond the Local Bank

## The basics of stocks, bonds, 401(k)s and swindlers like Ponzi

*Every family member should be trained in the principles of sound investing. This is critical for children because they'll eventually move away and be responsible for managing their own family's finances.*[72]

—Money Life Basic Series

Roger Orland didn't save much money in his life. He was busy raising his children, traveling to many places, and buying items for the family to enjoy. After the birth of his first grandchild, in the summer of his fifty-sixth year, Roger came to a horrifying reality. "My wife and I don't have money for retirement. Something has to change!"

In desperation to build a nest egg, Roger began to work six—sometimes seven—days a week. He maximized contributions to his 401(k) plan, loaded up on company stock, and accumulated half a dozen investment properties. Knowing the years were slipping by fast, he set out to accumulate riches quickly. He estimated it would take a hefty 20–30% return yearly to fund their retirement goals. Roger didn't know it then, but he was plunging into risky investments to accelerate the return on his money.

At first everything seemed to be going in his favor, according to plan. Profits were amassing on paper since he'd caught the upward motion of 2003 when the economy, thanks to the real estate bubble, was on the rise at warp speed. No one thought the momentum would stop. Roger saw no reason to put the brakes on. That is, until 2008 when the stock market took a nosedive in the opposite direction. All the subprime loans, imploding financial stocks, and equity losses turned his dream of riches into a dreadful nightmare.

Roger's family ended up worse off than before.

Debt acquired in the pursuit of wealth totaled more than the current fair market value of the properties. Now he was short $1,500 a month just to keep up with the mortgage payments. Financial stress was all around and hopes of equity gains were wiped out.

The immediate need was to salvage some cash from what few assets he had. That meant a quick sale of his shares of company stock.

To make matters worse, the downturn in the economy impacted his workplace. Because he was a sales representative who depended on customers being able to get financing, his income dropped by seventy percent.

In an effort to continue to make ends meet, Roger's credit card balances rose sharply.

## What Can Be Done Now?

Roger learned a hard lesson: Riches don't grow fast. Consequences of a shortsighted plan aren't easily erased. Sleepless nights crowd out rest, and tough decisions have to be made. Foreclosure and bankruptcy are not outside the realm of possibility. Driving past men holding up homeless signs adds fear. Listening to his wife's worries and seeing her in tears brought feelings of deep sadness and guilt. Not just one investment failed to perform well—all of them suffered loss. Roger came to Charlie desperate to know, "What can be done?"

Charlie commended Roger for taking the first big step in search of counsel. That act of alone opens the door to new ideas. Together they worked out a plan for Roger and his wife from the couple's existing financial information and the realistic formula below.

Get Counsel ⇨ Downsize ⇨ Restructure Goals ⇨ Maximize $ ⇨ Add No Risks

The dream of funding the golden years late in life with a get-rich-quick fix is not just unrealistic but risky. The five steps shown in the formula are necessary to progress from where you are to where you want to be.

1. Getting expert financial counsel is an important first step to amassing retirement money.

2. Downsizing is unavoidable. There isn't enough time between now and retirement to recapture what was lost. The monthly budget will need to shrink.
3. Set new goals. Write down what a realistic lifestyle in retirement will look like.
4. The next step is to maximize whatever money is left by tucking those dollars away in interest bearing accounts or an IRA. Sell whatever can be sold to accumulate more cash. In doing so, traction is found to secure a sustainable standard of living in the years ahead.
5. Make no more risky, too-good-to-be-true, purchases. If an investment promises more than the going rate of increase, risk is attached.

The most effective way to plan for retirement is to start as early as possible, take a conservative approach over time, and allow the benefits of compounding interest to take effect. But people like Roger shouldn't lose hope. There is still time to maximize both the dollars and the days that are left. Simply begin to put money where it can achieve its highest potential.

Because Roger and his wife listened to counsel, they wasted no time putting the plan in place. To their delight, their finances turned around, from gloomy to optimistic, as they followed through and made the necessary changes to prepare for retirement. Some of the things this couple did included:

1. Reviewing all assets and liabilities in detail.
2. Downsizing their lifestyle to a realistic level. They eat at home more often now.
3. Selling many household items, big and small, to create cash flow.
4. Giving the keys to their house back to the bank in lieu of foreclosure when they were no longer able to make the mortgage payments as before.
5. Renting a home took the pressure off their finances.
6. Facing the fact that the rental houses were costing them money each month—money they didn't have—and had to be sold. The housing market was not going to improve anytime soon.
7. Praying for God to lead them to the right decisions each and every day.

Best of all, Roger and his wife found a new perspective along the way. "We discovered peace of mind and contentment were the result of having less," Roger said, "and all the stuff we thought made us happy had really given us lots of anxiety and bills to pay. With money worries under control, a heavy load's been lifted off our minds. At last we're free to enjoy life."

## Accept Change

Know how much cash will be left after the losses are fully realized. Chances are there may be enough to start anew when salary, disability, and the sale of items is taken into consideration. It might not be possible to stay in the same house or neighborhood. In fact, grieving over this loss can be part of the process of letting go of those broken dreams.

Don't cling to what cannot be kept. Allow God to chart a new path for the future. Accept change as a good thing.

1. New beginnings are not geographically attached to a piece of property.
2. Depression is a counterproductive state of mind.
3. A positive attitude is necessary to take new steps and feel good about those decisions.

Money comes and goes throughout life's journey. Thankfully, our worth is not wrapped up in the dollars we do or do not possess. Personal value is our gift from God. Strong character is ours to build and always trumps wealth. In a crisis, character is what pulls us through and makes known our core values.

To know yourself better, ask the hard questions. How well do I cope when life turns sour? Do I make lemonade or spit seeds? Then ask someone who's known you for a long time (spouse, child, close friend, co-worker, relative) to tell how they've seen you react to life's issues. Compare their comments with your own assessment.

## Invest—But Be Careful Who You Trust

Ask Questions ⇨ Get Counsel ⇨ Research Products $ ⇨ Risk Tolerance ⇨ Invest

Scams abound. Anywhere there's money to be made there'll be con artists in the shadows. Over 4 trillion dollars sits in individual 401(k) accounts. Where is it invested? Most participating employees can't answer that all-important basic question with confidence.

No one else cares as much about preserving my dollars as I will. My money is of personal importance to me. When my cash is in the game, I want to win. So should you. That's why it's crucial to do some homework *first* before investing those hard-earned dollars.

The last thing we want to do is fall victim to a cunning money manager or dishonest financial advisor. A great resource provided by the U.S. Securities and Exchange Commission is http://www.sec.gov/investor/brokers.htm. This easy-to-navigate site tells who's who among brokers and investment advisers, who's licensed in good standing and who's on probation or without a license. The supreme goal is to protect our money. Every investor has to take it upon himself to know the good guys from the bad guys.

John Mauldin, President of Millennium Wave Advisors, LLC, is a respected Registered Investment Advisor. His weekly newsletter, *Investors Insights*, is a great resource. On January 12, 2009, in utter disgust over Bernie Madoff's Ponzi scheme, Mauldin penned his thoughts: *2008 gave us the ultimate of all rats: Bernie Madoff. The warning signs were there: people like Harry Markopolos wrote the SEC on numerous occasions, and yet nothing was done. In my opinion, Mr. Madoff has done more harm to the investment community than any single individual I can remember in financial history. Samuel Isreal, Ivan Boesky, and the eponymous Mr. Ponzi all pale in comparison to the economic, social, and trust destruction wrought by this single investment sociopath. In the Old Testament, the Bible speaks of the "Toevah," which is defined as "an abomination." On Bernard Madoff's tombstone, I hope they inscribe: "The Great Toevah."*

Well said! So many people were betrayed. Huge fortunes lost overnight. Charities that help vulnerable people had also been conned. There is not a good way to recover such a large amount of capital funding. What will happen to those in need?

Crook Madoff's gift of gab gave him a friendly access to those he targeted—individuals and organizations who had megabucks to invest but little savvy regarding investments. Their trust was blind, void of adequate knowledge or investigation.

The average employee does the same thing with 401(k) dollars. He or she buys a pig in a poke. I often overhear Charlie ask, "Can you tell me what's in your portfolio? Do you know where your money is invested?"

"No, I don't know," is the most common answer.

Don't accept not knowing where you've put your money. Know what is being bought and who you are buying from. The company behind the sales representative must be in good standing with the Securities and Exchange Commission (http://www.sec.gov/investor/brokers.htm) and be on sound financial footing. Be cautious. Ask questions until you get satisfactory answers.

To invest in a bond fund, choose a sector of interest and know what corporations are in the mix. A sector could refer to financial, housing, medical, and energy and so on. To purchase shares of stock, ask if a dividend will be paid. This research is called due diligence.

Feel enough danger before investing to get educated first. Realize there are lots of perilous places where you can be put at risk or ripped off. Another excellent site for the investor to make use of is the Financial Industry Regulatory Authority (http://www.finra.org). FINRA has many articles, interactive tools, and resources meant to protect investors from making uninformed decisions.

Investing is still a good thing to do. Just be a safe, smart investor—one who is streetwise enough to learn facts before letting go of the cash.

## Get to Know Ponzi

Madoff is only the tip of the iceberg. This kind of con is all too easy to pull off. All that is needed are a front man and gullible people. As long as the concept behind a Ponzi scheme is not understood, people will continue to be vulnerable marks.

The originator of the scheme, like Madoff, looks sharp, talks a good line and hangs out in prestigious places. He's convincing. Inexperienced folks with money to invest are looking for ways to make big bucks. These investors mistakenly believe the shares and bonds will actually be bought in their names. Not so. The truth is that *all* investments are held in one name—that of the con artist. This charismatic guy is the *only* legal owner. He's sweet-talked men and women of considerable wealth to entrust their fortunes to his care.

A Ponzi scheme is similar to a pyramid plan. Both use new investors' monies to pay earlier backers. They differ in that the Ponzi mastermind controls all the money brought in from new investors and distributes the dollars himself, while pyramid plans allow each investor to get a direct benefit based on how many new players are recruited. The person at the peak of the pyramid never has access to all the money brought in—the direct opposite of the Ponzi mastermind who has the whole pot!

Charles Ponzi, an Italian immigrant, lived in Boston. He is recognized as the first mastermind to run such a con game and thus the Ponzi scheme was named after him. According to history, Charles Ponzi came to the United States as a young man 1903. Seventeen years later, in the short span of six months, Ponzi went from anonymity to being a well-known Boston millionaire. His fame would have been widespread at the same time Charlie's papa was a teenager. If there's interest in learning more about Charles Ponzi, Wikipedia.com is a great place to find more history.

Madoff operated the game the same way Charles Ponzi had. His fraudulent plan targeted gullible friends and associates who were all too eager to find above-average returns on money invested.

To look legitimate, mastermind Madoff started his own company. By the end of 2008, when Bernard Madoff knew his Ponzi game had come to an end, he'd stolen an estimated $50 billion dollars from investors and perhaps millions more will surface.

In January 2009, another Ponzi artist, Nicholas Cosmo, was exposed having bilked investors of nearly $400 billion dollars using his company Agape World, Inc. as the front. How wickedly ironic he chose to name his business "Agape" which in church circles denotes unconditional love. Without a doubt, the flock was being preyed upon.

A bit more trivia surfaced from author Charles Dickens' day. In 1844 his book, *Martin Chuzzlewitt*, describes a Ponzi scheme more than seventy-five years before Ponzi was even born! Greed for a fast buck is an age-old sin ingrained deep in human history.

Learn to smell a rat and how to be suspicious of the front man. He's likable, trusted as a friend, possesses a gift of gab, and hangs out in prominent social circles. He knows who's who, fills ears full of big promises, brags of profits and interest rates well above the norm. The front man's job is to keep new money coming into the game. That's the only way the earlier chumps get paid. Ponzi schemes depend on a steady stream of fresh investors signing up. Otherwise, the party's over.

The day of reckoning always comes. It's impossible to keep up with the game play. The promises will fall short for the simple reason that real earnings are not large enough to sustain the promised pay outs. Without substantial capital behind the scenes, new money chases old money until it runs its course and dries up. Only early players see profits and even their payoffs stop when the game is over. On the day when investors choose to pull out their money, or when the authorities get wind of what's happening, there is not enough cash to go around. Even the principal money invested can't be found. Incurable financial loss falls heavy on the gullible suckers who fell for this con. Little recourse remains for angry investors.

Seeing the scam artist brought to justice is the only satisfaction that remains. Like Ponzi, Madoff was handcuffed and taken into custody. From the heights of indulgent wealth, the fool fell hard embarrassing his family, the community, and the world. Throughout history his name will invoke cursing and hatred. His unfortunate heirs have been handed a terrible legacy not easily dismissed. Extorting others for personal gain is a rotten thing to do. Those who've been swindled soon discover the future won't turn out as rosy as planned.

It's paramount to understand the con man's game because his impact is far reaching. This guy cleans out people and organizations who trust him. Fortunes are lost. Charitable contributions, operating capital, and retirement funds are not going to be recovered. Projects intended to go forward are suddenly brought to a halt indefinitely. Staff might have to be cut, hospital wings left unfinished, and private investors (who have grown accustomed to living with plenty) are abruptly confronted with a lower standard of living.

## Be an Investigative Investor

Never let loose of a dollar until you know where it's going. Don't turn money over to anyone who in turn invests the money in *his* own name. Madoff took money in *his* name. It is so important to hold the title to investments bought and not be legally known as a third party. Always write the check to a reputable brokerage house. As the Madoff scandal demonstrates, personal vulnerability and financial ruin await the inexperienced investor. Never ever hire a money go-between.

Two ways the average person can become investment savvy are to:
1. Acquire a basic knowledge. Read money magazines. Search the web. Dig deep for as much information as you can find on a company before buying any kind of stocks, bonds, options, or other financial instruments.
2. Buy a couple hours consultation time with a Certified Financial Planner. This individual has years of education in finances and economics and can see the bigger picture. The majority of sales personnel who call themselves financial advisors or planners are not certified. Their market knowledge is limited. And titles vary. Their

job is to sell lots of product to bring in commissions from clientele who purchase mutual funds, life insurance policies, annuities and the like. Most brokerage firms are limited to one, perhaps two, principal brokers on site. The majority of the sales staff holds a Series Six or Series Seven license which requires a minimal amount of career training to enter the workplace.

Seek counsel from a well-educated individual who has no dog in the fight. Talking to a broker who is primarily sales-driven should wait until financial objectives have been discussed with a planner who can design a strategy that suits your particular financial goals. A Certified Financial Planner (CFP) or a Certified Public Accountant (CPA), with an outstanding track record, is highly recommended. We suggest looking at www.kingdomadvisors.org. Kingdom Advisors was founded by financial specialist Ron Blue and provides a large list of qualified financial experts.

Research for investments is on par with how I sought out a competent physician to resolve a serious health problem in 2008. When tests confirmed I had a heart valve that needed replacing, I set about finding a top-notch heart specialist, not a pharmaceutical salesman touting the benefits of Coumadin. I wanted answers that I could trust. You should want the same. A CFP is a money specialist trained to thoroughly understand currencies, investments, and finances from the inside out with the same scrutiny I expected to find from a top-notch heart surgeon.

After the appointment is on the calendar, do some prep work. Since time is money, you'll want to maximize the hour in order to minimize the bill. No two families are alike. All investment strategies are case-sensitive and tailor-made to fit a client's need. Consider these things beforehand.

- ✓ Are you raising young children or caring for elderly parents?
- ✓ Are the children done with college?
- ✓ How many years are left before retirement?
- ✓ What is your total income and risk tolerance?
- ✓ What health issues or handicaps need to be taken into consideration?

Some questions the CFP might ask in order to create a client profile might be:

1. What are your career goals?
2. What is your current income? Is the job stable?
3. What future expenses need to be addressed for the children?
4. What are your current financial obligations?
5. How much do you anticipate needing at retirement?

6. Will pension money be available?
7. What do you want your lifestyle to look like?

After the intake session, a summary proposal is drafted and given to you with recommendations to consider. Look it over carefully—but don't act too quickly.

Next, ask for company reports. Good CFP's can produce reports on the profitability and sustainability of the companies under consideration. Take enough time to process what's been said, further investigate, and discuss the advice you've received. Does the plan line up with your family's goals? Are there any red flags? Google each company to find the latest stories of interest. Take time to pray. Now you've done what's required to feel confident in letting money change hands.

When the homework is done right, the plan should be a good one. Invest the time up front and you'll likely be blessed with success in the future. There's no need for a college degree. Listening to the experts, and putting wise actions in place, is strategy enough.

## Simple Lessons about Investments

**Stocks:** Those who own a stock are shareholders, holding partial ownership in the corporation. As the business operation grows and makes money, dividends are paid to stockholders. The reverse can also be true. A loss means the shares will be worth less. McDonald's is a good example of a corporation making money today. Their stock has a proven track record, even in a bad economy. Starbucks, on the other hand, has downsized by closing 300 storefronts in 2009.

When the economy shifts, stocks go up and down on the New York Stock Exchange. New companies are always forming that were not on the scene twenty or thirty years ago. Companies who used to be front-runners, like Bear Stearns, have met their demise.

Owning stock comes with a risk. A gain is not guaranteed. All investors should know how much risk they can tolerate. Evaluate in such a way that the family finances are not compromised.

Charlie favors a conservative approach to investing. He makes it a point to know which industries are growing—and the ones that are not—by doing plenty of research before buying. One place to get lots of information on stocks, bonds, mutual funds and a wide range of other investment products, as well as articles of interest is www.morningstar.com. This company researches and rates bond funds.

Owning stock in our portfolio made Charlie too nervous. He felt he needed to watch our accounts two or three times a day to know when to hold them and when to sell them. Owning stock doesn't affect everyone the same way. Some are quite happy to buy shares, hold them for years, and believe their worth will appreciate over time.

Know your emotional temperament. Invest in ways that allow peace to prevail after the money is put into good growth investments.

**Basket of Stocks:** Workers with 401(k)s or IRA pensions buy into a "basket" of stocks—some larger than others. A big basket could have 1,000 companies. A basket filled with sector investments will be a smaller one because its contents are isolated to a distinct sector such as utilities, health care, energy, financials, building, metals and so on. The average employee purchases a portion of a big basket full of small pieces from all sectors. Think of buying a bag of jelly beans, so many colors, flavors, and smells. In financial circles mixing investments together is called diversification. Mutual funds are a prime example.

A mutual fund is an investment fund that contains an assortment of companies. Diversification is at work so all the eggs (money) are not put in one basket while allowing the investor to buy one basket made up of many corporate holdings (lots of eggs). Be certain to scrutinize these funds for both historical and current earnings and future performance. Not all mutual funds are equal. There are bad eggs. Again, do the homework. Stay in keeping with financial goals.

Some funds are conservative while others are designed for faster, yet riskier, growth. Investigate facts at www.morningstar.com.

An employer offering retirement account benefits typically gives employees the freedom to pick from perhaps three available plans. The choice is commonly between a money fund, a conservative fund, and a fast-growth fund. The faster the growth, the more risk involved. The worker decides what best suits her needs or temperament.

This chapter should help the average employee understand how to confidently make retirement-dependent decisions. By asking the right questions and gathering reliable facts, we put a stop to the guessing game. Everything to do with investing has to do with practical thinking.

1. Does the business operate with a capital margin? Is there money held in reserve to tap?
2. What is the company's debt to asset ratio?

3. Who are the corporate officers? What is their character? What are their goals?
4. Is the product sustainable?

Answers to these questions should show up platinum apart from sudden illness or downsizing. Whether it's a family or a corporation both need to live with a margin in mind.

The added benefit when employees take part in a company's matching funds is huge. Employer contributions sweeten the pot, making it possible to take full advantage of every dollar that is put away.

**Bonds:** Owning bonds is different than owning shares of stock. Bondholders are lenders. Bonds have a day of maturity at which time the investor gets back his original investment plus the interest earned. Maybe a municipal bond was purchased in 2008 that matures in ten years. Growth happens while we sleep. Government bonds are also a good example to use. Money is put into government agency bonds, like Fannie Mae and Freddie Mac. Fannie and Freddie then put that money to work lending to others who want to buy homes. As borrowers pay their mortgage each month, bondholders participate in the profits.

Yes, foreclosures are on the rise. But the bond value remains. Despite the huge credit crisis taking place in our country, most mortgage holders continue to make their monthly payments and Fannie Mae and Freddie Mac are considered to be backed by an explicit guarantee of the United States government.

**General Obligation Bonds and Municipal Bonds:** State and city governments offer either general obligation bonds or municipal bonds for road building, schools, libraries, prisons, bridges, universities, education, infrastructure, and so on. Some corporations offer the same kinds of investment instruments. For instance, a hospital, ready to build a new cancer wing, seeks money from the public to make the work possible. Bonds are sold to build buildings, purchase equipment, make necessary improvements, and staff the new wing. People help to build the community at large when investing in general obligation or municipal bonds.

Wise men and women understand it's important for money to grow while they sleep. Investing and saving are the only ways to maximize a dollar's earning potential 24/7.

Generally speaking, the rate of return on bonds is more conservative than that of stock holdings because bonds are bought with a locked-in fixed-interest rate promising a profit at maturity.

Let's use an example with a maturity 10 years down the road. The purchase of a $5,000 bond today at 5% interest equals a return of $250 for each year up to the date of maturity. Ten years later $2,500 profit is made on that bond and we still have the $5,000 initially invested. Now there's $7,500 of real money is in our pocket. Not bad. The money was growing while we slept. That's the joy of bonds. There is no need to lose sleep or be glued to the fluctuations of Wall Street for fear of a big up or down cycle. A bond is considered a more secure investment.

Because interest rates fluctuate, laddering is a good way to maximize profits on bonds. Laddering simply means that the bonds bought do not all mature in the same year. They would perhaps be spread over two, five, seven, and ten years. It is our personal preference not to go more than ten years out so we can periodically make the most of changing market conditions.

Another word of caution must be mentioned—not all bonds are equal. Be careful to know the facts about any investment before buying. Some bonds are best to avoid. Some corporations are not solid and carry too much debt-to-asset ratio. Selling bonds before maturity could result in a loss depending on market conditions, interest rates, global crisis or national disasters. On the other hand, selling early could result in a nice profit depending again on interest rates on the day sold.

Use streetwise sense. There is no sure place to hide money. In an uncertain economy, things can change rapidly. Many states and municipalities are also finding it difficult to pay their bills. That problem could result in a downgrading of the issued bonds; do thorough research, get adequate counsel, know the bond's rating, and pray first before investing. Always keep in mind our top priority is to protect the family's financial future.

## How Bonds Are Rated

A rating on a bond is similar to a rating on a credit score. The higher the bond rating the easier it is to peddle the bond on the open market. There are three major bond rating companies:
1. Moody Bond Rating
2. Fitch Bond Rating
3. S & P Bond Rating

Governments, corporations and municipalities pay interest out according to the rating they are given. Bond-rating companies are hired to assemble an expert analysis of a given business operation: to know what kind of product is offered, how it competes, if the product is doing well, and whether bills are kept current and payrolls met in a timely fashion (or not). From A to Z the company is scrutinized. Rating companies want to know how each business compares with its peers in the marketplace. Then a rating is applied. From AAA all the way to DDD. Anything below a BBB is not investment grade. Anything above BBB is an investment grade product. The *higher* the bond rating the *higher* the quality of investment for the bondholder. Check bonds out at www.morningstar.com.

Wikipedia is also a great resource for the novice investor. Wikipedia charts the wide variety of bond ratings and then defines the investment grade (quality) that correlates to the letter ratings. Much can be learned by exploring http://en.wikipedia.org/wiki/Bond_credit_rating.

Contrast this rating concept with a FICO credit score. How do I pay my bills? Think of the corporation ratings in the same light. Ratings of AAA, AA, A, A1, A2, A3, BBB, BB, B, B1 are pretty good. Charlie follows a rule of thumb that everything below BBB is subprime. It's important to know what bond pool we are playing in. For us, we don't like a lot of risk. Our preference is to pick from those with a triple A rating.

*Warning:* In this uncertain economy, with recession all about, bond ratings are being downgraded after the point of purchase. This nasty little practice will continue to surprise investors. To make matters worse, we discovered the three bond rating companies weren't always on top of their game. A bond rated AAA when bought three years ago could now receive a new rating of AA, A, A2 or lower. Try not to panic. If the corporation was solid on the day of purchase, it's likely solid today and tomorrow also. Do some fresh research before selling.

Consider three things capable of producing a change in bond ratings. First, market conditions are pressing bond raters to lower their initial bond ratings. The consumer may feel distrust when this happens. A lot of banks and financial institutions have been hit hard by risky loans now known as toxic assets on their books. (See TARP below.)

Assume the rating at purchase point might not be today's rating.

Market conditions affect a bond's performance. A company's performance, a city's growth plans, and government programs could be going through a tough time right now. It's public knowledge that Cleveland, Ohio built home after home fast and furious during those boom years. Bonds connected with these mortgages sold with quality ratings above BBB. That's not so today. All have been downgraded to undesirable grade investments since the housing bubble burst leaving hundreds of homes, riddled by foreclosure, empty.

The backlash of abandoned homes is the growing number of displaced families and the shrinking number of tax dollars for city, county, and state budgets. It takes large sums of money to operate police and fire departments, schools, parks, libraries, and so much more. A shortfall in tax revenue has shrunk these much-needed programs and services in substantial ways. Most communities face tough decisions today because there is less money to work with. Serious decisions have to be made. Which employees can be kept on the payroll? Where is it possible to make cutbacks in operations and services while still taking care of the most important needs?

Second, government interference is a huge contributor to sudden changes in bond ratings. Governments can tip scales by backing a state, a city, or a bank. Governments won't bail everyone out but a small percentage will be guaranteed not to fail despite the financial downside being experienced. The government has chosen to cover the losses of Fannie Mae and Freddie Mac under the Toxic Asset Relief Program (TARP).

SPIC is the Securities Protection Investment Corporation that protects investments up to $500,000.

Third, **companies are allowed to *buy*** a better rating. Say what? Firms selling general obligation or municipal bonds can actually go out and find an insurance company to review their bond offering. For a price, the insurance premium makes it possible to keep that bond at AAA rating. The premium is deemed a small price to pay in exchange for a good rating. For the consumer, it's a smart move to only buy bonds backed by insurance.

Direct United States government-backed bonds are the closest thing to a guaranteed investment. Yes, they will pay the lowest rate of return but their risk of failure is construed as almost nonexistent. The full faith (or purse) of the United States of America backs these particular bonds.

The municipalities Charlie chooses for his clients to invest in have insurance *plus* the backing of the state of origin. These general obligation bonds are desirable because they are bought with more than one layer of protection. If the municipality doesn't pay, the State of Oregon, Pennsylvania, or New York will. Added layers of backing pay less interest but present less worry. Still, there is no guarantee. Many bonds have been downgraded lower than the value of the bonds.

## Vested in Retirement Accounts

Take retirement accounts seriously. Understand how yours works. Vesting means the company is partnered with you and also contributes a percentage of money into your account based on how much you contribute to the plan. The 401(k) is a widely chosen plan but not the only pension plan available. The vested portion on the statement refers to the employee's share of ownership. The rules governing this are always defined in paperwork accompanying the pension plan. Some businesses require people to work five years before all the money put in by the company reverts to the employee. Others can state a lesser or greater length of time. Outing earlier than the plan allows leaves the individual with say 40% of the money, or worse yet, nothing at all.

Businesses big and small know the average number of years an employee stays with a company. Vesting schedules are built from job statistics so not too much money leaves the company. Know the terms and conditions of the particular pension plan. Read the fine print to know what the benefits will be. Important! For sure be aware of the number of years required to work before those benefits belong to the employee.

A friend's dad got bamboozled out of his retirement dollars. Twenty years was the length of employment required before an employee could retire with full benefits. Larry was called into the office in the middle of his nineteenth year. To his surprise, he was let go with zero benefits! Suddenly there was the realization that there'd be no pension money to pay the way in retirement as he'd once envisioned; only a single payout of less than $10,000. There was no choice left but to go back to work. What could Larry have done differently? Hire on with eyes open, understanding the vesting schedule. But he could not have prevented them from letting him go one year shy of being fully vested. Apart from the business going under, it's hard to muster up sympathy for an employer who pulls such tricks. Shame on them!

Try to negotiate vesting when hired. This is appropriate and does happen. Weigh seriously whether it's beneficial to work for a company that states in writing an employee gets nothing if the company folds or lets them go prior to being fully vested.

A 401(k) worth $50,000 could be 50% owned by the company. The stated length of employment must be met for the total of that account to be ours. One size does not fit all. Every company adopts its own guidelines for retirement accounts. There are many ways to provide retirement plans.

Mary's employer matches her contributions to her 401(k) dollar-for-dollar and will be fully vested in three years. Husband John also works for a company with a 401(k) plan. He likes the perks and assumes his plan is the same as his wife's. He doesn't ask questions. Later he learns his employer matches just twenty-five cents for every dollar and he is not fully vest until he's worked for 15 years. Not the same kind of pension plan at all.

Investing makes good sense. Just make some streetwise moves along the way.

### The Bottom Line

- Research the financial stability of companies considered as investments but realize all stocks come with risk attached. Research through www.morningstar.com.
- Be on guard—Ponzi schemes and con games are everywhere. Weed out the bad guys through www.sec.gov/investor/brokers.htm.
- Bondholders are lenders.
- It helps to understand how bonds are rated.
- Seek counsel from a respected Certified Financial Planner. A list of experts can be found through Kingdom Advisors, www.kingdomadvisors.com.
- Know exactly where retirement money is invested.
- Figure out what it takes to be fully vested in your company's pension plan.

## Increase the Wealth Challenge

Make it a point to know where all personal money is invested. List the companies one-by-one. How has this investment grown or lost money since its date of purchase? Check www.morningstar.com to see if any of the bonds have been downgraded to a lower rating. Consider spending an hour with a Certified Financial Planner to gain professional insights and you'll sleep easier knowing you are getting the most from your hard-earned money as a streetwise investor.

## Common "Cents" Sense

*Money is put into risky investments that turn sour, and everything is lost. In the end, there is nothing left to pass on to one's children.*[73]

## Groom: \grüm, grüm\

To get into readiness for a specific objective

Merriam-Webster's Online Dictionary, 2007-2008, Merriam-Webster Incorporated

# Fifteen

## Pass Along Smart Money Habits

### Groom children to be streetwise with money

*Parents are not raising children; they are raising future adults. So, they must not allow their children to leave home without learning and understanding the basic principles of financial management. Anything less would be detrimental to their financial survival after they are on their own.*[74]

—Crown Financial Ministries

No loving parent deliberately sets their child up to fail. But when it comes to equipping one's own flesh and blood with the right tools for financial success, millions of dads and moms are not teaching the best lessons. Instead, a lifestyle of perpetual debt and constant caving in to the requests of the younger generation is modeled. Little Austin or Haley ask for all kinds of stuff—from things advertised on television to items brought to their attention by peers. Children are at the apex of marketing strategies. Added to the begged-for list is the cost of things parents believe a child should participate in:

**Entertainment**: movies, water parks, skiing . . . $$$
**Competitive sports**: baseball, soccer, football, tennis . . . $$$
(no longer offered free in the majority of public schools)
**Social activities**: birthday parties, prom night, graduation . . . $$$
**Private lessons**: music, karate, dance, swim . . . $$$

Life can spin out of control quickly. The dollars add up. It's not wrong to want to give a son or daughter every advantage. It's natural to want to bless those we love. But is the message being absorbed by the child one that screams, "I'm entitled to everything"? And is the family budget on overload? Groceries, gas for the car, and medical bills are far more necessary to family life than satisfying a child's request for another Nintendo DS game or fashion jeans.

Love is powerful enough to blur common sense. Going into debt is just one way hearts may get in the way of good judgment. When that happens, we allow feelings to override teaching moments. Neglecting to train boys and girls in the smart use of money carelessly lays down a foundation riddled with financial ignorance. Our children, whom we love more than anything in the world, will be ill-equipped to meet life's challenges.

Everyone is special. Birthdays should be celebrated. Blow out candles, sing "Happy Birthday," and applaud special milestones in life. But unashamedly party in a way that honors the pocketbook, too.

A lot of parents, many of modest means, are opting to host extravagant parties—whether they can afford it or not—to create crazy fun for the birthday boy or girl. The bar has been raised to include popular destinations, trendy food, limousines, shopping trips, dances, lavish party favors, bears to build, clowns, event tickets, and so on. All this over-the-top hoopla might be saying more about the parent than the child. We need to question whether the plans are an extension of how we want to be viewed by our peers. Do we feel obligated to keep up with party choices previously laid down by other parents?

After examining our motives, we are better prepared to make good decisions. Perhaps the result will be to celebrate in a grand style only on landmark birthdays like becoming a teenager or sweet16, or high-school graduation.

Simple celebrations are often the most memorable ones. A backyard or local park is the perfect setting for lawn games, giggles, and birthday cake excitement at a reasonable cost to the host family. In colder months take advantage of a family room, a garage, a church fellowship hall, or an office board room. Borrow or buy a book of party games. Create fun around items the family already owns like Wii or air hockey. Some of our funniest parties included an old Twister game while others centered on the juke box in the family room with guests attempting to do the limbo.

Plan in advance but keep the fun at a level that sends the right message to our children and won't threaten to blow up the family budget.

Ignore outside pressure. Arrange events based on what you can pay for with real money. Push aside any twinge of guilt. True friends, who accept our invites, already like who we are. They want to be at our parties—to laugh, to eat, and to hang out on our turf—no matter where we fall on the socioeconomic scale.

## Eighth Grade School Shopping

Our daughter Felicia found creative ways to help thirteen-year-old Saraya make some of her own spending decisions.

"When the time came to shop for school clothes, Saraya told Dad and me, 'I want to get stylish clothes this year. I don't want to shop at Target.'

"Ugh," I thought. "I knew we would be in for an argument since we had no plans to spend money for clothes from Abercrombie or Hollister where one shirt can run $40 and jeans $70. We had to keep in mind that extras like volleyball clothes and shoes would have to be purchased.

"We devised a strategy. Volleyball things (2 pairs of spandex shorts, 2 sports bras, and socks and athletic shoes) would not come out of her $200 clothes budget. Saraya was responsible to buy her jeans, sweaters, T-shirts—all the daily wardrobe items. The combined total spent would come to $300–$350 when the job was finished. This was the predetermined amount we were willing to spend.

"Saraya was agreeable to this idea. She wrote out her list, naming all the purchases she wanted to make. Then the three of us sat down to prioritize her list in order to create a plan for the next day's shopping trip.

"We asked her to take a second look at the list and narrow it down to what she really wanted or needed from what was nice to have. Next she decided where to shop.

1. The sports store
2. Shoe store
3. Target for basics
4. The mall for the stylish stuff

"Saturday arrived. The two of us set out to accomplish our mission in one whirlwind of a morning.

"Our first stop was the ATM machine where I withdrew $200 and had Saraya count it. This money was kept in my right pants pocket now called *the bank* and off we went to our first stop—the sports store. I found some truly amazing deals on her volleyball gear, and to her amazement she found some gym shorts and headbands to spend her money on. The shorts were only $7 each—what a bargain! Before heading to the register, I asked her to add up the cost of her items to know how much she was spending. Then we pulled money from *the bank* and counted out what she'd need at the register.

"This adding up prior to getting to the register really paid off at our first stop as one of the items rang up at regular price ($10 more than the sale price). This presented a great teaching moment. I asked the clerk to run a price check. Sure enough, not only had the price not rung up correctly, it was actually marked down even more than we'd thought. I looked at Saraya and she had a big smile on her face.

"'What happened?' she asked, 'Why did I get more money back?'

"This is the kind of moment a parent loves. I was able to explain why I like to have an idea of how much my things are going to cost before I get to the checkout counter. Then it's easy to know when something rings up wrong. I explained that it wasn't the store's fault. They weren't purposely trying to charge more, but when stores have sales all the time items sometimes get missed in the system. What made this lesson even more interesting was that it happened again at the very next stop!

"The next store was Famous Footwear. I told Saraya that we should go there because they were running their buy-one-get-one-half-off sale and she needed two pairs of shoes. When we got to the shoe store I knew we were buying the shoes and they would not be coming out of her $200. I also knew that I didn't want to spend much more than $65 for both pairs. Saraya found one pair she liked right away and then found another pricier pair that she absolutely loved. I told her they were pretty expensive and asked her to look around for another pair she liked just as much. She couldn't find one. Now we had a problem to solve.

"Quick thinking pays off. I presented an honest compromise.

"I planned on spending no more than around $65 on shoes. I told her that if she wanted that particular pair, the total would be $85. If she really, truly wanted those shoes, she would have to contribute to buying them from her clothing money.

"'OK,' she immediately agreed and handed over $20 from her fund. That money went into my left pocket☺ and not *the bank*.

"When we got to the register, the two pairs of shoes rang up $95. Again I had to have the price checked. Again the items had rung up incorrectly. The price was changed and off we went to continue shopping for the remaining items."

This story presents so many teaching moments in the midst of a parent and teen experience. But there's still more.

"Target was next. They'd advertised layering tank tops on sale for $5 each. Saraya immediately picked up eight of them and tried them on to make sure they fit. Next she found a pair of jeans she wanted that were also on sale. But, when we stopped to add up the total cost she quickly realized it wasn't going to leave her with very much money for the mall. She put back half of her tanks, remembering she already had some in the same colors. This decision left her with about $90 to spend at the mall.

"On the way to the Mall she asked me an interesting question."

"'Do you think I could get about ten shirts at the mall?'"

"Probably not. Abercrombie or Hollister shirts cost $30–40. But you might be able to buy one shirt there and find others at a less expensive store. We've got time to look around and see what you can find.

"'OK. Thanks.' She looked a little dismayed.

"After a quick bite to eat and a chat about the deals we had gotten that morning Saraya mentioned she wanted to go to a store called Wet Seal to look at their shirts. On the way to the food court we'd seen a sale sign. Sale signs meant getting more for the money. She came out of there with six Wet Seal shirts for $60! Not too shabby. She had $28 and change left.

"Where do you want to go now?" I asked. "You can find something for about $25 before tax.

"'I'd like to go to Aeropostale,' she said.

"Upon walking in the store she saw a sweatshirt that she absolutely loved. The original ticket price was $40, but it was marked half-off. A very cute T-shirt on sale for $5 that matched the sweatshirt perfectly brought the total to exactly $25. Up to the register we went. School shopping was done.

"This last purchase left less than a dollar in the clothing budget. She was one happy girl proud of the great deals she'd found. Her face was full of smiles."

## Recap the Teen Lessons

In unity the parents set appropriate boundaries and stuck with them. Their teen was taught several excellent lessons.

1. How to make a plan for school shopping
2. How to stick to a budget
3. How to prioritize what she really wanted/needed
4. Why it is important to know how much will be spent before getting to the cash register
5. Errors are often made on price tags that can and should be corrected
6. How to successfully negotiate a compromise
7. An appreciation for bargains without control issues taking center stage

By the end of the shopping experience, not one thing had been bought from Abercrombie or Hollister. Best of all, the parent could say, "There was never a single complaint the entire day, no arguments. We had fun!"

## Pass the Stewardship Baton

Money, when put to work as a tool to teach life lessons, is the best way to pass the baton of financial stewardship along to your child. Parents have a big responsibility to carry out—one that can only be fully taught by allowing boys and girls to gain an appreciation for what it takes to spend smart or save for a bicycle or a Nintendo game. Unless a young person is encouraged to give to the poor how will he grow a heart of compassion with his money? A parent must bring example and opportunity together in order to teach children life's most important lessons.

Showering young Austin or Haley with every possible advantage childhood has to offer, despite the cost, sets an unrealistic expectation in place that typically proves unsustainable when the young adult leaves home. Don't rob your children of a good financial foundation. Take advantage of the open window of younger years to teach life skills before the age of eighteen (preferably most of the groundwork should be in place by age sixteen) arrives for your son or daughter. Remember, parental influence sways a child's direction in life. Make it a goal to plant good seeds of money management in your Austin or Haley before they graduate from high school. These seedlings grow into repetitive habits capable of producing a sustainable lifestyle.

From the words of Howard Dayton, founder of Compass—finances God's way, and co-founder of Crown Financial Ministries: *Modeling, communicating verbally, and offering real-life opportunities will form within your children the discipline and habit they need to faithfully handle money their entire lives.*[75]

Kids learn in two ways: by example and through experience.

Observing the actions of parents will always speak louder than hearing their words. For the children's sake, be consistent and model successful money management. Childhood is boot camp for adult living. While in this training period, allow youngsters not only to see a working budget in the home, but also to participate in some of the decisions. Hands-on instruction works best. For instance, Dad goes to the dentist with a bad toothache. The dentist determines a root canal must be done and that it will cost $850. This item is well beyond the family's dental-care budget of $600. Where will the other $250 come from? Allow the children to help brainstorm solutions. Perhaps young Haley will offer to share some of her allowance money or Austin will decide not to go to the movies with his friends on Saturday. Unless boys and girls are given an opportunity to experience a budget's restraints, they will come up against an education deficit in adulthood, and most of them will be unable to live a disciplined money life.

Streetwise parents understand why stewardship with money is as important to life as crossing the finish line a winner. The baton of money management represents the difference between financial success and failure. When handed off well, this baton is caught by the next generation, who in turn puts the same sound money principles they've been taught into practice.

## Money Develops Character

Money is a significant gauge of character. A bent toward greed, generosity, selfishness, compassion and so much more can easily be seen in how a child spends, saves, or gives from his own piggy bank.

Parents know it's easier to pull the cash out of their pockets rather than engaging in a lengthy conversation with a son or daughter in order to convince that child to spend his or her own money, but the payoff later will be worth the discussion. Unless youngsters are expected to provide for some personal wants and a few basic needs (hairspray or notebook paper), they will not be prepared to manage money as an adult.

To manage money, there has to be money to oversee. An allowance, not linked to chores, is a good way to begin. These dollars are given simply because the child is a member of the family. The amount should be age-sensitive and moderate—not enough to provide everything he or she wants or needs. Parents give guidance for spending. Begin with simple categories. Three jars or boxes are all that is needed to teach basic budgeting. The first one is labeled *Saving*. The second *Giving*. And the third *Spending*. One way to divide up the money is to put fifty percent into *Savings*, ten percent into *Giving*, and forty percent into *Spending*.

Be sure to use currency that divides easily. For added fun, pretty up the containers with paints, markers, or stickers.

Add to the allowance an income stream earned from doing chores. It should be understood that all members of the family participate in the working order of the family like taking out the trash, setting the table, or picking up toys. Chores for pay are extra jobs like sweeping the driveway, pulling weeds, or washing the car—jobs made available as incentive to earn more cash. One dollar might be enough to sweep the front steps, $2–3 for pulling the weeds, and maybe $4 to wash the car. If the family owns a business, pay $20 to clean the office. Get creative about any number of jobs that might need to be done.

Remember the goal is to teach discipline in money management. It's natural to want to shower our children with good gifts. But what feels natural is not always beneficial to their growth and development. Money does not grow on trees or magically spit out of a box on the bank wall. There has to be an association between money and work that takes place in the child's mind. When a parent displays restraint, and does not pay for everything requested, the child's character begins to mature. He is put in a position to figure out another way to have what he wants—or not buy it at all. This pivotal moment turns into an all-important lesson in delayed gratification.

Treat kids with respect. Pay them in the same prompt way a boss would pay you. Pay when the work is done or at an agreed-upon day, such as Saturday morning. Don't pay for work that is not finished—or of poor quality. That gives the wrong message. Expect the job to be done well at an age-appropriate level of performance. A ten-year-old will not wash the driveway as thoroughly as his dad or sixteen-year-old sister. He's ten! The lesson being taught is one of work ethic, which prepares a young person to one day step into adult shoes in the workplace.

Be charitable. Youngsters should be encouraged to give. This habit is learned best by a parent's example. And, if children value giving, some even motivate parents to do more than they dreamed possible for others. One such guideposts.com story[76] is about Hannah, a teenager in Atlanta, Georgia. *After seeing a man driving a Mercedes on one side of the street and another man holding a sign asking for money for food on the other, she inspired her family to sell their home and give half the money to help others. Family talks over the course of a year resulted in the home being sold and hundreds of thousands of dollars strategically given to help needy villages in Africa, Asia and Latin America.*

The average family won't set such a big goal in motion. That's okay. But dare to dream big. Carry an attitude of anticipation. God can do great things when even small amounts are set aside to help others.

The best way to be streetwise moms and dads is to look for teaching moments. Children need to be motivated to appreciate the value of a dollar. Part of good parenting is to inspire kids to earn some money themselves. Later, when actions are put in motion, recognize the child's effort and speak praise. Hugs show approval. Praise builds confidence.

## College Education

The cost of higher education is mind-boggling. Four years at a college or university leaves the majority of graduates strapped with tremendous debt. Sixty percent of graduates in Oregon alone have student loans that average between $17,000 and $26,000. This accumulated debt has to be paid back. Remember, *average* is determined by counting all students; those who have no debt, those who have moderate debt, and those who carry crazy debt two, three, or four times the median.

Added to the problematic debt is a job market in the midst of a terrible slump. The Project on Student Debt, part of the Berkeley-based Institute for College Access and Success reports the national unemployment rates for college graduates ages 20–24 rose from 7.6 percent in 2008 to 10.6 percent in 2009. Our graduates face a huge problem!

What can be done will depend on where the student is in the educational process. Graduates have fewer options. The money has to be paid back. Bankruptcy is not possible. Look at deferment plans. See what it takes to qualify. One available choice is to give time and talents by enlisting with the Peace Corps for a couple years. As a word of caution, always research an organization thoroughly before signing up. Check out the good press and the bad being reported. These programs can prove valuable beyond deferring payments. Individuals gain experience and are able to build résumés that give them an edge later. Employers tend to be impressed with men and women who don't sideline themselves. Doing *something* good demonstrates proactive behaviors and work ethic.

The job market is tough, but stay the course. Continue to seek employment. Fill out those applications. A lot of graduates resolve to take whatever jobs they can get to get by for now. Others move back home with a parent while searching for suitable career positions. Doing nothing for months on end sends another message—one that says there is a lack of creativity, initiative, and survival skills.

High school students who have not yet entered the university are in a good position to take other choices into consideration. A concerned parent should not want a son or daughter to finish college weighed down by debt four years down the road. Some options are:

1. Keep up those grades in high school. Scholarships are worth the effort.
2. A year or two at a community college while living at home gets basic requirements out of the way at a lot less cost. Make sure credits transfer.

3. Make use of online courses offered by many universities. Make sure credits transfer.
4. Look at universities in other states. Tuition costs do vary state-to-state and school-to-school. Quality of education won't suffer.
5. The military is a way to both serve our country and get education funds.
6. Work during the day and go to school nights—or vice versa.
7. Delay college for a time while working to save money toward this goal.

Parents who plan ahead for college expenses send a positive message to a child. Even when the entire amount can't be put aside, having some money put aside helps. Start early. Think about college education right after birth. Look for educational funds that offer tax-free incentives from the government. Ask other family members to give for college in lieu of other gifts. Over the span of eighteen years the accumulation of interest can increase the amount deposited two-or threefold.

## Campus Credit Card Practices

The college campus is the friendly place where young naive adults are lured into the credit trap. Neither the students nor their parents are ordinarily familiar with affinity-card contracts. These contracts are between credit card companies and the college or university. Issuers encourage schools to sell students' contact information to credit card companies in exchange for attractive financial rewards kicked back to the school every time a student swipes the card. This practice is a very lucrative to campus life.

These contracts are often confidential and bond hundreds of schools across the country with credit-card companies eager to sign up undergraduates. For example, *students at the University of Michigan probably aren't aware that their e-mail addresses and contact information are worth a whopping $25.5 million. That's how much Bank of America (BAC) is paying the Michigan Alumni Assn. over an 11-year affinity-card contract to market school-branded plastic to students, alums, and sports fans. The Michigan Alumni Assn., which forged the deal, gets 0.5% of total.* [77]

Sounds like the alumni favor helping students forge a lifestyle of debt. Or, maybe these enthusiastic folks are simply looking to fund projects with their portion of the profits. Perhaps we should teach our students about responsible credit card use before sending them off on their own as unsuspecting fish tempted by the bait.

President Obama did sign a new law, effective February 22, 2010, that sets some layers of protection in place. Youth under 21 years of age will no longer be given a credit card unless they have proof of an independent income source or a parent willing to co-sign the application. This ruling only changes how the student gets credit. It does not dismiss the relationship between the school and affinity-card incentive programs. But it should bring more accountability to the process and alert young people to keep a tighter lid on debt.

So what happens to the student whose parents have terrible credit? What's this young adult to do? Three choices remain: 1) get a job and go to school as the money is available 2) keep grades up and be eligible for scholarship money 3) use a debit card or wait until his 21st birthday to use a credit card. Whatever the choice, be a smart student who possesses a healthy appreciation with the use of credit and a genuine uneasiness about debt.

## Groom for the Future

Parent with fiscal responsibility in mind. What is done now readies our sons and daughters for tomorrow. From infancy to college graduation, money plays an important role in grooming young minds. Never forget that today's children are tomorrow's adults. Equip those under your roof to be shrewd money managers.

### The Bottom Line

- Start financial training early; preschoolers understand the simplicity of a piggy bank.
- Observe your child's spending habits and take advantage of teaching moments.
- Create a way for boys and girls to have money to manage (allowance, chores, other sources).
- Children learn by example. Teach a child to save, give, and spend by carrying out these practices well in your own life.
- Saying "No" at appropriate times is part of good money management and helps keep the budget in balance.
- Plan well in advance for college; consider many options.
- Bless young adults by keeping student loans as a last option—not a first choice.

## Increase the Wealth Challenge

If you were to grade yourself on how well you are passing the baton of good money management along to your children, what kind of grade would you get? On a sheet of paper, identify the smart money habits that have already been caught and the principles that still need to be taught (review the information found in this chapter for ideas). After knowing the work left to do, get together as a family and do some brainstorming. What will it take to teach the remaining financial concepts to your children? The only way to prepare a son or daughter to be financially responsible as an adult, before he or she graduates from high school, is to put actions in motion. Ideas without actions attached cheat the children.

## Common "Cents" Sense

*Point your kids in the right direction—when they're old they won't be lost.*[78]

# Spread: \spred\

To distribute over a period or among a group; to become dispersed, distributed, or scattered

Merriam-Webster's Online Dictionary, 2007-2008, Merriam-Webster Incorporated

# Sixteen

## Spread Some Green Around

## Sharing with others produces a harvest of joy

*Don't judge each day by the harvest you reap, but by the seeds you plant.*
— Robert Louis Stevenson

Money, when planted in the right places, produces hope for those in need.

Twenty plus years ago Charlie and I began supporting children through Compassion International. Currently, our giving goes to two boys—one in Ethiopia—the other in Haiti, who would otherwise be desperate for the basic necessities of life. But the blessing goes two ways. Opening the mailbox and finding a handwritten letter from Yonas or Kenson is a bright spot in our day.

- *I pray for you. I wish you to be well.*
- *Thank you for the gift of the goat.*
- *I love you and feel I would like to live with you.*
- *I learn much about Jesus.*
- *Please pray for my studies. I like music and play the guitar. I would like to be good at it.*
- *I have taken a one-year training in construction and got a certificate. Thank you.*
- *Here's a verse for you: 1 John 2:3 (We know we have come to know him if we obey his commands.) I love you forever in quantity and in quality.*
- *I am sorry to tell you that I failed the $2^{nd}$ term exams and I was so sad for that.*
- *I took my exams and I promote to the superior grade.*

As we follow the lives of these boys from afar, knowing we'll likely never meet Yonas or Kenson face-to-face, there is a warm friendship that's been knit together. Learning how each one celebrates Christmas and Easter in his homeland opens our minds to other cultures.

Spreading a portion of our resources to help a good cause is a privilege, not a burden. Children around the world dream dreams just like boys and girls in America do. Every one of them likes to play and imagine who they will be one day. Will it be a farmer, a teacher, a singer, a fisherman, or a construction worker? But feeling loved and safe, having enough food to eat, drinking clean water, wearing shoes, receiving medical care, or being blessed with an education, or introduced to a relationship with Jesus should not be just a dream. Everything on this list is a basic need. If one of these important support systems is lacking, a child becomes vulnerable to the harsh realities of poverty, illness, and evil intent. That boy or girl is too young and too small to do anything but fall victim to what life dishes out—unless help comes from an outside source.

Children in third-world countries feel fortunate to have sponsors. The opportunity is not taken for granted. Supporting one of them helps their whole family beyond rice and meat by providing an education and Christian teachings that most other children in their communities are denied access to.

When we improve a child's life, hope spreads into the family, the community, and the nation. For $38 a month per child (the cost in American dollars of two large combination pizzas), lives are being changed. We would happily eat tuna gravy at home, or even skip a meal if need be, to shape future leaders. These boys are being equipped to achieve their own personal potential. Most sponsored children graduate from the program eager to advance the quality of life for their own people.

A word of caution: Always research a charity before giving money. Some use most of the money for administration and others pour the majority of dollars into field operations. The administrative end should not be the weightier of the two. Our personal goal is to help the needy get optimum benefit from our donations. At our house, we do not appreciate telemarketing calls digging for donations because a great portion of those monies go to the cost of manning phones. It's better to give directly to the charity instead of through the telemarketer. The exception could be if the organization is volunteer-driven. But always be alert. Con games and scam artists pretend to be legit charities, too.

## Unlock the Gift

"Discovering the things that you already have to give to others will unlock the gift of giving and let you enter into a joyous realm you have never known before." [79]

Charlie met Robert while heading up Compassionate Ministries at the Oregon City Church of the Nazarene. Like so many others, Robert needed some help. His family had fallen on hard times. He lived in a small apartment with his wife and teenage daughter. There were a few pieces of furniture but no groceries—and no job. Robert held a college degree but couldn't seem to find work.

For months the church stayed alongside Robert's family. Wanting to do more than just pass out food, Pastor Charlie also counseled and prayed with Robert. He encouraged him to keep trying while the ministry continued to assist his family. But the inability to provide for his family resulted in a serious depression. The doctor prescribed an antidepressant.

Robert also had trouble walking. Part of the problem was that his shoes were broken down. Even so, that didn't stop him from getting around. He showed up for groceries every Monday night. But he didn't just show up to take. He showed up, a smile on his face, willing to help out. People from nearby neighborhoods came to get free sacks of food and items of used clothing or household goods. Some of them weren't able to carry out what had been given to them. That's where Robert was happy to be of assistance.

Whoever needed a helping hand, he carried out what they'd been given. Time after time this big guy would be seen hobbling along, arms full of groceries, tagging along behind someone to a parked car or, if need be, to a home within a few blocks of the church—even in the rain.

One Monday night Charlie asked Robert, "Why do you spend your time down here every week? You've spent your whole day looking for work. Perhaps you should go home and be with your family?"

"I figured something out," Robert said. "Being here on Monday night is far better than Prozac."

"Explain that to me." Charlie said, wanting to learn more.

"I come here after having no luck all day and for a couple hours I feel good about who I am because I'm helping others—I'm giving back. By the time I get home, my attitude is upbeat, I sleep better, and I don't think about me for a while."

In time, and to his delight, Robert did start to land temporary work. But the greater joy for this man was to discover he had something worth giving to others even when he himself was in great need.

The ability to give cheerfully, expecting nothing in return, is the mark of a good steward. Giving with a pure heart lifts our spirits. Personal problems shrink in size for the sheer fact that giving is great therapy.

## Get Rid of Poor Attitudes

Dr. Adrian Rogers, 1931–2005, once said: "You cannot legislate the poor into freedom by legislating the wealthy out of freedom. What one person receives without working for, another person must work for without receiving. The government cannot give to anybody anything that the government does not first take from somebody else. When half of the people get the idea that they do not have to work because the other half is going to take care of them, and when the other half gets the idea that it does no good to work because somebody else is going to get what they work for, that my dear friend, is about the end of any nation. You cannot multiply wealth by dividing it."

The government tries to raise the lifestyle of the poor by taking from the wealthy. Robin Hood politics don't work as well as expected. It's not possible to legislate equality.

Poor attitudes about giving and getting exist on both sides of the economic spectrum. Those with little can stop trying to better themselves and choose to stay on public assistance. Those with plenty can resent letting go of what they've worked so hard to gain. One mind-set takes advantage of the generosity of folks. The other viewpoint is void of compassion for our fellow man.

Where do we go from here?

The best thing to do is to identify the truly needy. People with genuine needs will always be among us and might include widows, disabled persons, retirees on fixed incomes, children, or injured veterans. Their need is real.

Where will help come from? Real help will come from able-bodied people willing to share with those in need. There is an unspoken moral obligation to be charitable—to reach out and share from our resources when a legitimate need is brought to our attention. Americans, overall, are seen as a generous people. We might want to take a hard look at our prevailing attitudes regarding our giving.

1. Is there a desire to give? If married, does my spouse agree?
2. Are we willing to sacrifice to give to others?
3. Have we included the poor in our budget?
4. Are we generous within our community?
5. Do we tithe to a local church?

It's not a good thing to act as a closed-up reservoir collecting money only for personal use. Charitable individuals strategically plan to open the gate (the checkbook) and release a measured amount of water (a generous portion) into the river below. Those resources tumble downstream into tributaries that in turn irrigate crops, promote recreation, and maintain a balanced fish and wildlife ecosystem. Likewise, our gifts will, or should, pour forth to deliver needed blessings.

A measured amount is one that doesn't give away more than we have. Today a lot of charities and churches make contributing easy. The use of credit cards has become a common practice. If a contribution is in line with the family's spending plan, okay. When giving piles on greater debt for the family to bear up under, it's not a wise move. Emotions are determining our decision to give. The charity receives a blessing, but the family is on a slippery slope to insolvency. Don't allow a soft heart to displace good sense. The only good reason to bust a budget is for a real emergency.

A good rule of thumb is to live in such a way that there is room to spread some wealth (some green) around.

## The Bottom Line

- Openly discuss giving with the family.
- Generous giving goes beyond the tithe and exhibits a compassionate spirit.
- Those who share with others are happier people.
- Research an organization to validate its legitimacy before sending a contribution of money or time.
- Challenge personal attitudes: Do I feel entitled to something? Am I hoarding? Why?
- Find a way to donate time as well as money.
- Give thanks. The ability to give is a privilege—not an affliction.

## Increase the Wealth Challenge

Examine the family's spending plan. Make sure there is a giving category. Find a worthy cause in the community or around the world. Do your research first; then prayerfully commit a dollar amount to this cause—even if all you can give right now is $20 or less. Every dollar represents hope and help to someone in need and adds joy to those who give. This activity is a wonderful family project.

## Common "Cents" Sense

*The generous prosper and are satisfied; those who refresh others will themselves be refreshed.*[80]

# Hearse: \hərs\

A vehicle for conveying the dead to the grave

Merriam-Webster's Online Dictionary, 2007-2008, Merriam-Webster Incorporated

# Seventeen

## There's No U-Haul Behind the Hearse

## Living today with tomorrow's legacy in mind

*Legacy encompasses how to live and how to die, the passing on of one's core values. My legacy will be my personal answer to the question, "What has been the theme of my life?"*[81]

—Fred Smith, Sr.

Gary's life was anything but happy when he found himself out of work for a year and a half.

"During that time I became very bitter and blamed my situation on my past employer. I eventually sued the company. After a year-long court battle, my case was thrown out. I was buried in debt with a daughter in college and a son and wife at home. We'd sold all the big toys—the camper, the boat, and anything else we could do without just to get by.

"I'd pray to God for work, but no matter how hard I tried, no doors opened. This went on week-after-week, month-after-month, with no relief. My self-esteem felt lower than the drainage ditch that carries runoff water beneath the road. My pride ate away at me. I became very depressed when I couldn't even provide for my family.

"On the way to church one morning, my wife and I got into an argument about our son's future college and how we would pay for it. The thought of more college tuition on top of all the debt we already had was more than I could bear. I saw no way out. I got up, left my wife at church, and drove home planning to kill myself.

"I opened the cupboard where the pistol was kept and picked it up. My next thought was about what it would be like for my son, the boy I love with all my heart, to come home and find me dead on the floor. I just couldn't do that to my family. Thank God he caused me to think twice before acting.

"When my wife came home, I told her what I had tried to do. Desperate to find another answer, she called Charlie and Maxine to talk about our financial situation. That evening we went to their home and heard about Crown Ministries.

"Charlie had said, 'Your debt is not so bad that it is impossible to pay off. God's blessings will follow if you learn how to apply the principles of good stewardship with your money.'

"For the first time since this nightmare began I'd found hope to grab onto and reasons to believe our family could get out of debt. One week later we sat in a Crown class with others who also had financial problems. Knowing we were not alone was a real source of comfort. Together, our group learned financial principles and shared prayer requests.

"Life began to change. Finding out God talked about money in the Bible was a new concept. Until now we'd never thought about money being a spiritual matter. Now we were beginning to understand that handling money well could not be separated from our walk with the Lord.

"Miracles started to happen. Long before the course was over, I did land a good steady job. But one of the biggest answers to prayer was the unusual way we got a new roof for the house. The old one was so bad that on one side the felt could be seen under the shingles. But we had no money to fix it until after a severe hailstorm pelted both our car and our truck and left them badly dented bumper-to-bumper. This terrible act of nature became a blessing in disguise. The insurance company settled the claim using quotes presented by reputable body shops. Through word of mouth, we heard of a lesser known body shop that was willing to repair the damages much more cheaply. There was just enough money left over to put a new roof on the house.

"More than ten years have passed. My walk with the Lord remains strong and our bills are paid, even our home mortgage. I'm not a wealthy man, just a guy who wants to leave a respectable legacy behind. Had despair won out, and I had pulled the trigger that Sunday morning, my family would have been devastated. They'd have remembered me as a depressed selfish man who gave up. I wouldn't have walked my daughter down the aisle, seen my son marry, or known what it's like to be a grandpa to four amazing grandchildren. I'd have lost years of joy and memories with my wife. Thank God my life turned away from suicidal thoughts.

"What my family knows about me now is that I don't quit. Instead, I'll work hard to solve problems. Actions always speak louder than words.

It feels good to be an example of conquering trials and hanging onto faith. I won't lie and say getting out of debt was easy, but I will mention how humbled I am by how the Lord supplied every need (not want) and allowed my wife and me to stay focused and full of hope."

This is the kind of stuff that shapes a memorable good legacy for our families—ordinary people choosing the excellent path in life. Gary and Jean became two of our best Crown Ministries leaders. Because they walked through financial despair, they understand others in similar situations. They can tell a true story of how God lifts this heavy load.

## A Big Mistake

Don't allow debt to mess up legacy. Legacy is more important. Debt is temporary. Legacy lives on.

Because the world system creates such a persuasive sense of discontentment, it's easy for hordes of people to be lured ever deeper into debt for just about everything. Unfortunately, that impetuous lifestyle often results in a whole lot of consumers coming to a critical point in time when it's impossible to repay all that is owed. Life begins to crowd in on them. Feelings of desperation set in.

An acute financial crisis reveals one of the most overlooked mistakes a money manager can make. That mistake is to underestimate the sinister power gaining momentum behind the growing debt. Left unchecked this merciless devil takes otherwise good people to places they would not normally go—to dark irrational places. Some choose to steal, cheat, pimp themselves, manufacture drugs, or lie. Others start believing the only way out is to end their life. When financial pressure mounts, so does crime, hopelessness, and suicide.

Suicide is *always* a bad decision—an irrational thought, with no exceptions. It is the ultimate act of cowardice and selfish behavior. Suicide leaves a rotten legacy behind. To make matters worse, the debt doesn't go away. The family is left to figure out how to solve the money problems with one less wage earner.

Life insurance policies include a suicide clause with lots of fine print. A payout will only be made if the deceased has died within the stipulations set forth in the policy.

Remember, debt is a temporary condition. Speak up. Communicate inner struggles with a trusted partner or friend. Don't remain silent. Do the smart thing. Reach out for help. Make that phone call. Help is available.

Those who fall into despair lack contentment.

No one is born instinctively content. Everyone arrives demanding personal needs be met because feeling hungry and lying in a wet diaper is uncomfortable. Contentment is learned as we mature. In financial matters, this process means we only buy what is reasonable and affordable. That keeps budgets in balance and the blessing of inner peace in place.

Pastor and author Max Lucado defines contentment as: *A state of heart in which you would be at peace if God gave you nothing more than He already has.* [82]

## One Thing Carries Forward—Legacy

Rich or poor, whether we've amassed lots of material possessions or just have the shirt on our back, everyone checks out without a U-Haul driving along behind the hearse. Death is life's greatest equalizer. Our worldly treasures are left for someone else to use or throw away at their discretion.

Only one thing carries forward into eternity—our soul.

Only one thing stays behind to influence others—legacy.

Legacy impacts the family and those we've poured our lives into for generations to come. We will be remembered for something—good or bad. What will be the summation of our time on earth? What will be said about us when we're gone? It will depend on how we live today.

Leaving money and property for the heirs is an honorable thing to do but the essence of a memorable legacy goes beyond bank accounts and material goods. Legacy carries forward in a priceless timeless way. That heritage reminds the next generation of family values and lifetime accomplishments.

I'll never be a Pulitzer Prize winner, star basketball player, renowned pianist or hold a royal title. But I should desire to live life with my eyes on the finish line. That's something all of us can do. Asking ourselves a few simple questions brings perspective to light.

1. What are my priorities?
2. How am I loving my family?
3. How am I contributing to the community or the nation?
4. Am I creating good stories for my children, grandchildren, and great grandchildren to retell?
5. Is God relevant and my faith bold enough to be noticed?
6. Can I honestly say God is pleased with how I am living my life right now? What should I do differently?

## Maxine Recalls a Piece of Her Legacy

On a recent trip to the Saskatchewan prairie, I stopped at the Community Cemetery in Kenaston. This was my first visit to the graves of my grandparents and two uncles. Looking down on the lichen-covered headstones, I read the words "In loving memory." My mind easily drifted back to the summer vacations of 1959–1965 when our family—all six of us (Mom, Dad, and four kids) piled in the four-door sedan and headed north. The drive from southern Oregon seemed endless to us kids—four days each way, squished shoulder-to-shoulder.

I was ten years old when the Canadian vacations began. Spending a week with Grandma and Grandpa was always exciting. Grandpa loved to show his grandkids around the wheat farm. He'd dip his big sun-browned hand into the granaries, or pull a stalk of wheat from the field, roll the kernels between his skilled palms, and place the freshly hulled grain into our young hands. That's how I learned it took a whole lot of wheat to make a sack of flour!

Grandma was a petite woman who set boundaries, like making sure the hired hands fed the horses before sitting down to eat breakfast themselves. On the rare occasion when those rules were not taken seriously, the guy would be shocked to have his plate removed from the table and told to come back after the horses were taken care of.

From Grandma I learned it was okay to have cookies on the breakfast table every morning and that mixing yellow coloring into the oleo made it look like butter. At our house the margarine was already yellow when we bought it off the grocer's shelf. And I fondly remember how she used her seamstress skills, no doubt learned from her own father who was a tailor by trade, to help us girls make new dresses for school.

Years later, the smell of the grain, the flat prairie, the clear blue of the endless sky all mean a lot more to me. Within those precious memories I see a family legacy—full of good stories to hang onto. These relatives knew how to set down roots in a harsh land at a time when the government of Canada was looking for settlers eager to develop bare land in exchange for title to that property. Of course there were strings attached. Settlers were required to make the land productive before having it deeded over to them. Not an easy task for a young family in a harsh northern climate. Only the strong survived. There were good years of profitable crops and happy memories. And there were stories told of some years when severe drought caused the crops to fail and the harvest to be lost or of dreadful winter blizzards.

I understood the snow story better when I read a sign standing tall in the city of Kenaston that read: "Welcome to Kenaston, the blizzard capital of Saskatchewan." Enough said.

Children benefit by having a concept of who they come from. History uncovers virtuous qualities to grab hold of and repeat. A lifelong friend of my dad's family told me that my grandfather was admired by all the neighbors. "No one took care of his harness or team like Wopschall," Roy said. "Wopschall men and women lent a hand to a neighbor in need and turned no one away hungry. They were good honest folk who worked hard."

My dad lived this way and showed the four of us what it meant to work hard and help a neighbor. I also sense there's some prairie pioneer in me. I'm not afraid of a new adventure. Like those who have gone before me, I am practical, creative, and determined to persevere.

When I'm told I remind someone of my grandmother, I'm proud. This is a legacy I can appreciate and share. Not to tell this story would be a sad disservice to our family. This piece of our family's legacy should not fade unnoticed into the recesses of time.

## Something Left to Share

After my grandparents passed away, I received a modest inheritance from money divided among the five grandchildren. It was a surprise and just enough money for a down payment on my first house. I couldn't have owned a home so soon if it had not been for their gift.

The money disappeared fast. A teacup, a few tablecloths, and other small memorabilia remains. Those few possessions and the memories of time together live on. They represent what really matters. In my heritage are compassion, bravery, and integrity—qualities worth passing from generation to generation. They will never cease to be important values to possess.

I can see how my life and parenting skills were shaped by the family's imprint. For instance, Grandma once said, "You finish what you start." At the time I didn't like hearing this. It seemed like she was scolding me. But it was good for me to complete the job I'd begun. I came back in the house and finished baking cookies with her instead of running off to play. That's how a child's character develops—one lesson at a time. When I had my own children, it mattered to me that they also finish what they started. And now I watch them expecting the same character quality from their little ones, my grandchildren.

Streetwise people even continue to influence others from beyond the grave.

Tony Snow spent a great portion of his life in the public arena, most recently as White House Press Secretary until his death at age 53. One tribute to his life described him as:

*A great father, patriot, and professional, Tony Snow was loved and admired, respected, and listened to, not only in America but around the world. We loved him because he daily reminded us of what Americans could be: faith-filled gentle and compassionate souls who passionately love our families and America, speak the truth in love, genuinely care for everyone around us, thankful to God every day for our blessings, with humility and grace. We will miss him, but we will not soon forget him. Such is the legacy of his courage, character, and commitment.*[83]

Tony Snow wasn't a poor man, but it wasn't his income level that marked a life of integrity. Rich or poor doesn't matter. Dying dirt poor is nothing to feel bad about. Ending our days on a high note, admired by others, comes from living an honorable life day after day, one good personal choice after another.

## Lies Might Get in Our Way

Sometimes it's hard to think about legacy or believe we have what it takes to create a good one. Three nasty lies can keep the truth from being seen.

1. Placing too high an emphasis on our abilities, resources, or knowledge as the source of a good legacy. Legacy can certainly include these things but legacy is best developed when godly character is its most definitive quality.
2. Low self-esteem might be tripping us up, making us believe we've made too many mistakes, or lived in sin too long, to create anything good. But a bunch of poor choices are not the end of the story. While there is breath, there is time to confess wrongs, turn a new leaf, and bring forth beauty from ashes. Changed lives speak real loud and are admired. These people often leave incredible legacies in their wake. Consider Chuck Colson who went from being a prisoner to creating Prison Fellowship Ministries.
3. Buying in on the idea that having fun is what's most important in life. This dangerous lie diverts our attention away from chasing after great things to settling for a meaningless pursuit of pleasure. All people possess God-given abilities to leave the world a better place.

## Tying Up Loose Ends—Who Gets What?

End of life issues aren't much fun to talk about but they are important to discuss. Exiting in a good way means our estate is also in order. Wisdom, clarity, and sensitivity are needed to make these important decisions long before illness or death steals our opportunity to make our wishes known. This is one area where it's okay to be a control freak.

One solution won't fit all. Many outcomes need to be taken into consideration depending on the family's dynamics.

1. What will be the family's greatest needs after our death?
2. How will the assets be put to their highest use?

Forms for a simple last will and testament can be downloaded from the internet or purchased in a stationery story. It's good to meet with an attorney or paralegal to ask questions and draw up these ultra-important documents.

Some families will be better cared for with a family trust and a few might have good reason to create a foundation.

The *worst* thing to do is to do nothing. Heirs are better off emotionally when the deceased has made his wishes known. No one is left to imagine what he'd want to do. Having the details in place is something that can be done now to lessen drama later.

Burial is a big expense that won't get cheaper as the years go by. Charlie and I have already taken care of this cost. Our burial spot is already chosen. Our children won't have to figure out where to bury the parents when the day comes. The paperwork is in a file folder for them to refer to.

Appointing an executor for the estate is a serious decision. The best one to oversee the estate might not be a close relative. We need to choose someone who can be trusted to carry out our wishes after we are gone. If one brother is at odds with the other, or adult children do not have a good business sense, it might be best to choose an unbiased third party like a bank trust department or attorney to look after the estate.

Assigning beneficiaries is super-important. Life insurance policies, IRA accounts, stocks or trusts held in individual names, homes or automobiles (unless held jointly), must be assigned a beneficiary. At death, the beneficiary, or the joint owner (in most cases a spouse or an ex-spouse) is given the asset. It is our responsibility to make sure the beneficiary list stays current. If there has been a major change in marital status be sure to fill out new beneficiary forms and file the paperwork reflecting a transfer of titles.

Tampering with beneficiaries is a serious matter in legal circles. The rules governing beneficiaries no longer allow a husband to change an assigned beneficiary, such as his wife, without her acknowledging the change and signing off on the policy or account. In the past, some people were known to cheat a spouse out of everything, leaving her destitute and unaware of this nasty secret until the time came to divvy up the money.

Deciding who gets what is a big job. All our worldly possessions, properties, and everything else will be distributed either by us or the probate court. For sure the U-Haul will not be following along behind the hearse.

Inheritance issues can get real messy. It helps to lessen the drama as much as possible in advance of our death when possible. Another good reason to plan ahead is to keep the squabbling among the heirs to a moot point. The arguments can't be brought to us and will do them no good to fuss about either.

Some people label everything: *Martha gets the Thomas Kincaid painting, Donald gets the power washer, Evelyn gets the piano.* Others leave general broad instructions for the heirs to figure out how to share the stuff. A list is a good idea. Perhaps the bulk of the estate will be given to charity. If so, clarify the particulars of that contribution. Don't just leave money to the Salvation Army, Boys Club, or church denomination. Be specific. Include street addresses and cities so there is no mistaking which chapter of the Salvation Army, which Boys Club, which church is the recipient of those gifts.

Some people try real hard to distribute all the assets before they die. Their goal is to spend wisely but die broke. Since we can't accurately pinpoint the day of our death, this is an interesting choice to make. Actuarial tables define average life spans for any given year of birth, but *average* might not be accurate enough to predict our own last day.

Financial decisions made through the lens of outcome-thinking are typically wisdom-based. These choices take into consideration those who will be left behind, especially minor children and a spouse who would struggle to survive after our death. Be intentional with planning and realistic about end-of-life decisions. Keep in mind there is no U-Haul behind the hearse. We depart empty-handed. But our stamp on the next generation, our legacy, remains to influence and be carried forward by those who knew us.

## The Bottom Line

- Create a special folder, or file box, for all the important papers that's easy to find after death (life insurance policies, the will, investments, savings account information, etc.).
- Draw up a last will and testament; seek counsel if necessary.
- Select a trustworthy overseer for your estate.

- Know the character and needs of the heirs; disburse the estate accordingly.
- Consider charitable giving within the estate.
- Take care of funeral arrangements in advance of the need.
- Live a legacy-minded lifestyle.
- Spend wisely so you reach the finish line with money left over.

### Increase the Wealth Challenge

Reflect on your own ancestry. What kind of legacy did you inherit? What kind of legacy are you fashioning now? Then get practical. No more procrastination. Get your estate in order. Even a simple will spells out personal wishes, preserves family assets, and protects heirs. Touch base with an attorney or paralegal to take get this process underway. Proceed to draw up the will, or trust, that best suits your family's needs. Don't stop there. Continue to put end of life decisions in place. Make an appointment to speak with a local memorial park and get those funeral arrangements taken care of—long before the need arises.

### Common "Cents" Sense

*The boundary lines have fallen for me in pleasant places; surely I have a delightful inheritance.*[84]

# ACT: \ˈakt\

The process of doing; a state of real existence rather than possibility; to behave in a suitable manner

Merriam-Webster's Online Dictionary, 2007-2008, Merriam-Webster Incorporated

# Eighteen

## Feel the Urgency

## Act streetwise—know the players—know the talk

*The day of reckoning or of choice is upon us. You either purge the system of its excesses ...or you continue to stimulate with more dire consequences later.*[85]
—The International Forecaster

The above quote mentioned some additional alarming facts: *The 2010 deficit will range from 1.6 trillion and $2 trillion. That should push debt to 95% to 100% of GDP. It should be interesting to you all that Treasury debt is now higher than GDP at $14.3 trillion.*

Serious news like this should grab our attention like a house afire. But most often it doesn't. A whole lot of money chatter goes over our heads because it includes words that are not familiar or easily understood. A large percentage of us pay little attention to financial news because what is being said is not easily understood. This problem needs to be solved so a lack of comprehension doesn't weaken our ability to make the right moves at the right time.

Each profession has its own peculiar vocabulary. Finance is no exception. This chapter makes an effort to bridge the information flow between those who work in financial circles and those who do not. Lots of confusing words will be taken apart and explained in simple easy-to-understand ways—similar to a dictionary's format.

Why is this important? Ignorance is not bliss. To relate intelligently to what's happening in the economy requires an ability to grasp meaning from financial talk. Only then can current financial news be put to its highest and best use. A clear understanding empowers all of us to make informed decisions. Please invest the time to absorb what you read.

**Austerity Measures or Policies:** Austerity is a word that surfaces in desperate times. It is often the only way to avoid economic collapse. Or, as in World War II, when a massive amount of money was needed to protect our citizens, austerity measures made good sense. But back then people understood sacrifice and were proud to do what was best for the country. They had no choice but to accept ration coupons for sugar, gasoline, and so much more, as a way out of trouble.

And now, unsustainable debt is the great threat. Banks, or inter-governmental institutions such as the International Money Fund (IMF), may require that an indebted government pursue an austerity policy. This typically occurs when the government must refinance loans that are about to come due and the government does not have adequate resources to make those payments. To receive help, Greece has been told to implement austerity measures. A government may be asked to stop issuing subsidies and reduce public spending. Austerity measures cannot avoid creating some forms of hardship in order to bring budgets back to sustainable levels.

**Cap and Trade:** The Center for American Progress defines "cap and trade" as steadily reducing carbon dioxide and other greenhouse gas emissions economy-wide in a cost-effective manner. *The cap:* Each large-scale emitter, or company, will have a limit on the amount of greenhouse gas it can emit. The firm must have an "emissions permit" for every ton of carbon dioxide it releases into the atmosphere. *The trade:* More efficient companies, who emit less than their allowance, can sell their extra permits to companies that are not able to make reductions as easily. http://www.americanprogress.org/issues/2008/01/capandtrade101.html The end result of this bill will be a rise in the cost of energy to all of us and more restrictions on the amount of energy a product can consume (i.e. a light bulb, toaster, lawn mower, furnace, automobile, the list is endless.)

**Capitalism:** The United States is built upon capitalism. Capitalism is an economic system in which the means of production and distribution are privately or corporately owned. Growth and development is proportionate to the accumulation and reinvestment of profits gained in a free market. The free market operates on supply and demand to determine price points and how much is sold. The result is either a profit or a loss. The most innovative and efficient entrepreneurs come out winners.

**Consumer Price Index (CPI):** The Consumer Price Index measure estimates the average price of consumer goods and services sold throughout the economy during a particular month.

**Derivatives:** Only those steeped in financial expertise should dare play with derivatives. Investopedia.com, a Forbes digital company, defines derivatives as a security whose price is dependent upon or derived from one or more underlying assets. The derivative itself is merely a contract between two or more parties. Its value is determined by fluctuations in the underlying asset. The most common underlying assets include stocks, bonds, commodities, currencies, interest rates and market indexes, and even derivatives based on weather data, such as the amount of rain or the number of sunny days in a particular region. Most derivatives are characterized by high-leverage. Futures contracts, forward contracts, options and swaps are the most common types of derivatives. Derivatives are generally used as an instrument to hedge risk, but can also be used for speculative purposes.

**Gross Domestic Product (GDP):** Gross Domestic Product includes only those goods and services produced within the geographic boundaries of the United States, regardless of the producer's nationality. GDP tallies the total market value of all final goods and services produced in the USA in a given year, plus the value of exports, minus the value of imports. The GDP report, released at 8:30 a.m. EST on the last day of each quarter (March, June, September, December), reflects the economic increase or decrease of the previous quarter. This number is a standard monetary measurement used in international guidelines for economic accounting. GDP information facilitates comparisons between the United States and other countries.

**G20:** This group, representing 90% of global gross national product, 80% of world trade, and 2/3 of the global population, brings together important industrial and emerging-market countries from all regions of the world to discuss the management of the global economy. Argentina, Australia, Brazil, Canada, China, France, Germany, India, Indonesia, Italy, Japan, Mexico, Russia, Saudi Arabia, South Africa, Republic of Korea, Turkey, United Kingdom, United States of America, and The European Union, which is represented by the rotating Council presidency and the European Central Bank, are the 20 members of the G-20. For more information visit: http://www.g20.org/about_what_is_g20.aspx.

**G8:** The world's top eight richest industrialized countries (Canada, France, Germany, Italy, Japan, Russia, the United Kingdom, and the United States) are the members of the G8. The purpose of G8 is to discuss global matters.

**LIBOR:** The London Interbank Offered Rate is the rate one bank charges to another bank for lending money.

**Mark to Market:** A measure of the fair value of accounts which can change over time. Mark to market aims to provide a realistic appraisal of an institution's or company's current financial situation—its assets and liabilities. This accounting act records the price or value of a security, portfolio or account to reflect its current market value rather than its book value.

Problems happen when the market-based measurement doesn't accurately reflect an asset's true value. It's possible for this to occur when a company is forced to calculate the selling price of assets or liabilities during adverse or unstable times, such as a financial crisis. Washington Mutual is a good example of an institution whose liquidity fell sharply after the 2008 financial collapse. The selling price of the bank's assets dropped much lower than the actual value. The result was a lowered shareholders' equity. Mark to Market hasn't been used since March 2009 and is now referred to as Mark to Make Believe.

**M1, M2, M3:** All three refer to the money supply, including currency, checking deposits, savings deposits, time deposits, institutional money-market funds, money-market deposit accounts for individuals. M1 money supply includes only checkable demand deposits. M2 is a broader classification of money than M1. Economists use M2 to quantify the amount of money in circulation and to try to explain different economic monetary conditions. M3 includes M2 as well as all large time deposits, institutional money-market funds, short-term repurchase agreements, along with other larger liquid assets. This is the broadest measure of money; it is used by economists to estimate the entire supply of money within an economy. Answers.com at http://www.answers.com/topic/m3 offers much more information.

**Producer Price Index (PPI):** The Producer Price Index measures change over time in how much it costs to manufacture domestic products. The prices included in the PPI are from the first commercial transaction for many products and some services. Some of the costs of manufacturing are passed along to retail customers and others are absorbed by shrewd manufacturers who are able to sell at less.

**Redistribution of Wealth:** This course of action best reminds us of the adventures of Robin Hood. He'd rob from the rich to give to the poor. More precisely, this practice is the transfer of income, wealth or property from those who are deemed wealthy to those who are seen as less fortunate. This is progressive redistribution, from the rich to the poor. But redistribution of wealth has another meaning as well. It may also refer to regressive redistribution, which takes from the poor to benefit the rich.

The desirability and effects of redistribution are actively debated on ethical and economic grounds. Progressive redistribution argues that to take from the rich robs them of the incentive to create new jobs and products while giving too much to the poor robs them of an incentive to strive to do better. Regressive redistribution is more perilous. It robs from the poor in ways that purposely undermine life for hard-working people. Through excessive taxation or a lack of adequate food and education this redistribution can, at its worst, become a means of genocide meant only to strengthen the power of oppressive corrupt governments.

**Repudiation of Debt:** The arbitrary renegotiating of debt, especially by public authorities. This might play out as a failure to acknowledge a contract or debt or in reducing what is owed to a lesser amount in order to free up money needed to keep government services operational. Overnight, with the stroke of an Executive pen, all investors holding government debt could wake up to find nest eggs eroded to a fraction of what was promised.

**Sin Tax:** This kind of tax is placed on things that are deemed unhealthy or unnecessary for people to do. Cigarettes, alcohol, the tanning salon and so on. Yes, on July 10, 2010 a 10% tax went into effect for tanning salons. Coca Cola, or all cola-type drinks, are being discussed right now.

**Socialism:** This economic system is the direct opposite of capitalism. The production and distribution of goods is controlled substantially by the government rather than by private enterprise. Cooperation instead of competition directs economic activity. Some socialists tolerate capitalism as long as the government retains its dominant influence over the economy. Other socialists push to utterly abolish private enterprise; to make all things equal for all people. All communists are socialists. Socialism never succeeds economically.

**Surtax:** An extra tax is piled on top of taxes already required to be paid by individuals or corporations. Gasoline is one good example. What the consumer pays at the pump includes taxes levied on each gallon sold. From state to state the amount differs. Governments use these revenues to care for road repairs or community works projects. A few cents a gallon adds up to millions of dollars over a year's time. Another form of surtax is to add another tax in addition to the normal income tax imposed on those whose income goes beyond a particular dollar amount, say $250,000. And in some countries, a surtax is levied on specific luxury items that cost more than $1,000.

**Tort Reform:** Tort reform is a group of ideas and laws designed to change the way our civil justice system works. A great deal is being heard about tort reform as it relates to health costs. Tort reform law is designed to either limit the circumstances under which injured people may sue, or puts a monetary limit on how much money juries are allowed to award to injured people, or both.

**VAT—Value Added Tax:** VAT is common in many European nations already. A value added tax adds a tax at every level of manufacturing and distribution all the way from the raw materials to the consumer who buys the finished product whatever the product (i.e. tires, cereal, medical equipment, cosmetics, drill bits, everything). All commodities will cost more than they do right now. The only fair thing about this tax is that no one escapes paying their share.

**Velocity of Money:** The average rate of recurrence with which a unit of money is spent. If I spend $100 for vitamin supplements from my nearby merchant and she in turn spends $100 to buy books from me, the two of us have created $200 of our nation's gross domestic product. If we continue to do this once a month for twelve months, we've got $2,400 of annual GDP.

According to financial expert John Mauldin, gross domestic product is a function of not just the money supply but also how fast that money moves through the economy. Stated as an equation, it is $P=MV$, where P is the nominal gross domestic product (not inflation-adjusted here), M is the money supply, and V is the velocity of money. You can solve for V by dividing P by M. This is known as an identity equation. It is true at all times and all places, whether in Greece or the US. If the velocity of money does not increase, that means that on average each business is now going to buy and sell less each month. The prices of products fall. It's basic supply and demand. If the demand for corn increases, the price will go up. If Congress decides to remove the ethanol subsidy, the demand for corn will go down, as will the price. If velocity falls then money supply must rise for nominal GDP to grow. The Fed attempts to jump-start the economy back into growth by increasing the money supply.[86]

**World Bank:** The World Bank refers to a family of five international organizations that makes leveraged loans, generally to poor countries. Their lending focuses on developing countries in fields such as human development through education and health; agriculture and rural development such as irrigation ditches; environmental protection through pollution reduction; infrastructure by building roads, urban regeneration, and electricity; and the establishment of anti-corruption policies and legal institutions. Loans are provided at preferential rates to member countries, as well as grants to the poorest countries.

Many more financial words could be defined since the tentacles of the financial world are long and forever in motion as the economy ebbs and flows 24/7 day-in and day-out. Within these pages you've gathered enough forward motion to actively pursue financial excellence. Money matters are that important.

Never before has there been a better time to stop going deeper and deeper into insane peace-robbing debt. That bumpy road leads families into harm and threatens national security. The world is full of powerful financial players. But one common denominator has every player on edge—it's big unsustainable DEBT. There is movement afoot to usher in a one world government; a global governance. That's not a good idea. But it is a real threat to the freedom we've grown accustomed to.

It's time to be streetwise consumers who live within our means—who stop spending more than we earn as individuals, states, municipalities, and nations. Budgets need to be real, practical, and sustainable because the writing is on the wall. There will be less discretionary money to spend in the years ahead. Debt has run rampant far too long. Future generations are destined to live at a lower standard of living than did their parents. Homes and automobiles will be smaller. Taxes will be higher.

Knowing the economy could get much worse is a sobering thought.

But the good news is that those who've read this book are now prepared to achieve financial stability for their families. The future is full of hope and the baton is in your hand. Please don't drop it. Take deliberate control and become a proud COO (Chief Operating Officer) of your money.

## The Bottom Line

In summary, this book has prepared you to:
1. Live within your means.
2. Pay off debt.
3. Have a great credit score.
4. Avoid falling for the wealth effect.
5. Recognize and pass up a Ponzi scheme.
6. Stay clear of con artists and fast-talking marketers.
7. Invest with wisdom.
8. Earn money while you sleep.
9. Downsize and economize.
10. Prepare for an emergency.
11. Not fall victim to the gaming industry's seductive draw.
12. Teach children to appreciate the value of a dollar.
13. Look beyond the USA to see a global economy.
14. Give for the right reasons and to the right places.
15. Arrive at the finish line with some cash left over.
16. Have a layman's understanding of financial language.

Love shows up in tangible ways. That is especially true when making financial decisions. Love means caring enough to be wise money managers all the time, not just for ourselves today, but for those who will follow after us—the children, grandchildren, great grandchildren, and the list goes on.

Streetwise money managers don't upset the family's progress because they've eliminated unnecessary money arguments. They can say "No" to overtime hours and "Yes" to being home with the children. And, last but not least, these families are not robbed of the peace good financial management brings.

Today's spending habits can set the tone for an upbeat tomorrow—one dollar at a time—in spite of an uncertain economy.

### Increase the Wealth Challenge

Feel a sense of urgency. What is done today prepares your family for tomorrow. With prayerful consideration, sign the commitment statement and share that decision with a trusted family member or friend.

From this day forward (date) _____ my goal is to be a streetwise money manager who accepts the role of *Administrator* over all resources God places in my care. I am determined to practice good financial habits.
(signature) _____

### Common "Cents" Sense

*So then, let us not be like others, who are asleep, but let us be alert and self-controlled.*[87]

# Notes

### Chapter One: On the Brink of Financial Collapse
1. Larry Burkett, *Debt-Free Living*, Moody Publishers, ©2010 Crown Financial Ministries, p. 174
2. Bob Sullivan, "Why American Consumers Can't Add," Red Tape Chronicles, 12-20-09
3. "2010 worst year for bank failures since 1992," David S. Hilzenrath, *Washington Post* staff writer, December 28, 2010 http://www.washingtonpost.com/wp-dyn/content/article/2010/12/28/AR2010122803649_pf.html
4. William M. Welch, *USA Today*, "States May Hold Onto Tax Refunds for Months," 3-11-10, http://www.usatoday.com/news/nation/2010-03-11-tax-refunds_N.htm?csp=34&POE=click-refer
5. 1 Thessalonians 5:8, New International Version

### Chapter Two: After the Bubble Burst—Now What?
6. A. Gary Shilling, "We Haven't Seen the Worst Yet," October 11, 2008. Gary Shilling is president of A. Gary Shilling & Co., economic consultants and investment advisers. www.forbes.com/shilling
7. Phillip Lovell and Julia Isaacs, "The Impact of the Mortgage Crisis on Children," *First Focus*, May 2008, www.firstfocus.net
8. Psalm 20:4, New International Version

### Chapter Three: Four Words Show Up Big in the New Economy
9. John Mauldin, "Green Shoots or Dandelion Weeds?" May 8, 2009, *Thoughts from the Frontline* weekly newsletter. John Mauldin, best-selling author and recognized financial expert, is also editor of the free *Thoughts From the Frontline* that goes to over 1 million readers each week. For more information on John or his free weekly economic letter go to: http://www.frontlinethoughts.com/learnmore
10. Ibid.
11. Sy Harding, Street Smart School, 5/9/09, "Being Street Smart" http://www.streetsmartreport.com/school/Commentaries/My%20006%20Wish%20for%20, copyright 2005, Asset management Research Corp.

[12] Charles Hugh Smith, Of Two Minds, "The Unsettling Mystery Of Japan's Perpetual Debt Machine," 12-29-11, http://www.businessinsider.com/japans-perpetual-debt-machine-2010-12
[13] "About the Great Depression," Encyclopedia Britannica article
[14] "Consumer Borrowing Drops for 10th Straight Month," Associated Press, January 8, 2010, http://www.npr.org/templates/story/story.php?storyID=122370959&sc=17&f=1006
[15] Linda Stern, "Money Woes Can Make You Sick," Reuters, Feb 26, 2009, 17:44:51 UTC 2009, lindastern@aol.com
[16] Haggai 1:5-7, New International Version

### Chapter Four: From the Streets to Streetwise
[17] Suze Orman, *The Courage to be Rich*, Penguin Group, 1999, 2002, p. 5
[18] Proverbs 4:23, New International Readers Version

### Chapter Five: Marketing Slick Talk Sets the Trap
[19] May 2, 2006 Charles Hugh Smith, "Housing Wealth Effect Shifts Into Reverse," Charles Hugh Smith weblog
[20] Kathleen M. Howley, "Record 19 Million U.S. Homes Stood Vacant in 2008," Feb 3, 2009
http://www.bloomberg.com/apps/news?pid=20670001&refer=home&sid=a0IfdN5GEvcQ
[21] The Associated Press, May 29, 2009 6:00 AM "Record 12% of homeowners are behind on their payments," http://www.mailtribune.com/apps/pbcs.dll/article?AID=/20090529/BIZ/905290339&emailAFriend=1
[22] Cindy Perman, CNBC.com staff writer, "Housing Market Slips into Depression Territory," Tuesday, 11 Jan 2011 | 10:52 AM ET, http://www.cnbc.com/id/41019790/
[23] Proverbs 23:4-5, The Living Bible

### Chapter Six: What Creates a Bubble in the First Place?
[24] Brian J. O'Connor, "Bubble Bursts on the Wealth Effect," June 17, 2008 *Money & Life Editor boconnor@detnews.com* http://www.detnews.com/apps/pbcs.dll/article?AID=/20080617/OPINION03/806170350
[25] The White House, www.whitehouse.gov/news/releases/2007/06/20070601-13.html, June 1, 2007

[26] Robert Prechter CMT, "Ten Things You Should and Should Not Do During Deflation," Prechter is the world's foremost expert on and proponent of the deflationary scenario. Excerpted from: *Economic Deflation: How to Survive the Deflationary Depression, The Market Oracle*, June 21, 2009 Issue #48, Volume 3. (Prechter is the founder and CEO of Elliott Wave International, author of Wall Street best-sellers *Conquer the Crash* and *Elliott Wave Principle* and editor of *The Elliott Wave Theorist* monthly market letter since 1979)
[27] Romans 16:18b, New International Version
[28] Ecclesiastes 6:9, The Living Bible

**Chapter Seven: Know the Score**
[29] Mary Hunt, *Debt-Proof Living*, 1999, Broadman Holman, Nashville, TN, p. 175
[30] 2 Timothy 1:7, New International Version

**Chapter Eight: Cover Your Backside**
[31] Martin Crutsinger, "Consumer borrowing plunges a larger-than-expected $15.7B in April," 6/5/09, AP Economics Writer, http://www.usatoday.com/money/economy/2009-06-05-consumer-credit_N.htm?POE=click-refer
[32] Thomas Kostigan, "Market Watch," June 17, 2007, *San Jose Mercury News*
[33] Mark Whitehouse, "Low Interest Rates Crack Retirees' Nest Eggs," April 4, 2011, *Wall Street Journal*, http://www.smartmoney.com/personal-finance/retirement/feds-low-interest-rates-crack-retirees-nest-eggs-1301931823146/
[34] Dunstan Prial, "Credit-Card Company Cutbacks Might Be a Good Thing," FOXBusiness, July 10, 2009, http://www.foxbusiness.com/story/personal-finance/financial-planning/credit-card-company-cutbacks-good-thing/#
[35] Thelma Gutierrez and Wayne Drash, Santa Barbara, California (CNN), May 2008
[36] Nickel, "FDIC Extends $250k Insurance Limit Through 2013," http://www.fivecentnickel.com/2009/05/27fdic-extends-250k-insurance-limit-through-2013/ May 27, 2009
[37] Proverbs 21:21, New International Readers Version

## Chapter Nine: Count the Costs
38  Linda Stern, "Money Woes Can Make You Sick," lindastern@aol.com, Thu Feb 26 17:44:51 UTC 2009 Reuters
39  Proverbs 27:23, New International Version

## Chapter Ten: Why Games of Chance Are a Poor Bet
40  *Gambling Watch Global*, gamblingwatchglobal.com, 5/6/07 via the National Coalition Against Legalized Gambling
41  R.J. Bell, *Your Guide to Sports Gambling*, free newsletter, February 8, 2006
42  Brian O'Keefe, "Ten Things the Gaming Industry Won't Tell You," *Smart Money*, July 17, 2000
43  Ibid.
44  Bill Graves, "Loans up the ante for Gambling Addicts," *The Oregonian*, March 17, 2007
45  "Compulsive Gambling," Mayo Clinic Staff, January 16, 2007
46  Proverbs 21:5, New Living Translation

## Chapter Eleven: Families that Blend—Should the Money Merge?
47  Sharon Leigh, Janet A. Clark, *Financial Decision Making in Stepfamilies*, Revised and updated from GH 3507, Human Environmental Sciences Extension, MU Extension, University of Missouri-Columbia
48  Greg Stiles, "Foreclosure Comes Home," *Mail Tribune*, December 18, 2007, http://www.mailtribune.com/apps/pbcs.dll/article?AID=/20071218/NEWS/712180308&emailAFriend=1
49  Ezekiel 47:22, New International Version

## Chapter Twelve: Sharks in the Shadows
50  Sven Egenter, "Swiss topple U.S. as most competitive economy," WEF Sept 8, 2009, Editing by Andy Bruce, full report click on: www.weforum.org/gr, http://news.yahoo.com/s/nm/20090908/bs_nm/us_competitiveness_report_1/print,
51  "Fed Shuts Banks in Colo., N.M., Okla., and Wis.," January 28, 2011, http://www.cbsnews.com/stories/2011/01/28/business/main7295406.shtml
52  Barbara Kiviat, "How Americans Got Into a Credit Card Mess," 8-8-09, http://www.time.com/time/business/article/0,8599,1915015,00.

html, Charles Geisst is a professor of finance at Manhattan College and author of *Collateral Damaged: The Marketing of Consumer Debt to America*
53 Eric Dash, "Banks Trimming Limits for Many on Credit Cards," NYTimes.com June 21, 2008
54 Chris Pummer, "Cracking the Whip," January 1, 2008, *MarketWatch*
55 "New Debit Card Rules," by Julie Rainson, August 4, 2010, http://www.wisebread.com/new-debit-card-rules
56 Elizabeth Warren, "America Without a Middle Class," Dec 3, 2009, *The Huffington Post*, http://www.huffingtonpost.com/elizabeth-warren/america-without-a-middle_b_377829.html
57 Gail MarksJarvis, "Credit fix reduces interest in zero-percent financing," July 22, 2008, www.chicagotribune.com/business/yourmoney/chi-tue-gil-0722-jul22,0,7356352.column
58 "Consumers Tripped Up By Credit Card Fine Print, Says Survey," *MarketWatch*, Inc. June 12, 2007
59 James 3:13, New International Version

## Chapter Thirteen: All Eyes on a World Economy
60 Suze Orman, http://money.cnn.com/2008/06/19/pf/Suze_Orman.moneymag/index.htm?postversion=2008061909
61 Prashant Gopal, "The Credit Crisis Turns One," *Business Week*, August 1, 2008, 8:08 am ET
62 Mark Landler, December 2, 2007, *New York Times*
63 Geoff Colvin, "The next Credit Crunch," *Fortune Magazine*, August 27, 2008 http://money.cnn.com/208/08/18news/economy/colvin_next_credit_crunch.fortune/index.htm
64 Tom Raum, The Associated Press, 2007 ABC News
65 Peter S. Goodman, "Fear of Deflation Lurks as Global Demand Drops," November 1, 2008, *New York Times*
66 Martin Masse, "Bailout Marks Karl Marx's Comeback," http://network.nationalpost.com/np/blogs/fpcomment/archive/2008/09/29/bailout-marks-karl-marx-s-comeback.aspx
67 John F. Kennedy, 1960 Campaign
68 "9 thought dead as Minneapolis bridge collapses," msnbc.com staff and news service reports
updated 2:26 a.m. PT, Thurs., Aug 2, 2007, http://www.msnbc.msn.com/id/20079534/

[69] P.J. Huffstutter and DeeDee Correll, *Los Angeles Times* staff writers, "Urgency has buckled since Minneapolis bridge collapse," August 1, 2008, http://articles.latimes.com/2008/aug/01/nation/na-bridge1

[70] Jonathan M. Seidl, "World Amazing Video Emerges of China's 'Ghost Cities'", 3-29-11 http://www.theblaze.com/stories/amazing-video-emerges-of-chinas-ghost-cities/

[71] Psalms 60:2, New International Version

## Chapter Fourteen: Invest Beyond the Local Bank

[72] "Insurance and Investing," *MoneyLife Basic Series*, 2008 Crown Financial Ministries, Inc., p. 65

[73] Ecclesiastes 4:14, New Living Translation

## Chapter Fifteen: Pass Along Smart Money Habits

[74] Crown Financial Ministries, *Children and Finances Part 2*, www.crown.org

[75] Howard Dayton, *Your Money Map*, 2006 Moody Publishers, p. 223

[76] Megan Cherkezian, "The Power of Half,", *Guideposts*, February 2010, http://www.guideposts.com/story/power-half-salvwens-sel-house-for-charity?page=0%2C1&emaileid=NL_YWI_Sub+Category

[77] Jessica Silver-Greenberg, "New Rules for College Credit Cards," May 22, 2009, Businessweek.com, http://www.businessweek.com/bwdaily/dnflash/content/may2009/db20090522_377377.htm

[78] Proverbs 22:6, The Message

## Chapter Sixteen: Spread Some Green Around

[79] Jim Stovall, *The Ultimate Gift*, David C. Cook Publishers, p. 115

[80] Proverbs 11:25, New Living Translation

## Chapter Seventeen: There's No U-Haul Behind the Hearse

[81] Fred Smith Sr., *Breakfast with Fred*, Regal Books, p. 29

[82] Max Lucado, *Grace For the Moment Journal*, Countryman 2002, p. 353

[83] David Crowe, "Tony Snow: Quintessential American," July 13, 2008, Restore America, david@restoreamerica.org

[84] Psalm 16:6, New International Version

## Chapter Eighteen: Feel the Urgency

[85] "Sovereign Debt Crisis, Deficits, Speculation By Banks and the End of Monetization," *The International Forecaster,* 2/24/10, contributing story, http://beforeitsnews.com/storoy/199999/Sovereign_Debt_Crisis_Deficits,_Sp...

[86] John Mauldin, "The Implications of Velocity," March 13, 2010, *Thoughts from the Frontline* weekly newsletter. John Mauldin, best-selling author and recognized financial expert, is also editor of the free *Thoughts From the Frontline* that goes to over 1 million readers each week. For more information on John or his free weekly economic letter go to: http://www.frontlinethoughts.com/learnmore

[87] 1 Thessalonians 5:6, New International Version

www.ingramcontent.com/pod-product-compliance
Lightning Source LLC
Chambersburg PA
CBHW071307110426
42743CB00042B/1203